MERLEAU-PONTY,
HERMENEUTICS,
AND POSTMODERNISM

MERLEAU-PONTY, HERMENEUTICS, AND POSTMODERNISM

EDITED BY
THOMAS W. BUSCH
AND
SHAUN GALLAGHER

STATE UNIVERSITY OF NEW YORK PRESS

Published by
State University of New York Press, Albany

Printed in the United States of America

For information, address State University of New York
Press, State University Plaza, Albany, N.Y. 12246

Production by Diane Ganeles
Marketing by Dana E. Yanulavich

Library of Congress Cataloging-in-Publication Data

Merleau-Ponty, hermeneutics, and postmodernism / edited by Thomas W.
    Busch and Shaun Gallagher.
        p.   cm.
    Includes bibliographical references and index.
    ISBN 0-7914-1139-7 (alk. paper). — ISBN 0-7914-1140-0 (pbk.
    alk. paper)
        1. Merleau-Ponty, Maurice, 1908–1961. 2. Hermeneutics—
    History—20th century. 3. Postmodernism. I. Busch, Thomas W.,
    1937– . II. Gallagher, Shaun, 1948– .
    B2430.M3764M469   1992
    194—dc20   91-33857
                                                        CIP

10 9 8 7 6 5 4 3 2 1

Contents

Contents

Acknowledgments

We are grateful to Villanova University and Canisius College for hosting the meetings of the Merleau-Ponty Circle from which most of the material in this book was drawn.

We are also grateful to the editor of *Philosophy Today* for permission to reprint "Two Reversibilities: Merleau-Ponty and Derrida."

Abbreviations

AD   *Adventures of the Dialectic.* Translated by Joseph Bien. Evanston: Northwestern University Press, 1973. (*Les aventures de la dialectique.* Paris: Gallimard, 1955).

CAL   *Consciousness and the Acquisition of Language.* Translated by Hugh Silverman. Evanston: Northwestern University Press, 1973. ("La Conscience et l'acquisition du langage," *Bulletin de psychologie,* no. 236, XVIII, 3–6 (1964), 226–59).

HT   *Humanism and Terror.* Translated by John O'Neill. Boston: Beacon Press, 1969. (*Humanisme et terreur.* Paris: Gallimard, 1947).

IPP   *In Praise of Philosophy.* Translated by John Wild and J. M. Edie. Evanston: Northwestern University Press, 1963. (In *Éloge de la philosophie et autres essais.* Paris: Gallimard, 1953).

PhP   *Phenomenology of Perception.* Translated by Colin Smith. London: Routledge and Kegan Paul, 1962. (*Phénoménologie de la perception.* Paris: Gallimard, 1945).

PLS   *Phenomenology, Language, and Sociology.* Edited and translated by John O'Neill. London: Heinemann, 1975.

PrP   *The Primacy of Perception.* Edited by J. M. Edie. Evanston: Northwestern University Press, 1964.

PW   *The Prose of the World.* Edited by Claude Lefort. Translated by John O'Neill. Evanston: Northwestern University Press, 1973. (*La Prose du monde.* Edited by Claude Lefort. Paris: Gallimard, 1969).

S   *Signs.* Translated by R. C. McCleary. Evanston: Northwest-
           ern University Press, 1964. (*Signes.* Paris: Gallimard, 1960).

SB   *The Structure of Behavior.* Translated by Alden Fisher. Bos-
           ton: Beacon Press, 1963. (*La structure du comportement.* Paris:
           Presses Universitaires de France, 1942).

SNS   *Sense and Non-Sense.* Translated by H. L. Dreyfus and P. A.
           Dreyfus. Evanston: Northwestern University Press, 1964.
           (*Sens et non-sens.* Paris: Nagel, 1948).

T   *Themes from the Lectures at the College de France 1952–1960.*
           Translated by John O'Neill. Evanston: Northwestern Univer-
           sity Press, 1970. (*Résumés de cours: Collège de France 1952–
           1960.* Paris: Gallimard, 1968).

VI   *The Visible and the Invisible.* Edited by Claude Lefort. Trans-
           lated by Alphonso Lingis. Evanston: Northwestern Univer-
           sity Press, 1968. (*Le visible et l'invisible: suivi de notes de
           travail.* Edited by Claude Lefort. Paris: Gallimard, 1964).

General Introduction

When Merleau-Ponty's philosophical works first appeared they were naturally read as addressing those issues at stake in the philosophical conversation of the moment. The preface to his *Phenomenology of Perception* is a good indication of which of those issues were of most concern to him: phenomenology and the sciences, the relation of reflection to the unreflected, a fresh look at the question of rationality. Out of the pages of *Phenomenology of Perception* emerged a unique and original voice, contributing to the discourse of the time such rich and provocative notions as the body-subject, the nexus of motility and perception, the primacy of perception, ambiguity, original speech.

Subsequent to the *Phenomenology of Perception,* as the philosophical conversation, under the impact of structuralism, focused almost exclusively on language, Merleau-Ponty turned his attention to language, culture, history, and politics in such works as *The Prose of the World* and *Signs.* This change of focus, however, was not an abandoning of the work on perception, which endured as the sustaining metaphor for his thinking on the symbolic. The notions of inscribed subject, multiple perspectives, contingent meaning, and sedimentation, as well as the significance of social practices and lived experience frame his attitude on cultural matters. In his last writings, posthumously published as *The Visible and the Invisible,* he attempted to "deepen" and "rectify" his earlier work which now made him uneasy because of its traces of the "philosophy of consciousness" and its attendant subject/object viewpoint. His concern was to comprehensibly unite perception and language and he found in the structuralist model of diacritical and oppositional relations a paradigm for this project. Perception and language are reconsidered in the context of ontology, an ontology whose sketching out is as original and suggestive as it is enigmatic and underdeveloped. Merleau-Ponty appropriated structuralist elements within the terms of his own work on perception, employing his notions of indwelling, inscription, ambiguity. His ontology would have the distinctive mark of "incorporating," without reducing differences. It is in this sense that his ontological notions of flesh, reversibility, and chiasm must be understood.

These notions take on new meaning in relation to post-structuralism and postmodern hermeneutics precisely to the extent that when we read Merleau-Ponty's texts today they go beyond their original intentions. In new contexts we are able to read Merleau-Ponty differently. Throughout his writings, both early and late, many aspects of his thought are relevant to the concerns of hermeneutics and postmodernism. For example, a central preoccupation of Merleau-Ponty, throughout his works, is the question of rationality. Early in *Phenomenology of Perception* he writes: "The experience of chaos, both on the speculative and the other level, prompts us to see rationalism in a historical perspective which it set itself on principle to avoid, to seek a philosophy which explains upsurge of reason in a world not of its making and to prepare the substructure of living experience without which reason and liberty are emptied of their content and wither away" (PhP 56–57). As in hermeneutics' concerns with the interpretation of meaning and postmodernism's concerns with the dissemination of meaning, Merleau-Ponty explored a post-metaphysical approach to a reason "which has no guarantee in being." Merleau-Ponty's critique of reason is just one aspect of his thought which invites a new reading and a comparison with hermeneutics and postmodernism. Yet his works have been, unfortunately, all too often dismissed by post-structuralist thinkers within their sweeping condemnations of phenomenology. The readers and writers of Merleau-Ponty included in this volume, deeply sensitive to Merleau-Ponty's project, are able to bring his work into the sort of dialogue with hermeneutics and postmodernism which allows for both a better understanding and a productive criticism of these contemporary movements and of Merleau-Ponty's work.

Part One

Hermeneutics

1

Introduction:
The Hermeneutics of Ambiguity

ॡ ॡ

Shaun Gallagher

The chapters in the first part of this collection provide an explication of Merleau-Ponty's hermeneutics—an oblique theory of interpretation which shows how the perceptual world is "laid-out" by the embodied interpreter. This hermeneutics is "oblique" in two senses. First, Merleau-Ponty did not set out to write an explicit hermeneutical theory. His theory of interpretation is thus obliquely stated in what Gary Madison calls a "non-theory" of perception. For Merleau-Ponty, the primacy of perception is rooted in its interpretational nature. The starting point for his analysis is the hermeneutical fact that through perception we always find ourselves already immersed in meaning. Merleau-Ponty's hermeneutics is oblique in a second and more important sense: it veers off from the horizontal developmental line of the hermeneutical tradition. In this tradition the primary focus has been on textual interpretation where interpretation has been modeled on an internal mental reading of an external autonomous text. This tradition, as much as any epistemological one, has been a mix of the intellectualism and empiricism which Merleau-Ponty constantly criticized. Influenced by Husserl's insight that there is an interpretational schema operative in all consciousness, and following Heidegger's existentializing of the hermeneutical circle, Merleau-Ponty proposed a hermeneutical theory that identifies the embodied subject as the seat of interpretation.

For Merleau-Ponty, interpretation is no longer an erudite procedure located in an interior space called "the mind." Meaning "is not first of all a meaning for the understanding, but a structure accessible to inspection by the body" (PhP 320). Merleau-Ponty detoured

3

from the hermeneutical tradition by showing that the human body
acts as both an interpretational constraint and an enabling condition.
Through the performance of my body "I am at grips with [*en prise
sur*] a world" (PhP 303/349). The meaning of the world is not constituted on the model of a textual reading; rather, anterior to any intellectual process, the body schema both encodes and decodes the world
as a meaningful structure. We find ourselves always already surrounded by meaning, already in-the-truth of the world since "being-
in-truth is not distinct from being-in-the-world" (PhP 395/452).

That Merleau-Ponty's oblique hermeneutics is a hermeneutics of
ambiguity may be seen by focusing on the concept of perspective.
Ever since the eighteenth century when Chladenius introduced the
notion of perspective (*Sehe-Punkt*) into hermeneutical considerations,
a notion he rightly associated with the finite embodied nature of the
interpreter, the question of how to adjudicate between perspectives in
order to arrive at the objective truth of the situation has been a
central hermeneutical issue.[1] For both Chladenius and the Roman-
tics, differences of perspectives were resolved by employing logical
and methodological procedures which guaranteed that truth, in the
sense of *adequatio intellectus et rei* would be found either in the mind
(intellectualism) or in the objective thing (empiricism). For Merleau-
Ponty, however, perspectives never completely yield to methodological
procedures and cannot be reduced by logical adjudication. He proposes a hermeneutics in which truth is not found, but *brought into
being* (PhP xx). Yet the advent or realization of truth is never unambiguous; it is always incomplete and imperfect. How this truth is
brought into being, "the origin of truth," is an important question
addressed by Merleau-Ponty's hermeneutics of ambiguity. In regard
to the question of the adjudication of perspectives, Merleau-Ponty
proposed two answers, the terms of which—language and temporality—constitute central themes of his philosophy.

Gail Weiss, in her analysis of Merleau-Ponty's concept of perspective, explains why different perspectives can only be imperfectly adju-
dicated. Context and perspective are, Weiss explains, "interdependent, structural features of our experience" (below, p. 14). We find
ourselves always already within a perspective which is defined and
constrained by a context which itself is constituted by temporally
changing perspectives. In this sense, the relation between perspective
and context is reciprocal or dialectically circular. We have no perspective which is not constrained by a context; we have no context which
is not defined by past and projected perspectives. Our previous perspectives constitute a contextual background for our present interpre-

tations and the perspectives that we are capable of taking with respect to our current situation. Insofar as we also "reckon with the possible," our expectations and projections help to define our present context.

For Merleau-Ponty, the perspectival nature of perception is only partially explained in the *Gestalt* terms of figure-ground. Every perceived object is perceived within a spatial horizon, on a background from which it is distinguished. If *perspective* is capable of being defined in these terms, Weiss warns against identifying the *context* with spatial background or horizon. She proposes a significant correction to Merleau-Ponty's notion of context by suggesting that contexts have an essentially temporal rather than spatial nature. They operate in a diachronic manner which determines the meaning of the perceptual, synchronic background. Backgrounds, which are essential parts of any perspective, are "constituted out of a whole network of past experiences and future expectations which, on principle, are not part of the sensory field at any given moment" (below, p. 16). In this sense, contexts, which help to define perspectives, are not directly tied to the spatial model of figure-ground but more comprehensively reflect hermeneutical and social dimensions.

The explication of a context involves more than describing the lived space of perception; it requires an interpretation of why we perceive what we perceive. Diachronic contexts constantly condition the meaning of perspectival figures and grounds. By this contextual conditioning, perspectives merge into the 'perceptual field.' But this conditioning is not a one-way process. If we ask how contexts come to be shaped, we must answer that contexts are shaped out of our past perspectives. Contexts, which lend their hermeneutical stability to constantly changing perspectives, and which thus help tie together a meaningful world, are at bottom constituted out of the flux of perspectives. Moreover, one can understand a context only from within a particular perspective so that the possibility of gaining reflective, methodological control over those contexts which condition our interpretations and communications remains always imperfect and incomplete. We find ourselves always within the hermeneutical circle in which contexts condition perspectives and perspectives condition contexts. Every interpretation, every perceptual experience operates within this circular structure.

The insistence on hermeneutical ambiguity, which makes reflection always imperfect and incomplete, motivated Paul Ricoeur's critical questioning of Merleau-Ponty. "One can only wonder . . . how the moment of reflection on the unreflected, how the devotion to universality and truth, and finally how the philosophical act itself are possible if man is so completely identified with his insertion into his field of perception, action, and life."[2] Thomas Busch, in his chapter, takes Ricoeur's question as his starting point. Busch pursues the theme of perspective as perceptual finitude, and inquires into the possibility of escaping from the limitations of perspective. Following Ricoeur's suggestion, he explores the idea that *language* comes to the aid of embodied perception by allowing for a transgression of our own perspective by others. Merleau-Ponty himself accounts for the possibility of transgressing single perspectives through linguistic expression which is not, however, a purely intellectualistic accomplishment.[3] Expression, as Busch explains, "is founded on perception in the sense of taking up, sublimating, transfiguring, perceptual wholes. In the process the perceived world becomes imbued with language, plurality, ambiguity" (below, p. 28).

Busch proposes to locate the possibility of transgression in the conversational aspect of language. By focusing on conversation, Busch moves Merleau-Ponty in the direction of Gadamer. In contrast to Ricoeur's early emphasis on the semiotic aspect of language—treating language in terms of the factuality of signs and thereby giving priority to the textual paradigm rather than to speech—Gadamer identifies conversation as the essence of language and holds that in its conversational aspect language always goes beyond subjective perspectives. Thus, Gadamer claims that "to be in a conversation . . . means to be beyond oneself, to think with the other and to come back to oneself as if to another."[4] Precisely in this dialogue with others Busch locates the possibility of the transgression of one's own perspective. Since the other's perspective exceeds my perspective, dialogue establishes both the limitation of perspective and the possibility of a lateral universality. If Merleau-Ponty recognized that one's perspectives do not form a closed system (PhP 338), and that others "bring out the limits of our factual vision" (VI 143), still, he did not fail to acknowledge that language itself never escapes perspectivity. In contrast to the claims of Chladenius, we never resolve in a completely unambiguous way the hermeneutical *aporia* concerning the possibility of truth.

Michael Yeo, helps us to recognize the important ethical significance of just this *aporia*. Because a necessary prerequisite for a moral life is the recognition of others through their transgressions of our own perspectives Yeo calls our attention to the danger of not actualizing the hermeneutical possibilities of transgression. For Yeo, as for Busch, it is in relation to the question of language that we find the more promising possibilities of transgression. As Merleau-Ponty indicated "the interlocutor, to the degree that he understands, goes beyond what he already knows. The meanings involved in such a language are open."[5] In conversation (*la parole parlante*) our own perspectives get transgressed, and we transcend ourselves towards others. Conversation not only brings truth into being, but carries us beyond ourselves. Language, in its conversational aspects "is like a machine for transporting the 'I' into the other person's perspective" (PW 19).

Merleau-Ponty, in perhaps his most traditional of hermeneutical moments, offered the case of reading as a paradigm of this transgression. I not only carry something of my own to the text, but my encounter with the other through the text carries me beyond myself. There is a dialectic of assimilation and accommodation, of appropriation and transcendence (see PW 142). As Yeo puts it, "I can encounter the text only by assimilating its language to my ends, so to speak, but by so doing (and only by so doing) I open myself to experience something in the text that goes beyond what I put into it" (below, p. 47). The transcendence involved here is one which transforms the reader—one way or another—but without guarantees, since, as Yeo puts it, "it is not guaranteed that we will be respectful of otherness, and this contingency is the proper concern of ethics" (below, p. 49). If there is an ethical danger involved in failing to transcend our perspectives by opening ourselves to others, there is also a risk, as well as a responsibility involved in the attempt to do so.

Our experience with language in conversation constitutes the hermeneutical locus for the possibility of truth, but not a complete or absolutely objective truth. Gary Madison has noted that the "foundation of truth or rationality is this 'progressive experience,' the 'experience of agreement with myself and others.' "[6] But as Merleau-Ponty rightly remarked, this agreement is "hard to reach" (SNS 95). Language never guarantees a convergence to "the thing itself," a complete coincidence of different perspectives, or a necessary concordance with others. It involves us in uncertainty, non-coincidence, and the possibility of misunderstanding (see, e.g., VI 125; T 22). Merleau-Ponty here moved toward the postmodern emphasis on "wild language" which "has us" and which speaks itself. Here, if truth is possible, it is not a question of assimilating language to my own ends; "it is not we who speak, it is truth that speaks itself at the depths of speech" (VI 185). In this case, which is one of decentered subjectivity, our relations with others are always ambiguous. Speech and conversation, even if they do allow appropriate transgressions, do not neces-

sarily *"bring about* that concordance between me and myself, and
between myself and others . . ." (PhP 392).

If conversation and the ethical encounter with others allow us to
move beyond our own narrow perspective toward a lateral universality, Merleau-Ponty still insisted that this is never a perfect universality, a complete adjudication or unambiguous truth; one does not find
guarantees in conversation, since, as Gadamer would contend, we are
never in complete control of conversation. Yet for Merleau-Ponty there
is another possibility with respect to transcending isolated perspectives. A perspective is always involved in a "transitional synthesis"
(PhP 329). One perspective "merges into" another. Here the focus is
on temporality rather than language. My finitude is both what binds
me to perspectives (as my past limits my present) and what frees me
from my perspectives since from my present I can get a new perspective on my old ones—"my past *on the horizon* of my present" (PhP
338).

The temporality of experience, as Edmund Husserl has shown,
makes reflection possible. Only in so far as we retain our past, can we
review it, see it again from a new perspective, an ever-changing perspective, and thereby recognize the constraints that had been operative in those past perspectives. But even here Merleau-Ponty found
no certainty, at least not the type of certainty that either Descartes or
Husserl found in their own experience. Glen Mazis, in his essay on
temporality and reversibility, throws light on this other hermeneutical
possibility of transcending perspectives. By the concept of reversibility
Merleau-Ponty explicates what Mazis calls "the thickness of a temporality in which significant experiences, in their open indeterminacy,
are fated to return to themselves in never ending unfolding and enfolding" (below, p. 55). The working out of meaning is "always retrograde as well as progressive" (below, p. 55). It is not simply that our
past experiences condition our present perceptions and interpretations, but our present situations lead to reflective reinterpretations of
our past perspectives.

The conservative structure of continuity which one finds in
Husserl's concept of retentional consciousness is displaced in moments when the production of meaning transforms everything which
had gone before. In such interpretational moments the past and present
are interwoven, *"Ineinander,* each enveloping-enveloped" (VI 268). The
hermeneutical situation is composed of "one fabric" within a plurality
of differentiations (see VI 231). Insofar as time is an interweave of
pasts and missing presents ("the new present is itself transcended")
rather than one thread strung out in a straight line, one never com-

pletely escapes a perspective. As Mazis suggests, one simply improvises on it.

The fact that our past experience is both a constraining and an enabling principle for our present experience, *and* that our past is itself both constrained and enabled by our present, means that it is impossible to ever *absolutely* transcend a perspective, although we can always *ambiguously* do so. The text which Mazis cites from Joyce's *Ulysses* testifies to the ethical import of this situation. Michael Yeo reminds us of the danger involved if we fail to transcend our perspectives by opening ourselves to others; Joyce's text explicates the risk, as well as the responsibility involved in the attempt to do so.

Questions concerning language, reflection, and the possibility of achieving an objective viewpoint are central ones in the field of hermeneutics. In every instance the perspectives that call for hermeneutical reflection are biased by prejudgments, authority-structures, and distorted communication practices. The possibility of escaping such perspectives in order to obtain an objective consensus forms a central issue in one of the more famous of contemporary debates in hermeneutical theory: the Habermas-Gadamer debate which began in the late 60s and is still carried on in various commentaries. In the context of this debate I set out, in the essay "Language and Imperfect Consensus," to appropriate Merleau-Ponty's thoughts on language in order to show that whatever consensus might be found through conversation or critical communicative practice, it will always remain an imperfect consensus, short of perfect objectivity.

Merleau-Ponty's hermeneutics mediates between Gadamer and Habermas to the extent that he embraced a position which is *first,* akin to the hermeneutics of Gadamer, yet with more emphasis placed on the operations of power- and authority-structures; and *second,* akin to Habermas' concept of communicative rationality, but with more emphasis on the imperfection of any real consensus. With respect to language, Merleau-Ponty provided an account which would grant greater room for Gadamer's theory of the speculative nature of language but would not deny Habermas' project for communicative praxis. In my essay, however, I place Merleau-Ponty closer to Gadamer's side of the debate. This contrasts with Gary Madison's suggestion that rationality for Merleau-Ponty consists in a reasonableness which is "an attempt to reach uncoerced agreement with others by means of unrestricted dialogue," i.e., a rationality that comes close to Habermas' concept of communicative rationality.[7] My contention is that for Merleau-Ponty dialogue can never be completely unrestricted, and therefore, consensus can never be perfect. Merleau-Ponty helps to show that critique is possible, but only from within the ambiguous framework of language and the inescapable process of tradition. Since there is no absolute or external reflection, critique must operate within the hermeneutical bounds of interpretive understanding.

The imperfection of critique and the impossibility of perfect consensus are tied to the ambiguity of historical existence. We find ourselves already taken up into language, caught up in historical circumstances which are not completely of our own making. In attempting to get our bearings we cannot disengage ourselves from the larger social and linguistic processes in order to get an objective, neutral perspective. Nor can we completely adjudicate all perspectives in perfect consensus. Thus, our praxis cannot aim at a revolution which would result in absolute emancipation, or definitive solutions to human problems; rather, it must be a praxis of "unremitting *virtu*," because the ambiguity is unremitting.

If my essay measures Merleau-Ponty's contributions to critical hermeneutics, Gary Madison proposes, in the final essay of Part I, to move Merleau-Ponty into the context of the radical hermeneutics of postmodernity. Madison poses a surprising question in "Did Merleau-Ponty Have a Theory of Perception?" He answers it in an even more surprising way: No—despite his extensive dealings with the issue of perception. In Madison's view, Merleau-Ponty rejected the traditional concept of perception which, for both intellectualism and empiricism is a metaphysical construct—either a subjective activity or an objective natural event. Rather, for Merleau-Ponty, perception is a process of interpretation, a hermeneutical process which places the perceiver in the "phenomenal field" always in an indeterminate way. If the nature of theory is always to construct a determinate essence, then a theory of perception is, for Merleau-Ponty, impossible since perception itself is ambiguous or indeterminate.

Madison shows how Merleau-Ponty's insights into perception, interpretation, and language lead him in the direction of what was to become post-structuralism. In Merleau-Ponty's later philosophy, for example, the term 'flesh' signifies diacriticality or differentiation and approximates Derrida's non-concept of *differance.* Madison cites Merleau-Ponty at this point of approximation: " 'The flesh is not matter, is not mind, is not substance'. It is indeed nothing factual but is, rather, 'the possibility and exigency for the fact . . . what makes the fact be a fact' (VI 140). Like Derrida's *differance,* the flesh is a kind of primordial productivity. The 'origin' of both the visible and the invisible, the sensible and the sentient, 'the formative medium of the object and the subject' (VI 147)" (below, p. 96). The non-concept of flesh represents a radicalizing of Merleau-Ponty's notion of ambiguity and approaches Derrida's radical notion of play.

For Madison, Merleau-Ponty's postmodernism has a decided advantage over other, more recent versions. Merleau-Ponty never abandoned philosophy or humanism. "Merleau-Ponty remained a philosopher precisely because he did not believe in the 'death of man,' i.e., the human *subject*" (below, p. 98).

Perhaps we could express this advantage in a different way. Merleau-Ponty's message for postmodernism is that postmodern thought always must find its limits in the hermeneutical situation. Merleau-Ponty would challenge those postmodern thinkers—including Derrida, Foucault, and Lyotard—who quite frequently attempt to dissociate themselves from hermeneutics.[8] He would remind us that postmodernism can not afford to leave hermeneutics behind—even if that were possible. It cannot dissociate itself from hermeneutics precisely because even postmodern understanding is a human enterprise which is hermeneutically situated. As we see in these essays, human experience, insofar as it is perceptual, linguistic, and temporal is contextual and perspectivally limited, yet capable of both transcendence towards others and imperfect reflection on itself. Its hermeneutical situation is always ambiguous, regardless of whether one tries to repress the ambiguity, as in traditional theory, or radicalize the ambiguity, as in postmodern theory. For Merleau-Ponty, all thinking, whether traditional or postmodern, finds its limits in a hermeneutics of ambiguity, a hermeneutics which Merleau-Ponty started to work out between the extremes of traditional and radical hermeneutics.

Notes

1. See Johann Martin Chladenius, *Einleitung zur richtigen Auslegung Vernünftiger Reden und Schriften* (Leipzig: 1742), Ch. 8.

2. Paul Ricoeur, "Existential Phenomenology," in *Husserl: An Analysis of His Phenomenology,* trans. Edward Ballard and Lester Embree (Evanston: Northwestern University Press, 1967), p. 209.

3. In a similar context Dennis O'Connor has noted that with respect to transcending an embodied perspective the human body itself has a role to play. He suggests that by placing me "outside of myself," my body exposes me to interpretations by others, interpretations that I must come to terms

with in my own self-understanding. ("Addressing the Flesh: Teaching Carnal Subjects," paper read at the 14th International Conference of the Merleau-Ponty Circle, Canisius College, 22 September 1989).

4. Gadamer, *"Destruktion* and Deconstruction," in *Dialogue and Deconstruction: The Gadamer-Derrida Encounter,* eds. Diane P. Michelfelder and Richard E. Palmer (Albany: State University of New York Press, 1989), p. 110; also see pp. 106, 115–117. Gadamer also writes: "The mere presence of the other before whom we stand helps us to break up our own bias and narrowness, even before he opens his mouth to make a reply" (p. 26).

5. Merleau-Ponty, "The Experience of Others," trans. Hugh Silverman and Fred Evans, *Review of Existential Psychology and Psychiatry* 18 (1982–83), p. 57.

6. Gary Madison, *The Hermeneutics of Postmodernity: Figures and Themes* (Bloomington: Indiana University Press, 1988), p. 71.

7. Ibid., p. 72.

8. See, e.g., Jacques Derrida, *Of Grammatology,* trans. G. C. Spivak (Baltimore: Johns Hopkins University Press, 1976), p. 46. Michel Foucault, *The Archaeology of Knowledge,* trans. A. M. Sheridan Smith (New York: Pantheon Books, 1972), pp. 12, 109–110, 138–139, 202. Jean-Francois Lyotard, *The Postmodern Condition: A Report on Knowledge,* trans. Geoff Bennington and Brian Massumi (Minneapolis: University of Minnesota Press, 1984), p. xxiii.

2

Context and Perspective

ða ða

Gail Weiss

The notion of perspective is crucial to Merleau-Ponty's views regarding perceptual experience and yet, throughout his *Phenomenology of Perception,* the nature of perspective and the role it plays in perceptual experience remains somewhat unclear. On the one hand, Merleau-Ponty asserts that:

> I am not tied to any one perspective but can change my point of view, being under compulsion only in that I must always have one, and can have only one at once . . . (PhP 407)

Even while acknowledging the uniqueness of perspective, however, Merleau-Ponty also warns us that:

> I do not have one perspective, then another, and between them a link brought about by the understanding, but each perspective *merges into* the other and, in so far as it is still possible to speak of a synthesis, we are concerned with a 'transitional synthesis.' (PhP 329).

If, as Merleau-Ponty claims, I can only have one perspective at a time, but am also unaware of the precise point at which one perspective ends and another begins, this can only occur because the perspectives I have appealed to in the past or will take up in the future serve as the horizon for the present perspective that I have adopted. More specifically, previous perspectives I have taken towards a given object, person, or experience serve as a background or context for my present situation and the perspective I take up with regard to it. And, while it might seem less plausible that future perspectives also influence present perspectives, we should not lose sight of the fact that: "The normal person *reckons with* the possible, which thus, without shifting from its position as a possibility, acquires a sort of actuality" (PhP 109).

In this chapter I will examine the relationship between context and perspective, a relationship which is largely left unexplored in Merleau-Ponty's own work, and yet whose elucidation is necessary for a satisfactory understanding of how contexts and perspectives contribute to the meaning of our everyday experiences. My intention here is to make sense of this relationship from *within* Merleau-Ponty's own phenomenological framework and to explore some of the consequences that result from a description of context and perspective as interdependent, structural features of our experience.

Merleau-Ponty has characterized the continuity of our perspectival grasp on the world in terms of a "synthesis of horizons" that "merges with the very movement whereby time passes" (PhP 330). While most of us would readily acknowledge that the previous perspectives we have taken towards a given object, person, or experience (or which others have taken in similar situations) serve as a background or context for the present situation and the perspective brought to the situation, it is not always possible to assess the influence of these earlier perspectives on the present situation. If, for example, I am meeting someone for the first time, but have been told in advance that the person I am to meet is aggressive and confrontational, my perspective towards the upcoming encounter will most likely be affected by the information I have received. More specifically, the perspective another individual has provided me with regarding this new person, alters to some extent the context, perspective, and gestures that are relevant to the current situation. And, it is evident that my own past experiences with a particular type of person (e.g., other aggressive, confrontational people) will also help to determine the meaning of a specific encounter.

Undeniably, our future goals also give meaning to our present activity in a fairly consistent, and even predictable, fashion. If I am rushing out of my home to an appointment for which I am late, the sudden ring of the telephone will be perceived as an unwelcome intrusion that may result in my answering the telephone in an abrupt, semi-hostile fashion. If, however, I am expecting a call from a prospective employer regarding a job, I may view the telephone's ring as a summons to a new future. And, although the present perspective I have towards the telephone call may change from one situation to the next, in both cases it actively incorporates, albeit in a largely unthematized manner, expectations for the future as well as memories of the recent or more distant past.

A particular perspective, then, insofar as it is influenced by past experiences and possible future experiences, always invokes a broader context of significance that is not restricted to the moment at hand. Regarding the notion of context, Merleau-Ponty states that:

> If we turn back to the phenomena, they show us that the apprehension of a quality, just as that of size, is bound up with a whole perceptual context, and that the stimuli no longer furnish us with the indirect means we were seeking of isolating a layer of immediate impressions. (PhP 8)

Although, on Merleau-Ponty's account, it is evident that all perception takes place within an ever-changing context of significance, and moreover, that all perception is perspectival, it is not equally clear how the contexts that situate our experience and the perspectives that structure our experience develop in relation to one another. Furthermore, Merleau-Ponty's claim that perspectives are continually "merging" also raises a question as to whether or not we can even talk about *a* perspective or *a* context since our understanding of perspectives and contexts as distinguishable phenomena always seems to come *after* the fact. In Merleau-Ponty's words:

> We do not begin by knowing the perspective aspects of the thing; it is not mediated by our senses, our sensations or our perspectives; we go straight to it, and it is only in a secondary way that we become aware of the limits of our knowledge and of ourselves as knowing. (PhP 324)

Perspectives define the perceptual field insofar as they orient us toward an object, person or situation, and they are "invisible" to the extent that this object, person, or situation occupies the field of our concern. Indeed:

> The object-horizon structure, or the perspective, is no obstacle to me when I want to see the object: for just as it is the means whereby objects are distinguished from each other, it is also the means whereby they are disclosed. (PhP 68)

Since perspective, for Merleau-Ponty, is a matter of how a particular object reveals itself against a given background, and since an object changes in accordance with changes in its background and vice-versa, the figure-ground relationship must be the starting point for understanding the influence that context and perspective have upon one another.

If perspective is not solely a matter of the object or horizon taken in isolation, but involves the system that is formed out of their dynamic interaction, it may at first glance be tempting to identify a perceptual context with the horizon itself. Thus, we might claim that embedded within every perspective is a context of significance that changes relative to a particular perception since, "An initial perception independent of any background is inconceivable" (PhP 281). Under this account, the context would be integral to the perspective since it would serve as the background for our individual perceptions, and would have a ubiquitous function in our everyday experience. And yet, there is a concreteness or spatial presence of the background in the figure-ground structure that can be lost sight of if we identify a perceptual background or horizon with the more encompassing notion of context. Moreover, by equating context with the background in the figure-ground structure, we run the risk of subordinating context to perspective and it is not clear that context is so subordinated to perspective in our daily life.

Merleau-Ponty refers to the background for our individual perceptions as being both perceptible and constituted out of a whole network of past experiences and future expectations which, on principle, are not a part of the sensory field at any given moment. This produces a tension in his discussion of perspective and of the figure-ground structure of perceptual experience since the indeterminacy of the background is twofold: on the one hand it is the obverse side of the perceptual clarity of the figure which requires a spatial background in order to manifest itself as a distinct entity, and, on the other hand, it is due to the nature of the attitudes, experiences, and expectations which also combine to form the background and which defy explication since they possess a generality that transcends the immediacy of the present situation.

If we view the perceptual background as a primarily spatial phenomenon, then we can understand the indeterminacy of the background in relation to the corresponding determinacy of the figure, and can even explore the influence and extent of this indeterminacy in particular situations. Such an investigation was, in fact, a predominant concern of the Gestalt psychologists, and their experiments along these lines are referred to by Merleau-Ponty and others who have worked on perception. Once we turn to the second type of indeterminacy, however, the notion of background itself becomes obscured and we begin to lose sight of the relation of the background to a specific figure. And, as mentioned earlier, this second type of indeterminacy is a function of the unthematized fashion in which my former and future experiences "color" my present situation and help to present it in one light rather than another.

While I agree with Merleau-Ponty that our previous and anticipated experiences certainly influence the course of our present action, there is a need to locate this influence at a different *level* of experience than that provided by the figure-ground structure. Just as Merleau-Ponty refers to the varying spatial levels through which we build up our own sense of spatiality, there is a corresponding variety of contextual levels which help to determine the perspectives we take up towards objects, other people, and the situation as a whole. With regard to the varying contextual levels that are operative in any given situation, it is our memories and our expectations that serve as the parameters within which our perceptual experiences are defined and understood. And yet, as parameters that are themselves continually *re-constituted* out of a continuous perceptual framework, they are subject to the same ambiguity and indeterminacy that Merleau-Ponty has found to be inherent in all structures of the perceptual world.[1]

The unique, temporal nature of our memories and expectations contribute significantly to the richness of the contexts that help to situate our perceptual experience. Specifically, it is the cross-temporal aspect of the varying contexts we bring to our everyday experiences which allows us to transcend the spatiality of the physical figure-ground relationship with which we are actively confronted. These contextual levels themselves are a reflection of previous social situations and hence have also taken place within a particular spatial configuration. However, insofar as the context I bring to a particular situation stems from experiences I have had before or will have after that situation, it is not directly tied to the spatiality of the present situation as is the figure-ground structure.[2]

Because Merleau-Ponty fails to distinguish the contribution of a more general context of significance from the immediate spatial situation as it is revealed in the relationship between figure and ground, he is unable to account for the continuity that is revealed across different perspectives, a continuity that derives from similarity of context rather than similarity in the figure-ground structure.[3] That is to say, although all perspectives presuppose the presence of a figure outlined against a ground, these perspectives themselves often attain a type of permanence that is not characteristic of the shifting figure-ground structure.

The figure-ground relationship is primarily efficacious at the level of individual gestures since these latter are spatially grounded in the present and emerge as distinct phenomena that motivate our action. It is individual gestures rather than perspectives that are responded to as meaningful figures manifested against a particular social, spatial, and temporal background. A perspective, on the other hand, can only be indirectly indicated in a specific gesture since the

significance of the perspective derives from a more general context
that is never fully revealed. Individual gestures are usually not perceived as isolated entities, but rather are integrated into a particular perspective or point of view as they become part of what George
Herbert Mead has called the "conversation of gestures."[4]

Gestures are the medium through which we communicate with
one another, but it is the perspectives we form in and through them
that tie individual gestures together into meaningful wholes. And,
since these perspectives are developed spontaneously and not according to a prearranged law, the scope and relevance of a particular
perspective will shift over time. Changes in perspective are expressed
through modifications of gesture; however it sometimes happens that
our gestures may change before we are even aware that the change
conveys a difference in perspective.[5]

The context we bring to a particular situation, influenced as it is
by a multiplicity of past and future experiences, cannot be expressed
as easily in the present situation as can a perspective which is more
directly tied to a specific set of gestures.[6] Perhaps the reason it is so
difficult to make context the explicit focus of a particular situation is
because context is precisely what constitutes the situation *qua* situation for me. It is, in fact, because past and future are also implicated
in the present situation (in the form of memories, attitudes, and
expectations), that there will always be aspects of the situation that
are not revealed in the present moment, but which nonetheless comprise a horizon of significance that enables me to adopt a particular
perspective towards a given experience. In Merleau-Ponty's words:

> What needs to be understood is that for the same reason I am
> present here and now, and present elsewhere and always, and also
> absent from here and from now, and absent from every place and
> every time. This ambiguity is not some imperfection of conscious-
> ness or existence, but the definition of them. Time in the widest
> sense, that is, the order of coexistences as well as that of succes-
> sions, is a setting to which one can gain access and which one can
> understand *only by occupying a situation in it, and by grasping it in
> its entirety through the horizons of that situation.* (PhP 332; empha-
> sis mine)

In this passage, Merleau-Ponty attributes to the situation the
power of revealing the temporality of my existence. That is, it is
through inhabiting a situation that implicates past and future as
well as the present that I come to discover the temporal dimension
of perceptual experience, and, furthermore, it is through the discovery of the horizons that surround each situation that I learn how to

transform my situation and change my perspective. The situation and its horizons are, therefore, always already presupposed in the perceptual process and serve as the framework for the individual gestures that express my own response to the world. Inhabiting a situation means that I am at once "present and absent" because to be immersed in the situation entails taking up a perspective towards that situation, a perspective that relies on a context of significance that projects beyond the facticity of the experience at hand. It should not be surprising then, that self-knowledge also must occur through the situation, for: "I know myself only in so far as I am inherent in time and in the world, that is, I know myself only in my ambiguity" (PhP 345).

And yet, although Merleau-Ponty acknowledges the importance of the situation for self-understanding as well as for an understanding of temporality, he never clarifies the role that context plays in differentiating one situation from another.[7] Instead, Merleau-Ponty focuses more on the notion of a perceptual field than on the way in which these fields combine to form a unique situation. He discusses how each of the five senses constitutes a field of perceptual activity, but he does not describe sufficiently how these shifting fields bring about continuity in our perspectives—a continuity that is provided by an ongoing context of significance which helps to determine when one situation has ended and another has begun.

Regarding the function of the perceptual field, Merleau-Ponty asserts that:

> We now begin to see a deeper meaning in the organization of a field: it is not only colours, but also geometrical forms, all sense-data and the significance of objects which go to form a system. Our perception in its entirety is animated by a logic which assigns to each object its determinate features in virtue of those of the rest, and which 'cancel out' as unreal all stray data; it is entirely sustained by the certainty of the world. (PhP 313)

Here, Merleau-Ponty distinguishes the significance of objects from their colour, geometrical form and sensory properties, and views all of the above as mutually constitutive of a perceptual field. And yet, at the end of the *Phenomenology of Perception* we are still left wondering how all of these aspects of the thing relate to one another and to the individual perspectives we continuously take up towards new situations. If, on the other hand, we take context to be the ongoing framework that gives each situation its own peculiar focus, we can better understand why each situation is made up of experiences, attitudes and half-articulated expectations that are not the property

of any one person alone. The indeterminacy and ambiguity that are
so characteristic of the perceptual process, are themselves located
within a particular context and make possible the transition from
one situation to another without any corresponding change in my
physical orientation. Within any given situation, past, present, and
future are incorporated in a fluid totality that achieves its primary
determinacy through the immediacy of a spatially-oriented, figure-
ground structure. This latter structure, in fact, continually 'fills in'
the indeterminacy of the situation in the fullness of the present
moment, and the perspective that results out of a series, or conversation of gestures, in turn becomes part of the context for our future
experiences.

By failing to distinguish the contribution of a more general context of significance from the immediate physical "presentness" of the
situation as it is revealed through the relationship between figure
and ground, Merleau-Ponty remains unable to account for why it is
that when we recall an earlier incident, we appeal more to the
context for the experience rather than the actual spatial setting of
the incident itself. In addition, if the context was simply the immediate horizon or background for a specific experience, it is not clear
why one would emphasize the social setting which gave rise to a
particular encounter over and above the actual content of the discourse as often happens when we recount a previous experience to a
friend. Here, what is most important to us is recreating the situation
that gave rise to a particular conversation so that our friend too will
understand why we acted the way we did at that point in time. That
is to say, we look to the context to help supply the *reasons* for our
action and this context, when viewed from a later perspective, incorporates our own responses as well as the responses of the other
person to us.

The importance of context for understanding our everyday experiences does not extend just to situations that have already taken
place, but also applies to situations that we anticipate will take
place in the future. Thus, if I expect a certain letter to arrive by next
Tuesday, I concentrate not only on what the letter might or might
not say, but also on the attitude and expectations of the person
sending the letter, as well as on my own possible attitude and response to having received it. While it is certainly the case that these
attitudes and expectations form a horizon for the interpretation of
the letter when it actually does arrive, they are not rooted to the
present situation in the way that the color of the notepaper, the
handwriting, and the scent of the paper are. Instead, these attitudes

and expectations together comprise the basic context out of which a specific perspective towards the letter develops, and the figure-ground structure, by contrast, refers to the way in which the meaning of the written words themselves form a pattern against the background of the written letter as a whole.[8]

A good example of how our perspectives are influenced by the more general context within which our action takes place has to do with the way we view drivers when we are pedestrians and the way we view pedestrians when we are driving. Both pedestrians and drivers have places to go and each views the other as an occasional obstacle in arriving at a final destination. When I am driving, I resent the sudden appearance of a pedestrian cutting across the street in front of me *even though* I myself always cut across the same street whenever I see an opening in the stream of traffic. I silently curse the smug street-crosser and am angered when he or she causes me to miss my timing on the next light. When I, as a pedestrian, am waiting to cross the street, however, and a car speeds up to prevent me from crossing in time to avoid a whole onslaught of vehicles arriving from the previous light, I am furious at the driver's impatience and can become quite haughty about the respect due me as a pedestrian. After all, I am simply a fragile human being, without the protection of a honking mechanical monster at my disposal to make others jump to do my bidding. The second I step into a car, however, the situation changes, and I am the one angrily wondering what the hell those people are doing calmly crossing, crossing, crossing the street long after my light has turned green and they no longer have the right of way.

Just as the phenomenal field remains continuous over time and across space, there is a continuity in the contexts we bring to different situations, and, as Merleau-Ponty so often notes, it is the continuity of the world and of our bodies as physical entities within the world that is responsible for the unity we find within our experience. On the other hand, the contexts that we bring to situations themselves only emerge through those situations; the context that is invoked when I am driving differs from the context that is involved when I am a pedestrian. More specifically, the difference between these two contexts and the different perspectives to which they give rise has to do with the specific nature of the task at hand. Driving a car is a different type of activity than walking and hence carries with it a different set of attitudes and expectations which I implicitly make use of to isolate my own perspective as driver from that of the pedestrian. And, as long as I am driving, I can successfully maintain a division between my own perspective and that of the pedestrian despite those features of the situation that we share in common. If my car breaks down, however, or if I reach my destination, my own perspective as driver immediately gives way to a new perspective that is in turn related to a new activity. Moreover, the context that underlies my perspective is not merely a reflection of my spatial situation, but instead, serves to motivate the particular spatial organization that I give to the field of my concern. As a driver, the pedestrian cutting in front of me is an *obstacle;* as a pedestrian, the overanxious driver is a *threat.*

Although a context of significance cannot be said to precede the individual perspectives which give it its content, we find a given context always already operative within our experience, and, if we want to change our perspective on a given issue or problem, we must first come to terms with the context that has helped to present this issue or problem to us in a certain light. Context, then, is the measure of our perspectives, and our perspectives allow us access to the broader context of significance within which we give meaning to our lives. Moreover, it is in the interaction between context and perspective that we must seek to locate the significance of our individual gestures. And, as Merleau-Ponty notes, we can accomplish this by recognizing:

> around our initiatives and around that strictly individual project which is oneself, a zone of generalized existence and of projects already formed, significances which trail between ourselves and things and which confer upon us the quality of man, bourgeois or worker. Already generality intervenes, already our presence to ourselves is mediated by it and we cease to be pure consciousness, as soon as this natural or social constellation ceases to be an unformulated *this* and crystallizes into a situation, as soon as it has a meaning—in short, as soon as we exist. (PhP 450)

Notes

1. Ambiguity refers to the possibility of perceiving any given situation (or aspect of the situation) in more than one way. Indeterminacy is a related, albeit distinguishable phenomenon, and refers to the fact that the perceptual process conceals some aspects of the situation at the same time as it reveals other aspects of the situation to us. That is, it is impossible for *everything* contained in the perceptual field to be perceived in a determinate fashion. If perceptual experience is indeed *both* ambiguous and indetermi-

nate this suggests that 1) there will always be more than one possible interpretation of any particular experience and 2) these individual interpretations are incapable of being fully articulated—a limitation that is due not to a flaw in the communicative process, but rather, to the indeterminacy of the experience itself.

2. This is not to say that the figure-ground structure is merely a spatial phenomenon, but rather that the figure-ground structure is directly tied to a *particular* spatial situation in a way that a context is not.

3. Merleau-Ponty does claim that an individual's style gives continuity to perceptual experience, however, continuity of style is something that exists across different gestures, perspectives, and contexts and so is too general to account for continuity of perspective. Moreover, it is possible for several different styles to contribute to the formation of a singular perspective.

4. Mead uses the term, 'conversation of gestures' quite broadly to include dogfights as well as nonlinguistic and linguistic conversations between two or more individuals. Since gestures rarely occur in isolation, but most often arise in response to a specific situation and evoke a subsequent response from that situation, the meaning of an individual gesture needs to be understood in light of the conversation of gestures in which it occurs. Furthermore, it is the perspectives through which two individuals view a given situation that primarily affects the way they view the conversation of gestures they have initiated with one another.

5. The relationship between gesture and perspective becomes especially complex at the level of linguistic or symbolic gestures where the gesture itself becomes 'invisible' insofar as it serves as a kind of 'window' through which a perspective can be revealed.

6. Even a perspective resists precise definition since it evolves out of a series of gestures that are not always contiguous in time and space. However, we more frequently attempt to communicate our perspective on a given issue, problem, or experience through our gestures than the context out of which they have emerged. On the other hand, when disagreements or misunderstandings arise, context may indeed become the center of our attention.

7. In fact, it is Sartre rather than Merleau-Ponty who explicitly discusses the notion of situation as an existential "structure," and who assesses the implications of being "situated" for human freedom and responsibility.

8. It must be noted that the figure-ground structure also operates at several levels in giving meaning to perceptual experience. When I read the letter, squiggles become individual letters of the alphabet, letters become

words, words become paragraphs, and the paragraphs themselves ultimately become the ground for the situations they describe. Of course, once we have learned how to read, this whole process takes place immediately, and unless we have trouble reading a particular word or letter, we do not isolate out any of the factors that culminate in our own response to what we are reading.

3

Perception, Finitude, and Transgression: A Note on Merleau-Ponty and Ricoeur

≈▲ ≈▲

Thomas W. Busch

Paul Ricoeur once claimed that Merleau-Ponty was "the greatest of the French phenomenologists."[1] On those occasions, however, when he commented at any length on Merleau-Ponty, he was severely critical. One case in point occurs in his essay "Existential Phenomenology":

> In Merleau-Ponty . . . the description of the 'owned body' is entirely in the service of a philosophy of finitude or of an exorcism of standpointless thinking; ultimately it is in the service of a philosophy without an absolute. *The Phenomenology of Perception* should be followed from one end to the other without reference to the true object, seen from nowhere, which would justify the possibility of perception, even without ever denying the inherence of consciousness in a point of view. . . . One can only wonder . . . how the moment of reflection on the unreflected, how the devotion to universality and truth, and finally how the philosophical act itself are possible if man is so completely identified with his insertion into his field of perception, action, and life.[2]

In the light of these remarks, it is possible to read the opening chapters (devoted to perception and finitude) of Ricoeur's *Fallible Man*[3] as an extended critique of Merleau-Ponty's project of a philosophy of finitude (although Merleau-Ponty is not mentioned by name).

The thrust of Ricoeur's reflections on finitude is that "we must speak of infinitude as much as of human finitude" (FM 7). The experience of finitude originates with the body: "every experience of finitude refers back to this unusual relation I have with my body" (FM 29). The body's primacy in experience lies in the "percept" where there occurs a "primary appearing" of meaning which is foundational for all subsequent "secondary strata." Within perceptual experience finitude is identified with perspectivism: "Finitude is identified with the notion of point of view or perspective" (FM 35). The perceived object has an "insurmountable and invincible property of presenting itself from a certain angle," so that the "object is never more than the presumed unity of the flux of these silhouettes" (FM 32). Correlatively, the perspectives of the object refer back to the mobile body of the perceiver. At this point Ricoeur asks: "All perception is perspectival. But how could I recognize a perspective, in the very act of perceiving, if *in some way* I did not escape from my perspective?" (FM 40).

His answer invokes speech.

> If I now note that to signify is to intend, the transgression of the point of view is nothing else than speech as the possibility of expression, and of expressing the point of view itself. Therefore, I am not merely a situated onlooker, but a being who intends and expresses as an intentional transgression of the situation. As soon as I speak, I speak of things in their absence and in terms of their non-perceived sides (FM 41).

Language here comes to the aid of the body. "Thus I judge of the entire thing by going beyond its given side into the thing itself. This transgression is the intention to signify. Through it I bring myself before a sense which will never be perceived anywhere by anyone, which is not a superior point of view, which is not, in fact, a point of view at all but an inversion into the universal of all points of view" (FM 41). The intention to signify (here language) brings about a transcendental unity of the various perspectives, which allows the latter to be significant: "We need the 'name' to give a ground to the meaning-unity, the non-perspectival unity of the thing . . . Language, in so far as it penetrates all the sensory appearances of the thing, causes perception to be significative" (FM 45). Given this essential relation between signifying and perception, "the project of a phenomenology of perception, wherein the moment of saying is postponed and the reciprocity of saying and seeing destroyed, is ultimately untenable" (FM 42). Human reality is both body (perspective) and speech (word), intelligible only in terms of a dialectic of finitude/infinitude.

Ricoeur's critique goes to the heart of Merleau-Ponty's project for it challenges the attempt, begun in *The Structure of Behavior,* to overcome the traditional discourse of understanding and sensibility that permeates Ricoeur's views in *Fallible Man.* In *The Structure of*

Behavior, Merleau-Ponty defines a thing as "a concrete unity capable of entering into a multiplicity of relations without losing itself" (SB 118). The "concrete unity" was to be understood as a *gestalt,* a whole whose parts are mutually implicatory and express one another. In a thing, the significance and the material are inseparable. However, in *The Structure of Behavior,* Merleau-Ponty attributes the appearance of things to "symbolic behavior," unfortunately evoking intellectualist terminology. In the *Phenomenology of Perception* there is no such bad ambiguity, for he clearly attributes the appearance of things to perception and perception to the body: "I perceive with my body" (PhP 326). The primary datum of perception is the "spontaneous arrangement of parts" (PhP 58). The thing "is correlative to my body," and "is not first of all a meaning for the understanding, but a structure accessible to inspection by the body" (PhP 320). The significance of the thing "inhabits that thing as the soul inhabits the body" (PhP 319). The significance he refers to is not "a certain idea of the ash-tray which co-ordinates its sensory aspects." Rather, there is a style or "symbolism in the thing which links each sensible quality to the rest" (PhP 319). The linkage, merging, reference, expression of one aspect to another is a "transitional synthesis," a sensible logic that the body comes to understand. The body, dwelling among things, catches on to their style, which becomes a "familiar setting." "To have a body is to possess a universal setting, a schema of all types of perceptual unfolding and of all intersensory correspondences . . ." (PhP 326). Thus, "the perceived thing is not an ideal unity . . ." (PhP 16).

Recall Ricoeur's position: "I anticipate the thing itself by relating the side that I see to those that I do not see but which I *know.* Thus I judge of the entire thing by going beyond its given side into the thing itself. This transgression is the intention to signify" (FM 41). Ricoeur's sense of "know" in this text is, in terms of Merleau-Ponty's position, intellectualistic, for Ricoeur's sensibility is impoverished to the point of standing in need of deliverance by the understanding. For Merleau-Ponty, the thing is understood by the body, in the sense that the unseen sides are grasped as co-present.

> I grasp the unseen side as present, and I do not affirm that the back of the lamp exists in the same sense that I say the solution of a problem exists. The hidden side is present in its own way. . . . It is not through an intellectual synthesis which would freely posit the total object that I am led from what is given to what is not actually given; that I am given, together with the visible sides of the object, the nonvisible sides as well. It is, rather, a kind of practical syn-

thesis; I can touch the lamp, and not only the side turned toward me but also the other side; I have only to extend my hand to hold it (PrP 14).

There is in perception a paradox of immanence and transcendence: "immanence, because the perceived object cannot be foreign to him who perceives; transcendence, because it always contains something more than what is actually given" (PhP 16). The body deals with these objects through familiarity with them and they are correlates of the body as "I can," a mobile system of virtual powers. The body itself grasps the "absent," the "invisible," as the very style of things. Thus, for Merleau-Ponty it is not necessary to interject an "ideal" meaning into the sensible to constitute it as significant.

Ricoeur was right to be concerned with the issue of the transgression of individual perspective, for a cluster of problems are implicated, including not only the possibility of philosophy and universal truth, but also the possibility of self-understanding, critique, self-transformation, and ethics. While I believe that Merleau-Ponty, as opposed to Ricoeur, was right to insist that perception already involves transcendence, it is also true to say that Merleau-Ponty raised the issue of "transgression" of perspective in his own way. In the Preface to the *Phenomenology of Perception,* he recognized that "our existence is too tightly held in the world to be able to know itself as such at the moment of its involvement, and that it requires the field of ideality in order to become acquainted with and to prevail over its facticity" (PhP xv). He later referred to speech as "the surplus of our existence over natural being" (PhP 197), indicating that it is through expression that finitude is transcended, or somehow "prevailed over." Merleau-Ponty insisted, however, that there is no "view from nowhere" in the sense that Ricoeur suggested. Speech can create that illusion and is in that way dangerous. Speech is founded on perception in the sense of taking up, sublimating, transfiguring, perceptual wholes. In the process the perceived world becomes imbued with language, plurality, ambiguity. This leads to a distinction between perception narrowly defined, "natural perception," and perception more widely and richly defined, as including the differentiations of sexuality, language, the cultural in general, which make perception "ambiguous." A tension is created in the *Phenomenology of Perception* between a nostalgia for a primitive contact with a world already given and "the laying down of being . . . like art, the act of bringing truth into being" (PhP xx). In any case, the "surplus" of language never escapes the mark of the perceptual structure of figure/ground. "Mental" or "cultural" life "borrows structures from natural life and the thinking subject must have its basis in the subject incarnate" (PhP 193).

It seems to me that Merleau-Ponty's position on perception (as opposed to Ricoeur's) is correct, but that his appeal to ideality to prevail over facticity, and thus to thematize it for truth and universality (and self-critique) falls short in *Phenomenology of Perception.* My expression as such does not exceed *my* perspective. What does exceed my perspective is the Other's perspective. Dialogue, in which we come to recognize a difference of perspectives, establishes both the limitation of individual perspective and the possibility of critique and of universality. Only occasionally does this social transgression make its appearance in *Phenomenology of Perception.* For example, in the chapter on "The Thing and the Natural World," Merleau-Ponty discusses communication with a person who hallucinates.

> There is no privileged self-knowledge, and other people are no more closed systems than I am myself. . . . I misunderstand another person because I see him from my own point of view, but then I hear him expostulate, and finally come round to the idea of the other person as a centre of perspectives. Within my own situation that of the patient whom I am questioning makes its appearance and, in this bipolar phenomenon, I learn to know both myself and others. . . . I am sitting before my subject and chatting with him; he is trying to describe to me what he 'sees' and what he 'hears'; it is not a question of either taking him at his word, or of sticking to my own point of view, but of making explicit my experience, and also his experience as it is conveyed to me in my own, and his hallucinatory belief and my real belief, and to understand one through the other (PhP 338).

Contrast this to his more usual preoccupation.

> . . . we are trying to describe the *phenomenon* of the world, that is, its birth for us in that field into which each perception sets us back, where we are as yet still alone, where other people will appear only at a later stage, in which knowledge and particularly science have not so far ironed out and levelled down the individual perspective. It is through this birth that we are destined to graduate to a world, and we must therefore describe it. (PhP 256)

While the role of social transgression remains undeveloped in *Phenomenology of Perception,* it becomes thematic and a central concern in some of his subsequent writings. For example, "The Child's Relation With Others" attempts to fuse "corporeal and social conditions." He tells us that "in reality the two orders are not distinct; they are part and parcel of a single global phenomenon." One's sense

of self (including "relations of understanding" and "relations of being") is shown to develop through stages of mirror-image and of
social, linguistic, relations. This allows the self to transform itself
and enter into a universal dimension. The child will use the word "I"
Merleau-Ponty tells us

> when he has become conscious of his own proper perspective, dis-
> tinct from those others, and when he has distinguished all of the
> perspectives from the external object. . . . The *I* arises when the
> child understands that every *you* that is addressed to him is for him
> as an *I;* that is, that there must be a consciousness of the reciproc-
> ity of points of view in order that the word *I* may be used (PrP 150).

In his essay on Levi-Strauss he speaks of an access to the universal
"no longer the overarching universal of a strictly objective method,
but a sort of *lateral universal* which we acquire through ethnological
experience and its incessant testing of the self through the other
person and the other person through the self" (S 120). This move in
the direction of expression and communication was what he referred
to in his "Prospectus" as the "major topic of my later studies . . . the
general problem of human interrelations" (PrP 9).

Meanwhile, Ricoeur's thought was taking the hermeneutical turn.
No longer for Ricoeur would language be a "view from nowhere," but
rather it would be an expression of being-in-the-world and thus always situated. His earlier antinomy of finitude/infinitude would be
transposed as belonging/distanciation. He asks, in regard to
Gadamer's hermeneutics: "How is it possible to introduce a critical
instance into a consciousness of belonging which is expressly defined
by the rejection of distanciation?"[4] This distance will be lateral, not
vertical:

> Wherever there is a situation, there is an horizon which can be
> contracted or enlarged. We owe to Gadamer this very fruitful idea
> that communication at a distance between two differently situated
> consciousnesses occurs by means of the fusion of their horizons,
> that is, the intersection of their views on the distant and the open.
> Once again, an element of distanciation within the far and the
> near, the far and the open is presupposed. This concept signifies
> that we live neither within closed horizons, nor within one unique
> horizon. Insofar as the fusion of horizons excludes the idea of a
> total and unique knowledge, this concept implies a tension be-
> tween what is one's own and what is alien, between the near and
> the far; and hence the play of difference is included in the process
> of convergence.[5]

"Transgression" of perspective for Ricoeur no longer means the supple-
mentation of bodily perspective by language, but the encounter with

the Other's expressed perspective. This is accomplished through an interpretation of expressions, a task involving a number of distanciations, distortions, and methodologies.

When Ricoeur, in taking the hermeneutic turn, abandoned his earlier Kantian/Husserlian phenomenology, and when Merleau-Ponty went on to develop an expanded perception (social, linguistic, cultural as opposed to purely "natural" perception), the basis of their earlier difference about perception/transcendence gave way and common ground formed around problems of expression and communication. In *Signs,* in which Merleau-Ponty is urgent about dialogue in philosophy, politics, and social sciences, this is apparent, especially in the deep resonance between its "lateral universality" and Gadamer/Ricoeur's "fusion of horizons." Of course, in his late works, *Eye and Mind* and *The Visible and the Invisible,* Merleau-Ponty did not plunge ahead into the problem of human interrelationships. Instead, he paused to reconsider his work as a whole, in something of a fresh start, with an ontology in mind. How did this "new" thinking bear upon finitude, the transgression of perspective, and the issues which have defined the Merleau-Ponty-Ricoeur relation?

First, the later works, in my judgment, convincingly put to rest the nostalgia for origins (and the notion of "natural" perception) which haunted *Phenomenology of Perception.* "A lost immediate, arduous to restore, will, if we do restore it, bear within itself the sediment of the critical procedures through which we will have found it anew; it will therefore not be the immediate" (VI 122). What appears to us is not a "brute world," but an "elaborated world" requiring interpretation. There is no "fusion" or "coinciding" with things or with the past.

> And likewise there is no real coinciding with the being of the past: if the pure memory is the former present preserved, and if, in the act of recalling, I really become again what I was, it becomes impossible to see how it could open to me the dimension of the past. And if in being inscribed within me each present loses its flesh, if the pure memory into which it is changed is an invisible, then there is indeed a past, but no coinciding with it—I am separated from it by the whole thickness of my present; it is mine only by finding in some way a place in my present, in making itself present anew (VI 122).

Second, ideality is the invisible of the visible; it is "directly in the infrastructure of vision" (VI 145). Universality is present in the "hinges" or "dimensions" of our experiences. The notion of "reversibility," applied to fact and essence, perspective and speech, precludes the separation of facticity and ideality which, in *Phenom-*

enology of Perception, was to provide the distance necessary for a discourse on finitude. However, the universality implicit in one's situation does not of itself thematize one's perspective. This requires the Other. "Visions other than our own . . . bring out the limits of our factual vision, they betray the solipsist illusion that consists in thinking that every going beyond is a surpassing accomplished by oneself. For the first time I appear to myself completely turned inside out under my own eyes" (VI 145). While I and the Other set limits to our visions, the plurality of viewpoints takes place within the context of Being: "we are moments of the same syntax . . . we belong to the same Being" (VI 83).

This linkage of "syntax" and "Being," constitutes a third relevant consideration. Merleau-Ponty appropriates in a radical, ontological fashion the diacritical, oppositional, relative, system of linguistics. The model of symbolic systems becomes the model of thinking about Being, which includes the dimensions of sense, history, and culture. All "positivities" are understood as divergencies, oppositions. In this sense "transgression" is built into ontology as the differences constitutive of things.

These ontological considerations indicate that a common core of the thought of Merleau-Ponty and Ricoeur remains undisturbed, but that a new point of difference appears. Lack of coincidence of self with self, with things, with the past, with Others, the very condition of finitude, calls for an interpretation of expressions, traces, signs, by an interpreter who is herself enmeshed within the fabric of body, discourse, tradition, Being. The embeddedness of the interpreter in a finite perspective (albeit implicitly universal) is revealed through Others opening up the question of truth. On the other hand, their respective understandings of the "lack of coincidence" at the basis of hermeneutics differ sharply. Lack of coincidence, for Ricoeur, is *distanciation,* which he tells us is "a fundamental characteristic of the very historicity of human experience, namely, that it is communication in and through distance."[6] He links distanciation to objectification: "interpretation is the reply to the fundamental distanciation constituted by the objectification of man in the works of discourse, an objectification comparable to that expressed in the products of his labor and his art."[7] Merleau-Ponty bases his hermeneutics (although he does not use that name) upon the distance, which he calls *écart:*

> It is therefore necessary that the deflection (*écart*) without which the experience of the thing or the past would fall to zero, be also openness upon the thing itself, to the past itself, that it enter into

their definition. What is given, then, is not the naked thing, the past itself such as it was in its own time, but rather the thing ready to be seen, pregnant—in principle as well as in fact—with all the visions one can have of it, the past such as it was one day *plus* an inexplicable alteration, a strange distance—bound in principle as well as in fact to a recalling that spans that distance but does not nullify it. What there is is not a coinciding by principle or a presumptive coinciding and a factual non-coinciding, a bad or abortive truth, but a privative non-coinciding, a coinciding from afar, a divergence, and something like a "good error" (VI 124–25).

Their conceptions of non-coincidence, Ricoeur's "objectification" and Merleau-Ponty's "strange distance," are quite different. The difference is a result of their respective appropriations of linguistics. Ricoeur limited the oppositional, diacritical, relative logic of Saussurean linguistics to *la langue* and objective thought in general (explanation). The event of speech (*la parole*) was located in the discourse of historicity of Gadamer and an existentialized Hegel. Merleau-Ponty, however, came to see the logic of Saussurean linguistics as "characteristic of Being," and employed it to understand subject/object, sensory, intellectual, and cultural dimensions of existence. Distance is not the product of objectification, but the condition of finite existence as such. "Transcendence is identity within difference" (VI 225). All positivity is shot through with difference. Individual beings are formed by "segregation." "Distance," he tells us, "is not the contrary of . . . proximity, it is deeply consonant with it . . ." (VI 135). Time itself, for Merleau-Ponty, belongs to Being and its fleshy style of difference and entertwining.

In light of the fact that Ricoeur characterized the Saussurean linguistic model as immobile, self-enclosed, and determined, it is important to note that Merleau-Ponty considered Being (modelled on the Saussurean system) to be contingent and open to transformation (much as Ricoeur viewed "tradition"). Thus Merleau-Ponty (exhibiting his own traces of Hegel) spoke of the "hyper-dialectic" which brings about surpassings . . . concrete, partial . . . saddled with deficits," but "progresses" nonetheless (VI 95). It is characteristic of Merleau-Ponty's later work that surpassing and transformation are attributed to Being. This is in complete contrast to the *Phenomenology of Perception* where such "transcendence" was the definition of subjectivity itself, the "irrational power which creates meanings" (PhP 189). Indeed, the fate of the subject is unclear in the later work, as Merleau-Ponty often strongly suggests abandoning entirely the discourse of subjectivity, consciousness, etc. Ricoeur, on the other hand, while shying away from formulating an ontology, has consistently worked within, and appeared comfortable with, the discourse of the subject. He developed a philosophy around what he referred to as "a new theory of subjectivity,"[8] a subjectivity decentered and humbled, but productive as well. A good deal of his later writings are devoted to practices of self-formation and critique centered around the notion of a situated and social imagination.

In the course of developing their philosophies of finitude, Merleau-Ponty and Ricoeur crisscrossed common ground such as perception, body, language, and for a time, their paths seemed convergent. However, whereas the focus of finitude for Ricoeur was the delimited subject, Merleau-Ponty, especially in the "Working Notes" of *The Visible and the Invisible,* began to seriously rethink finitude in terms of the logic of semiological difference. Within this newly appropriated discourse the perceiver becomes "a certain fundamental divergence, a certain constitutive dissonance" (VI 234). The subject is nothing positive: "In reality there is neither me nor the other as positive, positive subjectivities" (VI 263). What this harbingers is unclear. At the time he wrote these texts there were proclamations in the air concerning the deaths of the subject and of humanism. A remark Merleau-Ponty made in his essay "Everywhere and Nowhere" indicates that, while his philosophy might move beyond subjectivity, it would not constitute a death of the subject. "There are some ideas which make it impossible for us to return to a time prior to their existence, even and especially if we have moved beyond them, and subjectivity is one of them" (S 154).

Notes

1. Paul Ricoeur, "New Developments in Phenomenology in France: the Phenomenology of Language," *Social Research,* 34 (1967), p. 1.

2. Paul Ricoeur, "Existential Phenomenology," in *Husserl: An Analysis of His Phenomenology,* trans. Edward Ballard and Lester Embree (Evanston: Northwestern University Press, 1967), p. 209.

3. Paul Ricoeur, *Fallible Man,* trans. Charles Kelbey (Chicago: Regnery, 1965). Hereafter FM.

4. Paul Ricoeur, "The Task of Hermeneutics," in *Hermeneutics and the Social Sciences,* edit. and trans. John Thompson (Cambridge: Cambridge University Press, 1981), p. 61.

5. Ibid., p. 62.

6. Paul Ricoeur, "The Hermeneutical Function of Distanciation," in *Hermeneutics and the Social Sciences,* p. 131.

7. Ibid., p. 38.

8. Paul Ricoeur, "Appropriation," in *Hermeneutics and the Social Sciences,* p. 182.

4

Perceiving/Reading the Other:
Ethical Dimensions

≈ ≈

Michael Yeo

I borrow myself from others; I create others from my own thoughts. This is no failure to perceive others; it is the perception of others.[1]

—Maurice Merleau-Ponty

Catch only what you've thrown yourself, all is mere skill and little gain.[2]

—Rainer Maria Rilke

I

Alterity has emerged as a dominant theme in contemporary continental philosophy. Emmanual Levinas is an exemplary figure here, but numerous others—Jacques Derrida, John Caputo, and Mark Taylor to name only a few—could also be cited. Insofar as ethics has to do with respect for others, or more precisely, respect for the otherness of the other, this concern with alterity has an ethical dimension. This dimension is quite explicit in Levinas, but is more or less present in others who make alterity thematic, including Derrida, who ironically has been criticized on moral grounds by self-appointed moralists.[3]

Merleau-Ponty does not figure prominently in contemporary discussion about alterity, in part no doubt because he addresses alterity in terms of a phenomenology which has become somewhat unfashionable. This neglect is unfortunate because he opens up a

37

promising path along which to think about alterity in ethical terms, even if he did not himself explore this path very far. Because Merleau-Ponty nowhere frontally approaches the issue that concerns me, my analysis must be somewhat indirect and highly interpretive. I will be rummaging through several texts of what might be called his middle period,[4] between the *Phenomenology of Perception* and the unfinished *The Prose of the World,* picking up here and there on certain passages that, sometimes only very obliquely, throw light on my chosen theme.

I begin with Merleau-Ponty's analysis of perception and show how (perhaps surprisingly) ethics appears as a problem at this level. I bring this problem to light with reference to what he calls "the paradox of immanence and transcendence." How is it possible to experience the other as other—as really transcendent—given that I cannot but experience her in relation to my own immanent frame of reference? In Merleau-Ponty's own words: "The spectacle begins to furnish itself a spectator who is not I but who is reproduced from me. How is it possible? How can I see something that begins to see?" (PW 135).

This problem, I go on to show, has an analogue in Merleau-Ponty's analysis of language. There is a commensurability between perceiving and reading the other such that examining what Merleau-Ponty says about reading illuminates and deepens his analysis of alterity at the level of perception. The paradox of immanence and transcendence described at the level of perception reappears in connection with reading as a variation of the hermeneutic circle. Merleau-Ponty's analysis of this circularity in reading throws light on the ethical dimension of perceiving or experiencing others.

II

Alterity has always been an important theme in phenomenology, but typically the matter has been framed in a horizon projected by concerns primarily *epistemological.* The scene is dramatically altered if, extrapolating from some remarks in Merleau-Ponty's works, we frame this theme in *ethical* terms. From this point of view our focus becomes not the perception of others *per se,* but more precisely the perception of the *ethical* other: the other as a being to whom we stand in an ethical relationship, as a being whose difference commands our respect.

I am borrowing the phrase "the ethical other" from the discussion that ensued following Merleau-Ponty's address to the *Société française de philosophie* in November 1946.[5] Accusing him of "relativism" and "protagorism," Emile Bréhier challenged Merleau-Ponty on explicitly ethical grounds:

When you speak of the perception of the other, this other does not even exist, according to you, except in relation to us and in his relations with us. This is not the other as I perceive him immediately; it certainly is an *ethical other;* it is not this person who suffices to himself. (PrP 28; emphasis added)

Although he never developed a systematic account of ethics, Merleau-Ponty was certainly a morally engaged thinker and believed that the phenomenological philosophy he advanced was at least consistent with his moral commitments. "It was never my intention to posit the other except as an ethical subject," he responds to Bréhier, "and I am sure I have not excluded the other as an ethical subject" (PrP 30).

However, before elaborating on Merleau-Ponty's response, it will be helpful to situate what is at issue here in the broader perspective of the phenomenological tradition, since phenomenology is the ultimate target of Bréhier's challenge. What would it mean to "exclude" the "ethical other," and why might phenomenology be especially vulnerable to this charge? Husserl's *Cartesian Meditations,* the canonical phenomenological work on the perception of others, will serve to introduce the problem.[6]

Husserl begins the "Fifth Meditation" by considering a "grave objection" to phenomenology, an objection based on implications about the perception of others that seem to follow from the reduction. It takes the form of a *reductio ad absurdum,* the key premise of which he states as follows: "Transcendental reduction restricts me to the stream of my pure conscious processes and the unities constituted by their actualities and potentialities" (CM 89). It seems to follow from this "restriction," however, that the other is reduced to being something (or someone) within my stream of consciousness, something (or someone) I constitute. This runs counter to what might be called 'common sense' about the other, and, although Husserl does not say it, to the sense of the other as a being commanding our respect: to be other is to be independent—not simply constituted, but constituting. Fleshing out this objection, Husserl asks: "But what about other egos, who surely are not a mere intending and intended *in me,* merely synthetic unities of possible verification *in me,* but, according to their sense, precisely *others?*" (CM 89). Is the other, transfixed within my noema and made relative to my consciousness, properly speaking the other at all?

Husserl is here playing ventriloquist for transcendental realism, which he uses rhetorically to set up the central problem of his text: "How can my ego, within his peculiar ownness, constitute under the name, 'experience of something other,' precisely something other" (CM 94). Whether and to what extent he succeeds in answering this question (and the realist's objection) is the subject of ongoing debate, which I will not prolong here.[7] Instead, with this background I want now to explore how this issue turns up in Merleau-Ponty's address to the *Société francaise de philosophie,* which prompted Bréhier's charge.

Speaking about the perception of otherness in general, Merleau-Ponty refers to the matter here in question as a paradox. "There is a paradox of immanence and transcendence in perception," he says, echoing the language of the *Cartesian Meditations* (PrP 16).[8] Phenomenology speaks of immanence, he elaborates, "because the perceived object cannot be foreign to him who perceives." The phenomenon is always organized in a perspective which ultimately leads back to a seer. Whatever is perceived is set within a context or horizon, assimilated in relation to the terms of reference of a perceiver.[9]

This recognition of immanence or horizonality is what gets the paradox off the ground in the first place, and what puts phenomenology at odds with realism (transcendental or otherwise). Realism, however, (mis)takes phenomenology's acknowledgement of immanence to amount to solipsism, to the denial of alterity or transcendence. This is because, captive to dualism, realism posits a transcendent that would be the negation of immanence, a transcendent on the hither side of all horizons, an invisible that would have no sensible sign or trace in the visible. Throughout his philosophy, Merleau-Ponty is concerned to undo the powerful spell of this polarizing either/or: to avoid juxtaposing immanence and transcendence along the familiar lines of inside and outside, subjective and objective.

Merleau-Ponty emphasizes that phenomenology does not oppose immanence and transcendence as mutually exclusive terms. It speaks rather of 'transcendence in immanence.' Transcendence has nothing to do with some unknown or unknowable 'x' on the hither side of all horizons but is a feature of phenomena as they announce themselves within a horizon. "Transcendence," Merleau-Ponty continues his elaboration of the paradox, means that what is perceived "always contains something more than what is actually given" (PrP 16). At the limit, this "something more" escapes or resists assimilation, remains wild with respect to our attempt to capture and encompass it in our horizon. The phenomenon (and human phenomenon above all) has the capacity to talk back as it were, to surprise us, to explode our horizons. The paradox of immanence and transcendence expresses this two-sidedness of phenomena.[10]

This is not to state the matter in ethical terms, however, and, a few brief sentences on the possibility of morality notwithstanding,

Merleau-Ponty does not explicitly approach alterity from the angle of ethics in the Address.[11] Bréhier's challenge, therefore, somewhat shifts the ground upon which Merleau-Ponty's analysis moves, and opens a more or less untried perspective from which to consider the problem of alterity. If, as phenomenology teaches, the other comes into being for me relative to my horizon, in a lighting that discloses only what in a sense I have been prepared to see, the "exclusion of the ethical other" is indeed a problem, and moreover a practical problem. Does not horizonality menace the other with what Levinas calls "the neutralization of alterity," whereby "a transcendence revealed is inverted into an immanence, the extra-ordinary is inserted into an order, the Other is absorbed into the Same?"[12] Indeed this menace is real, and the "neutralization of alterity," "the exclusion of the ethical other," is always possible. Undoubtedly—and one need not look very far—there is such a thing as blindness to the other, to what in the other is other, and this blindness comes under the auspices not of optometry but of morality.

To disclose the possibility of such blindness is not to create the problem in the first place, however. "From the simple fact that I make morality a problem," Merleau-Ponty continues his response to Bréhier, "you conclude that I deny it. But the question is posed for all of us. . . . It is not the phenomenological method which creates this problem" (PrP 30). If the possibility of blindness to the other is seen as a moral problem, a problem "for all of us," it is manifest that phenomenology did not create this problem. However, and Merleau-Ponty fails to admit this, neither had phenomenology addressed alterity as an explicitly moral problem.

Husserl, at least, approached alterity more as an epistemological than a moral problem. Beginning from the fact that we do perceive others, he undertook to account for this in phenomenological terms. However, the sense in which he established that and how we do perceive the other, and that solipsism is an unworthy position, is much too general. Just as he distinguished the perception of cultural objects from the perception of natural objects, and the perception of human beings from the perception of objects in general, it should be possible to distinguish the perception of the ethical other from the perception of the other *per se*. The silent other presupposed throughout the *Meditations* is a minimal other: more than a mere 'hat and coat' passing under Descartes' window but less than the interlocutor who might protest to us that we have failed to listen or to see. There is a moral equivalent to solipsism—a kind of blindness to the ethical other, or to the other as other—that goes unremarked in Husserl, and that is only marginally recognized in Merleau-Ponty's phenomenology.

Further analysis along these lines might disclose the perception of the ethical other to be somewhat extraordinary. Perhaps, to express the matter in ethical terms, it is not the norm but a task, not something given but something to be accomplished. Merleau-Ponty points in this direction in his response to Bréhier: "When Brunschvicg said that the 'I' is achieved by reciprocity and it is necessary that I become able to think the other as reciprocable with me, he meant that morality is not something given but something to be created" (PrP 30–31). The perception of the ethical other, we might interpret Merleau-Ponty to mean, is not guaranteed by virtue of our having functioning perceptual organs but is further contingent on what we do, or fail to do. In these terms, the moral task would then turn on avoiding the danger of failing to perceive the ethical other.[13]

III

Unfortunately, Merleau-Ponty does not develop his suggestive remarks about alterity and ethics in *The Primacy of Perception*.[14] He does not spell out what it is, as Bréhier awkwardly puts it, to "exclude the ethical other." At the risk of a certain exegetical violence, I want to elaborate this danger of exclusion in terms of what Levinas calls "the imperialism of the same and the I." Levinas describes the mechanics of this imperialism as follows:

> The foreign being, instead of maintaining itself in the inexpungable fortress of singularity, instead of facing, becomes a theme and an object. It fits under a concept already, or dissolves into relations. It falls into the network of a priori ideas, which I bring to bear so as to capture it.[15]

On this account, to exclude the ethical other would be to reduce the other to the same, to assimilate her under some taming category according to which her individual difference(s) would be dissolved. The other gains entry into my world only at the price of surrendering such difference or otherness as does not fit into my "network of a priori ideas." Whatever does not obey the laws of my imperial understanding, whatever cannot be brought to order in the stability of my horizon, is excluded.

This interpretation is at least compatible with some remarks Merleau-Ponty makes in "The Experience of Others," a text compiled from lecture notes to a course he gave at the Sorbonne in 1951 to

1952.[16] "Other people," he says, "are always menaced by the possibility of a stereotype within which the role encloses them. They can thereby disappear and leave only their role" (EOA 57). In these terms, to exclude the ethical other would be to confine them in such ready-made concepts as might be at our disposal, to see the other only *as* an instantiation of some type at the expense of being blind to whatever about them might not conform to our imperial projections. The stereotype, like what Levinas calls the "concept" or the "network of a priori ideas," would function to "neutralize" the other, to make the other the "same."

Merleau-Ponty's remarks about stereotyping are extremely basic, however, the stuff of an introductory psychology course almost, and they advance our understanding of these matters very little. Moreover, he is sketchy about what, in positive terms, it is to perceive the ethical other. "Within this whole analysis," he announces, "we will emphasize that the perception of other people is the perception of a freedom which appears through a situation" (EOA 57). This announcement, however, is not fulfilled in the remainder of his text.[17]

What is interesting about this text, however, is not so much what Merleau-Ponty says about perception directly but rather a very fertile analogy he makes between perception and language. "Psychoanalysis," he says, gives us the insight that "to perceive other people is to decipher a language" (EOA 45). Taken by itself, this could mean just about anything, but later he explicates it in connection with stereotyping:

> One cannot help but notice how much the perception of other people becomes increasingly comparable to language. Indeed, a language [*un langage*] in danger of becoming stereotypic can be distinguished from fertile language. (EOA 57)[18]

Whereas Merleau-Ponty never develops the distinction between 'stereotypic' and 'freedom-respecting' perception (let us say, between the perception of the other *per se* and the perception of the ethical other), he does say a great deal about the distinction between stereotypic and fertile language. To be sure, not much of this is said in "The Experience of Others," but, as we shall see, what little is said is enough to connect with a rich discussion of language that runs throughout his writing, and in terms of which the issue I am teasing out of Merleau-Ponty comes into view in a more promising way.

In the final analysis perception proves to be too narrowing a focus for analyzing our experience of others. Even in Merleau-Ponty, the analysis of perception has been dominated by the paradigm of the gaze, which is woefully inadequate for capturing our experience of others. Along these lines, the other who appears at the terminal point of the gaze is almost always silent, and the initiative is placed on the side of the beholder. Given the role language plays in our dealings with people, this is a remarkably bizarre way to stage the scene of our encounter with the other, and it is only to be expected that analysis which finds its point of departure in the gaze should be severely restricted. When, on the other hand, we consider the other as someone who speaks, and who speaks to us, the problem of alterity is radically transformed.

With this in mind, let us return to Merleau-Ponty's distinction between fertile and stereotypic language in "The Experience of Others." Fertile language, he elaborates, "employs signs which follow some as yet unconfirmed rules. The interlocutor, to the degree that he understands, goes beyond what he already knows. The meanings [*signification*] involved in such a language are open" (EOA 57). What is here called fertile as opposed to stereotypic language is approximately what, in other places, he variously calls speaking language (*le langage parlant*) as opposed to sedimented language (*le langage parlé*); originary speech (*la parole originaire*) as opposed to secondary speech (*la parole secondaire*); or again, the speaking word (*la parole parlante*) as opposed to ready-made language (*le langage tout fait*).[19]

The distinction between stereotypic and fertile language (or its rough equivalent) first arises in the *Phenomenology of Perception*. Stereotypic, sedimented, secondary, or ready-made speech (he is constantly shifting his terms) is there described as follows:

> We live in a world where speech is an *institution*. For all these many commonplace utterances, we possess within ourselves ready-made meanings. They arouse in us only second order thoughts; these in turn are translated into other words which demand from us no real effort of expression and will demand from our hearers no effort of comprehension.... The linguistic and the intersubjective world no longer surprises us,... and it is within a world already spoken and speaking that we think. (PhP 184)

Stereotypic language then is the reserve of ready-made meanings at our disposal: what has already been said, meaning already constituted, already become commonplace. With Levinas, we might think of these ready-made meanings as the "set of a priori ideas" in virtue of which we "neutralize alterity." Much of speech is idle talk captive to the stereotypes, cliches, stock meanings, and commonplace utterances of ready-made language.[20] Nothing new is said or heard. Everything is more of the same, a repetition of what has already been said before.

Originary, constituting, or fertile language, on the other hand, is open to alterity and brings new meaning into existence. It "formulates for the first time"; as does, for example the speech of "the child uttering its first word, of the lover revealing his feelings, of the 'first man who spoke,' or of the writer and philosopher who reawaken primordial experience anterior to all traditions" (PhP 178–9 n.1). Fertile language goes beyond meaning already constituted and "succeeds only by bending the resources of constituted language to some fresh usage" (PhP 389).

IV

Wherever Merleau-Ponty draws this distinction, and whatever the various terms by means of which it is expressed, the issue is always the same: how is it possible for the new to emerge in our experience? What is it for a speaker or writer to express something new, to use language creatively to bring new meaning into existence? Or, alternatively, what is it for a listener or a reader to learn something new, to win from the speech of the other something more and perhaps different than one puts into it? This latter formulation of the question in terms of the listener or reader turns out to be quite similar to the question I have been exploring in connection with the perception of others: "the same difficulty is involved in understanding how words arranged in propositions can signify anything else to us except our own thought, how the movements of a body patterned into gestures or action can present us with someone else other than ourselves, how we are able to find in these spectacles anything other than we have put into them" (PW 139). This passage from *The Prose of the World* (despite being fragmentary and unfinished, it gives the most complete and sustained analysis of reading in Merleau-Ponty's works), proves to be wonderfully rich in resources for rethinking the theme of alterity and ethics that we originally examined at the level of perception.

Fundamental to this analysis is a distinction between "sedimented language" [*le langage parlé*], "language after the fact, or language as an institution," and "speech" [*le langage parlant*], "language which creates itself in its expressive acts" (PW 10).[21] The emergence of new meaning in reading, the genuine encounter with the other, occurs, if at all, in a dialectical movement between these two terms, which I shall try to describe.

"Sedimented language," Merleau-Ponty elaborates, "is the language the reader brings with him, the stock of accepted relations between signs and the familiar significations without which he could never have begun to read" (PW 13). It is the body of stereotypes or "network of a priori ideas" in terms of which we appropriate what we read; more generally the horizon we project upon the text and into which we place what we read.[22] In order to be able to read Merleau-Ponty, for example, the words and phrases he uses must awaken in me thoughts which were mine to begin with. At least some passages must gear onto what I already know (or at least think I know). Reading takes place not upon a *tabula rasa* but in the setting of a horizon.

If this were the whole story—if, as Merleau-Ponty puts it, the words of a text limited "themselves to vibrating like chords the listener's machinery of acquired significations or to arousing some reminiscence" (PW 142)—I should never be able to learn anything. The text would be but an empty sign reminding me of what in some sense I must already have known. I could get out of the text only what I put into it. There would be nothing new, but rather always more of the same. Communication would be an illusion, and solipsism the order of the day.

Of course, as we shall see, the hermeneutical fact that the reader necessarily brings a "network of a priori ideas" to bear upon the text, must project her prejudices upon it, is not the whole story. Nevertheless, practically speaking, it is possible for reading to take place as if this were the whole story. Undoubtedly, there is such a thing as a solipsistic reading of a text, a reading that catches only what it throws, that is blind to anything it cannot catch in its net of "a priori ideas" or readymade meanings, that excludes whatever cannot be comfortably included in the reader's sphere of immanence. Undoubtedly, there is such a thing as an imperialistic reading—analytic philosophy furnishes abundant examples—that sentences whatever does not obey its (merely contingent) laws to such terms as "nonsense," "charlatanism," "nihilism" and the like: a good part of Plato, half of Kant, most of Hegel, continental philosophy, and so on. Probably more than anyone else, Derrida has sensitized us to the forces at work in this kind of reading. I believe that such sensitivity—moral sensitivity I would venture to say—is what informs the current interest in alterity in continental philosophy.[23]

Sedimented language being the source of the danger here, the answer to the problem of imperialism or solipsism would not be its negation, the empty head of the realist, let us say, or an absolute silence before the other. The source of the danger is also integral to its resolution. As Merleau-Ponty says with regard to perception (and it is remarkable how much he sounds like Gadamer talking about prejudice): "That everything which exists for me should be mine, and not qualify as a being for me except on condition of being framed in my field, does not prevent the appearance of the other—on the contrary, it makes that appearance possible . . ." (PW 138).

In connection with perception, we saw that immanence and transcendence are two complementary sides of the perceptual phenomenon. A similar complementarity obtains in language. Sedimented language, which pulls the other into the orbit of our horizon and threatens to reduce the other to the same, is complemented by speech, which Merleau-Ponty defines as a power of transcendence: "speech [contrasted with sedimented language] is the operation through which a certain arrangement of already available signs and significations alters and then transfigures each of them, so that in the end a new signification is secreted" (PW 13).[24] Note that this creative power of language makes use of and requires sedimented language. The new emerges, if at all, as a reconfiguration of the old. The book "makes use of everything I have contributed in order to carry me beyond it" (PW 11), Merleau-Ponty says. Sedimented language does not prevent the appearance of new meaning—on the contrary, it makes it possible.

There is a certain circularity between the two sides of language or reading, a circularity that echoes the paradox of immanence and transcendence. I can encounter the text only by assimilating its language to my ends, so to speak, but by so doing (and only by so doing) I open myself to experience something in the text that goes beyond what I put into it. This circularity recalls the hermeneutic circle. And, as Heidegger says, "What is decisive is not to get out of the circle but to come into it in the right way."[25] But what does it mean to come into it "in the right way?"

It means at least to keep the circle open, to be aware and vigilant about the possibility of closing the circle (solipsism) and excluding the other. The problem posed by this circularity is not a theoretical problem to be 'solved' by yet another rewrite of the *Cartesian Meditations* but a practical problem to be lived: a "task" as Heidegger puts it. Nevertheless, theory and description are important insofar as they enable a better understanding of the task and the danger. Merleau-Ponty's work is helpful in this regard. For Merleau-Ponty, reading becomes a metaphor for the experience of the other, and his illumination of the task of reading throws light on the task of experiencing the other as truly other.

V

By way of concluding (and tying together some of the threads running through this analysis) I will elaborate this chiasm between reading and experiencing the other with an interpretation of an extraordinary passage from *The Prose of the World*. In this passage Merleau-Ponty distinguishes two moments in the experience of alterity:

> My relation to a book begins with the easy familiarity of the words
> of our language, of ideas that are part of our makeup, in the same
> way that my perception of the other is at first sight perception of
> the gestures and behavior belonging to "the human species." But if
> the book really teaches me something, if the other person is really
> another, at a certain stage I must be surprised, disoriented. If we
> are to meet not just through what we have in common but in what
> is different between us—which presupposes a transformation of
> myself and of the other as well—then our differences can no longer
> be opaque qualities. They must become meaning. (PW 142)

"Surprise and disorientation" interrupt our attempts to situate the
text/other in terms of already-acquired meanings. Surprise is surprise only relative to anticipation—a surprise is always something
different or other than expected. Disorientation, likewise, is the loss
of orientation. The text/other is surprising and disorienting insofar as
it does not fit into our "network of a priori ideas," deviates from the
norms of our sedimented language.[26]

But for Merleau-Ponty this difference as deviation is not yet a
genuine experience of the text/other. The difference, he says, must
become meaning. He continues:

> In the perception of the other, this happens when the other organ-
> ism, instead of 'behaving' like me, engages with the things in my
> world in a style that is at first mysterious to me but which at least
> seems to me a coherent style because it responds to certain possi-
> bilities which fringed the things in my world. Similarly, when I am
> reading, there must be a moment where the author's intention
> escapes me, where he withdraws himself. Then I catch up from
> behind, fall into step, or else I turn over a few pages and, a bit later,
> a happy phrase brings me back and leads me to the core of the new
> signification, and I find access to it through one of its "aspects"
> which was already part of my experience. (PW 142–3)

"The book really teaches me something," "the other person is really
other," only when understood, and understanding is the reintegration
of difference.

Such reintegration, however, is different from the integration or
assimilation that takes place in imperialistic reading. Whereas imperialistic reading reduces the text/other to the same, here the text/
other is at least initially an enigma or anomaly relative to the 'same':
both the same and the other are transformed in the moment of
reintegration (in what Gadamer would call 'a fusion of horizons'). The
horizon into which the other is reintegrated is no longer the same;
the reader is transformed.

Of course, false synthesis is always possible, but this is all the more reason to be vigilant. In any event, it is not guaranteed that we will be respectful of otherness, and this contingency is the proper concern of ethics. In the passage just cited Merleau-Ponty tells the story with a happy ending, but, as he knows very well, this ending is contingent: "*If* the book really teaches me something"; "*if* the other person is really another; "*if* we are to meet not just through what we have in common but in what is different between us." Wherever there is an "if" there is an "if not," and the story could also be told in these terms. The circle of interpretation *can be* quite vicious. For example, it is possible to be so blind as not to be "surprisable." Or, having been surprised or disoriented, it is always possible to manage the disorienting text/other in such a way as to preserve our horizon intact by assimilating it under such catch-all categories as "incoherent," "nonsense" and the like.

Merleau-Ponty does not elaborate on the relationship between the "if" and the silently implied "if not," but the conditional invites us to ask what the conditional is conditional upon. To the extent that the answer to this question involves something like 'human freedom,' the conditional—the difference between the conditional "if" and "if not"—names a task. How we respond to this task is a measure of our moral integrity.

Notes

1. Merleau-Ponty says this in the context of a discussion about reading Husserl in "The Philosopher and His Shadow" (S 159).

2. This is taken from the poem cited on the front page of Gadamer's *Truth and Method,* trans. Garrett Barden and John Cumming (New York: The Seabury Press, 1975).

3. Richard Bernstein gives several examples of this kind of moralizing, and moreover succeeds in bringing out a neglected ethical dimension in Derrida's thought, in "Serious Play: The Ethico-Political Horizon of Jacques Derrida," *The Journal of Speculative Philosophy* 1, no. 2 (1987): 93–117.

4. During this time Merleau-Ponty was becoming increasingly interested in language, and was thinking about perception in terms of language, and language in terms of perception.

5. This has been published in English under the title "The Primacy of Perception" (in PrP).

6. Edmund Husserl, *Cartesian Meditations,* trans. Dorion Cairns (The Hague: Martinus Nijhoff, 1977); hereafter, CM. Merleau-Ponty had studied

this work as early as 1935, and gives his most detailed analysis of it in *Consciousness and the Acquisition of Language* (CAL 40–48).

7. M. C. Dillon's analysis of this issue in Husserl is very instructive, especially since he approaches it in the context of a study of Merleau-Ponty. *Merleau-Ponty's Ontology,* (Bloomington, Indiana: Indiana University Press, 1988), pp. 114–129.

8. Dillon builds his interpretation of Merleau-Ponty around this paradox and convincingly demonstrates how vital it is in Merleau-Ponty's thinking. See *Merleau-Ponty's Ontology,* especially pp. 1–50.

9. Heidegger described this horizonality in terms of the "as-structure" of understanding. We always (except in cases of privation) perceive something as something. The phenomenon, as a condition of being a phenomenon, is grasped according to the forestructures of understanding, and so on. For example, see *Being and Time* (seventh edition), trans. John Macquarrie and Edward Robinson (New York and Evanston: Harper and Row, 1962), pp. 187–92.

10. The "wild" dimension of the phenomenon becomes increasingly accented in Merleau-Ponty's later philosophy. Later on, when in place of "the phenomenon" he speaks of "the flesh," this two-sidedness will be expressed in terms of "intertwining" and "reversibility." Things are given, but only half-given—what presents itself has depth, pregnancy, latency. There is transcendence, to be sure, but for Merleau-Ponty the transcendent always has a sign. Thus the invisible of which he speaks is not the absolute other to the visible (as transcendental realism would have it) but is "hinged" to the visible. The visible is not altogether visible, not a full plenitude, but only half-open. The invisible is not a sheer nothing but a determinate invisible, the invisible of *this* visible.

11. He makes a few remarks about morality on p. 27, but the little he says does not go very far.

12. Emmanual Levinas, "Meaning and Sense" in *Collected Philosophical Papers* (The Hague: Martinus Nijhoff, 1977), p. 103.
    I borrow from Levinas to help set up the problem I see emerging in Merleau-Ponty, but do not mean to extend the comparison between Levinas and Merleau-Ponty very far. I think it could be extended considerably, especially around the theme of the "rehabilitation of the sensible," but there are also important points of contrast. Most notably, I think that while Merleau-Ponty would accept what Levinas has to say about "imperialism," he would reject his account of the genuine experience of others as being too mystical; as presupposing an undialectical notion of transcendence.

13. Merleau-Ponty himself licences me to speak of "danger" in this connection. He writes: "I would like to answer briefly one of M. Bréhier's remarks—namely, that it is 'serious' to posit the other in his relations with us

and to posit him in the world. I think you mean to say 'ethically *dangerous*' " (PrP 30).

14. Certainly he never did so in the *Phenomenology of Perception*.

15. Emmanual Levinas, "Philosophy and the Idea of Infinity" in *Collected Philosophical Papers*. The phrase "imperialism of the Same and the I" appears on p. 55, but the quotation is taken from p. 50.

16. Maurice Merleau-Ponty, "The Experience of Others," trans. Hugh Silverman and Fred Evans, *Review of Existential Psychology and Psychiatry* 18, nos 1, 2, 3: 33–63. Hereafter EOA.

17. Of course, it must be kept in mind that this text is transcribed from lecture notes, and it is impossible to say what might have been lost (or found) in the transcription.

18. In the text Merleau-Ponty distinguishes speaking language (la langue) and communicating language (le langage), which is somewhat puzzling and anomalous. I believe there must have been some lines crossed in the transcription.

19. Whatever Merleau-Ponty's virtues as a writer, terminological consistency is not one of them. A whole series of roughly equivalent distinctions come and go throughout his texts. A partial list of shifting terms in the *Phenomenology* would include: *la parole originaire* (first-hand or originary speech); *la parole authentique* (authentic speech) vs. *la parole seconde* (secondary speech); *la parole parlante* (speaking word) vs. *la parole parlée* (spoken speech); *la parole originaire* (originary speech) vs. *la parole secondaire* (secondary speech). In *The Prose of the World*, he typically expresses this as a distinction between *le langage parlé* (sedimented language) and *le langage parlant* (speech) [e.g., p. 10]. In *The Visible and the Invisible*, he often uses the following terms: *le langage tout fait* (ready-made language) vs. *la parole parlante* (speaking word); *la parole constituée* (constituted speech).

These distinctions all amount to more or less the same thing in Merleau-Ponty's writings. What is expressed in them is also very similar to what is expressed in Richard Rorty's distinction between "normal and abnormal discourse" (which is itself a "generalized" version of Thomas Kuhn's distinction between "normal and abnormal science"). For example, see Rorty's *Philosophy and the Mirror of Nature* (Princeton: Princeton University Press, 1979), p. 320.

20. Compare with Heidegger's distinction between Idle Talk (*Gerede*) and Saying (*Sagen*).

21. Of course, this is more or less the same distinction as we have already examined in terms of fertile and stereotypic language.

22. In this text, Merleau-Ponty often uses the language of projection and introjection to describe communication. For example:

"Whether speaking or listening, I project myself into the other person, I introduce him into my own self. Our conversation resembles a struggle between two athletes in a tug-of-war. The speaking "I" abides in its body. Rather than imprisoning it, language is like a machine for transporting the "I" into the other person's perspective." (PW 19)

He is very careful about this terminology, however, and sensitive to a bad use of projection, as in dualism, as where "projection" indicates meaning externally imposed upon an empty sign. "Thus we must have another idea of projection, according to which the other's speech not only awakes in me ready-made thoughts. . . ." (PW 118)

23. Derrida makes a number of interesting remarks linking deconstruction and the concern to respect alterity. For example, see "Deconstruction and the Other: Dialogue with Jacques Derrida," in Richard Kearney, *Dialogues with Contemporary Continental Thinkers* (Manchester: Manchester University Press, 1984). Two revealing passages: "Deconstruction is, in itself, a positive response to an alterity which necessarily calls, summons, or motivates it. Deconstruction is therefore a vocation—a response to a call" (p. 118); and, "Deconstruction is not an enclosure in nothingness, but an openness towards the other" (p. 124).

24. I have not quoted the preceding sentence in which Merleau-Ponty speaks about prejudice in a way that is easily open to misinterpretation: "Speech is the book's call to the unprejudiced reader." It is clear from what Merleau-Ponty says in other places that by "unprejudiced" he cannot mean "without prejudices" but rather something more like "open-minded."

25. *Being and Time,* p. 195. Heidegger elaborates at least this much about "the right way": "To be sure, we genuinely take hold of this possibility only when, in our interpretation, we have understood that our first, last, and constant task is never to allow our fore-having, fore-sight, and fore-conception to be presented to us by fancies and popular conceptions."

26. One could identify a genre of writing that is dialectically structured in such a way as to protect itself (at least to the extent that writing can) from imperialistic misreading. Here one could articulate a strategy of evading the reader's "network of a priori ideas": for example, Nietzsche (with his hammer carefully aimed at the readers image of him); Kierkegaard (who plays hide and seek with the reader through his pseudonyms); and Derrida (who writes in such a way as to challenge the conventions of reading).

5

Merleau-Ponty and the "Backward Flow" of Time: The Reversibility of Temporality and the Temporality of Reversibility

ba ba

Glen A. Mazis

> In order to see in reflection a creative deed, a reconstruction of past thought which was not prefigured in it and which yet validly particularizes it, because it alone furnishes us with an idea of it and because the past in itself is for us as if it had never been—it would be necessary to develop an intuition of time to which the *Meditations* only contain a brief allusion. (PhP 44)

The work of Merleau-Ponty is not only an attempt to articulate a new understanding of the way in which we are embodied beings, to affirm the ambiguity of a nondualistic philosophy, to inaugurate an indirect ontology that uncovers "the flesh of the world" within which the oppositions of being and nonbeing, the one and the many, identity and difference are seen to be intertwinings, and to describe the place of language within an expressive context of perception, but it is also primarily an attempt to think through seriously the primordiality of time as itself an ongoing becoming and not merely the containing structure of becoming. In this task, Merleau-Ponty carried further the project of his predecessor Henri Bergson in articulating the "within-timeness" of things. The notion of reversibility, which Merleau-Ponty articulated towards the end of his life, can only be fully understood if one understands its founding on Merleau-Ponty's radical understanding of time. Merleau-Ponty came to realize that it was the radical enmeshment of perception within temporality that was at the heart of the reversibility of perception, a theme imbedded within his work but not easily appreciated.[1] Merleau-Ponty also realized that time itself was chiasmatic, was reversible, and it was only *as such* that it was *the heart* of the reversibility of perception. This insight, however, had been haunting the pages of Merleau-Ponty's text throughout his work. The notion of *Fundierung* which is central to Merleau-Ponty's description of perception and its possibilities for expression in the *Phenomenology* already contains within it, the seeds of the notion of reversibility. Not surprisingly, it also already casts a radical reconsideration of time that Merleau-Ponty is still working out even in his last "working notes," gathered and published in *The Visible and the Invisible.*

In the passage cited from the *Phenomenology of Perception,* Merleau-Ponty suggests that Descartes' thought, that the omnipotent deceiver could never make it be the case that Descartes had never existed at this moment when his pronouncement makes him certain of his existence, contains an allusion to a notion of time that Descartes avoided exploring. It is that intuition of *experience within time* that provides the certainty that Descartes experiences in the cogito, but it is an intimation of a different sort of certainty than that which Descartes sought. As Merleau-Ponty puts it, "Reflection is not absolutely transparent for itself, it is always given to itself in an *experience*" (PhP 42). It is that experience which provides our certainty as given by time: "The experience of the present is that of being assured of his existence once and for all" (PhP 44). Descartes interprets this certainty as lying in the "presentness of the present, which posits it in advance as an indubitable 'former present' in the series of recollections" (PhP 44). In other words, for Descartes, there is projected a reflective wresting of an essence from the ongoing temporal existence: a return from a vantage outside time to the lived experience that will yield the moment as a static and certain being. From the standpoint of mental substance, there is an intelligibility that can be rescued from the chaos of becoming that provides certainty. In quite the opposite manner, Merleau-Ponty discovers an understanding of time in which we find a certainty in the enveloping richness and indeterminacy of ongoing becoming. The moment gives itself as having-been-*originating* in the unfolding of time, as continually becoming an ineradicable source of later unfoldings and transformations, and this experience of temporality is at the heart of what Merleau-Ponty called "perceptual faith."

Descartes' assertion remains only an allusion to an "intuition of time," an intimation of a different type of certainty, since it is one of those instants in which Descartes is describing an *experience* that his own theoretical interpretation of this experience invalidates. The experience is of the "lived certainty" of perception in the becoming of time. It is this certainty that is the founding of a different sort of truth than Descartes sought, but which is Merleau-Ponty's starting and end point: "We are in the realm of truth and it is 'the experience of truth' which is self-evident" (PhP xvi). This experience is one in which the open indeterminacy of the moment has its own kind of certainty, its distinctive self-evidence, in its undeniable hold upon us as inseparable from its enrichment and transformation in time. This is why in this passage Merleau-Ponty calls reflection a "creative deed": it is a working with the unfolding of *sens* within the becoming of time which calls forth an understanding "which was not prefigured in it and which yet validly particularizes it" (PhP 44). The "reflected" was not simply "there," as static, but within time *becomes* with reflection. For Descartes, who sought a mathematical certainty that was clear and distinct, or in other words, determinate and transparent, this lived certainty within experience was discounted. Descartes sought to find a certainty outside of time, to wrench experience into a graspable *ur*-experience "beneath" or "outside" the flow of time, the flow of experience, that would provide a firm foundation. However, Merleau-Ponty saw there was no indubitable source of experience "beneath" experience. Experience has its own certainty: an indeterminate, open, evolving "thickness" that is undeniable in its ensnarement and relentless development and transformation.

The certainty of this moment for Merleau-Ponty is in the fact that the future will return to this moment to find it as it was and yet as it never had been until that moment. Merleau-Ponty wants to explicate the thickness of a temporality in which significant experiences, in their open indeterminacy, are fated to continually return to themselves in a never ending unfolding and enfolding. This temporal surge and return is the becoming of these significant experiences, which, from within the palpable presence of a haunting yet elliptical future, they never were and yet had always been. This is the *sens* of a perceptual life within a perceptible world in which the flux and flow of unfolding meaning derives from the temporality of the body, which itself participates in the same flux and flow so that it cannot completely show itself gathered into a point of intelligibility. The working out, which is always retrograde as well as progressive, is the flesh inaugurating a depth of weavings and returnings, so that the continuous movement opens "the circle of the touched and the touching . . . of the visible and the seeing" (VI 142). This encirclement of perception, I hope to show is the play of time, the circularity of time, returning to its depths. Equally significant, and perhaps more so, are the rare

moments in which the chiasm of time jolts forth, palpably transfiguring worlds: moments worthy of description as being the fever pitch of
this always operative movement.

When one thinks in what sense perception could be thought of as
reversible—that one is seen in seeing and that in this doubled movement lies the nascence of one's seeing, and equally that the seen is in
some sense seeing in being seen—one tends to think the sense of this
expression in spatial terms as vectors or directionalities going one
way then another. Not only that, but the sense of space that one
tends to employ is that of a grid of positions within a neutral contain-
ment housing discrete, determinate "objects"—a Cartesian space. If
in thinking through Merleau-Ponty's philosophy, one slips into this
way of thinking, then the notion of reversibility is either nonsensical
or at best "poetically metaphoric." Only within the *becoming* of perception, thought, and speech, within the world's ceaseless "coming to
be" does the sense of reversibility emerge.

Reversibility is an achievement within time. Reversibility is an
historical achievement. Cartesian mental substance as outside space
and time could never be "caught" within reversibilities. When Cezanne
points to a heightened sense of reversibility emerging between him,
the painter, and Mount St. Victoire, the painted, in which he is now
painting the mountain painting itself through him, seeing him as he
sees it and seeing itself through his seeing it, there is a folding back
on itself of an unfolding encounter within time. Reversibility is the
temporality of the body as a 'working through' of its engagement with
what is perceived within an enveloping world. Within the temporal
thickness of acts of perception and expression a span is realized where
there had been gaps, a span which reaches backward to transform
the meaning of past gaps, which still remain, but are now electrified
with the charge of later connections. Certainly, during ten years of
painting that mountain, there are moments when Cezanne is lost to
himself, become more mountain than man, his flesh rocklike within a
strange resonance in which the perceiver is called as potentially perceptible in the same ways as the perceived. Such moments, and other
moments of displacement that we will explore, become part of a temporal thickness which alters both previous and later moments of
experienced disconnection, that otherwise might emerge as starkly
non-reversible, but will instead resound with such deeper instants of
resonant decenteredness essential to reversibility. The reversals of
reversibility are temporal and spatial, or rather such a distinction
itself is undermined by reversibility. Only when the sense of space is
understood on the basis of radical temporality in the way Merleau-

Ponty understood it, and only when time itself is seen as reversible, is the reversibility of perception, of the flesh of the world, understandable.

The Reversibility of Temporality

In Merleau-Ponty's early descriptions of perception, he uncovered a different sense of depth that increasingly became the key to his understanding of his new "indirect ontology" as eventually expressed in *The Visible and the Invisible* and "Eye and Mind." As articulated in the *Phenomenology of Perception,* depth is:

> This being simultaneously present in experiences which are nevertheless mutually exclusive, this implication of one in the other, this contraction into one perceptual act of a whole possible process, constitute the originality of depth. It is the dimension in which things or elements of things envelop each other, whereas breadth and height are the dimensions in which they are juxtaposed (PhP 264–5).

Experiences which are mutually exclusive, which should open gaps in our experience, which considered logically should cause spaces and times to be juxtaposed in their separateness, are instead enveloping, enjambing, of one another in the thickness of a present (of depth). This "going together" of incompossibles is the mutual envelopment despite difference in time and space which gives perception a primary depth out of which other dimensions emerge. By the time of the writing of the *The Visible and the Invisible,* Merleau-Ponty has come to see the perceiver as perceiving "by dehiscence of fission of its own mass" (VI 146); furthermore, the perceived "is not a chunk of absolutely hard, indivisible being . . . but is rather a sort of straits between exterior horizons and interior horizons ever gaping open" (VI 132). The perceiver and perceived are "two vortexes . . . the one slightly decentered with respect to the other" (VI 138). Rather than being destructive to sense, this dispersion of perceiver and perceived as open and enveloping is sense's depth as reversible and chiasmatic. Like the strands of a chromosome that constitute its being in their encircling chiasm, their folding over one another, the decentering of the perceiver within the world and the world within the perceiver leaves both as a "turning about one another" (VI 264). This depth of perception in which perceiver and perceived are both gaping open, not totalizable, means one is seen in seeing and the seen comes to see. Depth, for Merleau-Ponty, arises within dehiscence, contralogically across gaps, and these jostlings are not merely spatial, they are equally temporal.

In Merleau-Ponty's notes of the fall of 1960, where he understands "time as chiasm" (VI 267), he comes to see time as having a depth in which it "leaps" gaps in order to be one flow: "a point of time can be transmitted to the others without 'continuity' without 'conservation' " (VI 267). These flashings of time in which one moment comes to others "without continuity" suggest how moments of time can transform a past across gaps, as "sudden reversibilities." In addition to a temporality of reversibility in which the past keeps becoming itself through unfoldings which transform it, the temporal flow takes on an even greater depth in its own chiasmatic reversals, foldings back, which are of a more wild or brute sort. Husserl's sense of a flow of time consciousness that unfolds in its unity of protentional and retentional syntheses is rejected for a time more chiasmatic, more brute, more "tufted." When time is seen to be found within the unfolding of the body's perceptual explorations, one sees the ways in which, held within the landscapes, there are depths which cause the perceiver's time to burst, to reverse, to be released into the "straits gaping open" within things, landscapes, that hold us in holding them. Merleau-Ponty has moved from Husserl's analysis of progressive time to one "without fictitious 'support' in the psyche" (VI 267), to a time *lodged within the world* in its savage or brute being.

Merleau-Ponty, in opening the depth dimension of time, points to part of the phenomenon of time in which its overall flow is transfixed and transformed, irradiated from within by leaps and lateralizing flashes of *sens* which emerge at that moment in a manner different than the development which emerges from the conserved retentional significance in its continual unfolding. This jolting point of institution of a new meaning is one which transforms the entire previous developmental unfolding until this point is a chiasmatic one, in which time not only leaps up in transformation, but also reverses its flow. This is the temporality that Merleau-Ponty has sought throughout his work, inspired by Bergson but surpassing him, a temporality that functions according to what he now calls the "barbaric principle":

> It is a question of finding in the present, the flesh of the world (and not in the past) an 'ever new' and an 'always the same'—A sort of time of sleep (which is Bergson's nascent duration, ever new and always the same). The sensible, Nature, transcend the past present distinction, realize from within a passage from one into the other (VI 267).

At this point in his thought, Merleau-Ponty realized that there were differing dimensionalities within the upsurge of time. Time, itself, was not unitary in its internal structurations, but rather its unity was seen to be the presumptive unity of "perceptual faith." This is the "unity in depth" of incompossibles which nevertheless "go together." The past is itself present, not just through the latter's retentional reverberations or the former's protential reach, but also as a bursting of the world in tufts [*en touffe*][2] outside the realm of intentionalities and acts. The present itself could be seen to be located within a past of lateralizing, flashing reversals that are part of the verticality of Being, the "passages from one into the other" between temporal ecstaces that are leaps, "barbaric," and aside from the eidetic laws of unfolding phenomena.

For Merleau-Ponty, part of the understanding of how the seeing-seen, touching-touched, perceiving-perceived dichotomies had to be overcome in an autochthony in which "activity = passivity" (VI 265) is to see that the reversibility of the flesh is the reversibility of past and present: "Then past and present are *Ineinander,* each enveloping-enveloped—and that itself is the flesh" (VI 268). Although the sequential unfolding and resonating of time as articulated by earlier phenomenologies expressed part of the sense of the perceptual world as temporal, these characteristics were not exhaustive. Time, as the unfolding within one another of the perceiver-perceived, itself folds back across itself, *both* in sudden enfoldings, conflagrating "reversals," *and* within larger temporal rhythms of the becoming of becoming [which we will explore in the next section].

These moments when past and present flash forth in transformative bursts of enveloped-enveloping, are moments when what Merleau-Ponty had from the *Phenomenology* (PhP 70) through the *The Visible and the Invisible* (VI 194) called the "Memory of the World," comes to re-member us, taking us into its body as our body, opening depths of time. It is a heightened coming forth of the reversibility of the flesh:

> That is, that the things have us, and that its not we who have the things. That the being which has been cannot stop having been. The "Memory of the World." (VI 194)

We are brought back to ourselves, to the depths of our past, through being caught up in the sense of perception, the body's sense as a fold in the flesh of the world. The landscape, its things, are not mute: memory is "lodged" there, held, housed, kept, and in the "membering" openness of perceiving-perceived, where the landscape and its things become one's limbs or elongations, one is suddenly re-membered through the landscape to upheavals in time. These "burstings" of time, or "chiasmatic leaps," these "reversings" outside unfolding are of another possibility of time held within the landscape:

> In what sense the visible landscape under my eyes is not exterior
> to, and bound synthetically to ... other moments of time and the
> past, but has them really *behind itself* in simultaneity, inside itself
> and not it and they side by side 'in' time (VI 267).

The depth of the landscape, its things and horizons, hold chiasmatic
possibilities for sudden reversals which short-circuit the usual temporal unfolding.[3]

We can find some help in understanding Merleau-Ponty's conception of the reversibility of temporality in a fictive variation. If we look
at Margaret Atwood's novel, *Surfacing*,[4] we follow the journey of becoming of the narrator as she enters her abandoned childhood Canadian wilderness landscape in search of the sense of her life. From the
first line of the novel, when she states, "I can't believe I'm on this
road again, twisting along past the lake where the white birches are
dying" (9), in search of her missing father, until one of the last lines,
after she has encountered what he has become for her and she states,
"I am part of the landscape, I could be anything, a tree, a deer
skeleton, a rock" (218), there is an exploration of embodied self
refinding its depths in the perceptual world. The entire narrative
hinges upon certain key instants of perception in which time crosses
back upon itself to become something transformed with "new" depths
of both past and present emerging from sudden reversibilities of perception within these chiasms of temporality as held by the landscape.
These fevered moments occur as the narrator moves towards a heightened sense of being caught up in "the flesh of the world" of this
Canadian landscape: "I am not an animal or a tree, I am the thing in
which the trees and animals move and grow, I am a place" (213).

The novel strikes even the casual reader with its intense sense of
the bodily depths of thought, memory and imagination; its exploration of how the body is inseparable from its landscape; and its star-
tling collapses of our sense of the sequential unfolding of time. The
novel evokes a sense in which the meaning of the narrator's understanding of her life and her body is "held" or "buried" within the
backwoods Canadian landscape, the abandoned cabin, the haunted
garden, the dark lakes and the bloated corpse. Also within the recalci-
trance of things, even old Indian things, like rock paintings, there is a
key to a deeper time that suffers oblivion by the signifying power of
the flow of events in a more progressive time. The temporal depths,
still present within the layers of meaning of the landscape and within
ancient and natural objects, are repressed by the sense of sequential
time. However, the body opens a conflagration that undermines this
effacing flow. Deep underwater, beneath her canoe, the narrator is

shattered by the open-eyed vision of death that is her father's corpse, that instantaneously is also the dead fetus scraped out of her womb years before, that simultaneously is also the death in the eyes of her mother in a Canadian wilderness: in this scorching moment time leaps, becomes lightening, past flares in overwhelming presentness and into other promiscuities, present fires out into a past at the heart of moments long gone out but always fated to burn in this instant of passing, agonized slippage. Time past, present and future will always be different for the narrator, yet these transforming reversals trail their own fragility, will themselves keep becoming for her.

Although such moments, such "tufts" of *sens* are rare, they are part of the power of the reversibility with the landscape, within temporality. The narrator describes how she imagines that for her father and now for her, there were things within this perceptual field, there were landscapes, that could suddenly alter the sense of one's world, one's history:

> He had discovered new places, new oracles, they were things he was seeing the way I had seen; at the end, after the failure of logic. When it happened the first time he must have been terrified, it would be like stepping through a usual door and finding yourself in a different galaxy, purple trees and red moons and a green sun (171).

We may keep such heightened instants of chiasm and transformation at bay, but the barbaric principle is an originating depth within landscapes. The reader of Merleau-Ponty who then reads Atwood is not surprised that in the novel a temporal slippage is entwined with a slippage in perception and being between the narrator and a forbidding Canadian landscape. At such openings of the sense of one's enmeshment, which is time, the reversibility of the landscape does become palpable, and the narrator sees that "the forest leaps upward, enormous . . . everything is made of water, even the rocks . . . I lean against a tree, I am a tree leaning" (212). In time's shattering transfigurations, its reversing and lateralizing, the sense of the world that the narrator sees, has become seen through the narrator's becoming seen within her depths. These depths had long been rendered invisible. Lodged within the night of her repression, she was not a woman who had ever suffered an abortion, nor was she the student cast aside by her professor-seducer. She had been the divorced women who had left a child somewhere, somehow. In this moment of vision, she becomes what she had always been in the depths of those past (repressed) moments, which might have never come to be without the power of the landscape to blaze this instant of time's chiasm. Caught up with the fabric of this world, the narrator has seen aspects of herself that were uniquely evoked by standing within the vision embedded in this landscape and its objects that she came to see and did finally get to see. Seeing it, she has become seen. Seeing it, she has entered a new time. She has become. The past has become. This is what Merleau-Ponty meant by "the flesh" and its "reversibility."

It is not surprising that Merleau-Ponty abandoned the Husserlian analysis of temporality for several reasons central to his notion of flesh and its reversibility. Merleau-Ponty noted that "Husserl's error is to have described the [temporal] interlocking starting from a *Präsensfeld* considered without thickness, as immanent consciousness" (VI 173). Husserl failed to articulate the "time of the body." For Merleau-Ponty, the missing "thickness" of Husserl's understanding of time is inseparable from his retreat into immanence and his sense of the "interlocking" nature of time-consciousness. As Merleau-Ponty puts it: "Mythology of a self-consciousness to which the word 'consciousness' would refer—There are only *differences* between significations" (VI 171). We will not get beyond the traditional dichotomies, nor articulate the worldly character of the phenomena until we cease to think of consciousness and its "acts," reject the notion of subject, and think the "promiscuity with Being and the world" (VI 239). Merleau-Ponty decentered and detotalized the emergence of significance from a consciousness of syntheses to one within a fluctuating but equilibrating world: the correlative notion of time had to be altered too.

The Temporality of Reversibility

Within the world seen in its verticality, there is not an exhaustive space or a time that is spread out before us and behind us, but rather we find things which speak to us, which touch us, which strain to become visible just as we are seen within an interplay of divergences and dehiscences, joinings and couplings, which always pulls us into the depths of what the things in our world have come to mean. For example, I may be taken up within the thickness of how that particular sofa in its blue, broken-legged, paisley, puffiness has become a particular manifestation of the failure of a relationship in my life as well as my naive hopes which were its space and time. The *sens* of this constellation of hope, failure and pain is still only vaguely present in its self-contradictory moments of present meaning, and was always becoming so in a past that came to be what it was, and in certain moments flared up and forward through the present and its new projections into the past to become that history, although even then, still never quite being so determinately.

The recognition of the perceptual field, as this jostling, bustling summons to see, touch, perceive the *sens* of one's life, as the voices of these many things, seducing one's body into their vortices of significances, coming together in the midst of their difference, is itself the becoming of the play of time, and leads Merleau-Ponty to replace Husserl's diagram of temporality:

> The structure of the visual field, with its near-bys, its far-offs, its horizon, is indispensable for there to be *transcendence,* the model of every transcendence. Apply to the perception of space what I said about the perception of time (in Husserl): Husserl's diagram as a *positivist* projection of the vortex of temporal differentiation. And the *intentional* analysis that tries to compose the field with intentional threads does not see that the threads are emanations and idealizations of one fabric, differentiations of the fabric. (VI 231)

We are in the world in which both, myself and world, are at depths, at interplays, which come together in their incompossibility in the enlacement of time. I come back to myself from the world, whether from the river outside my window, the blue sofa, the Bach violin concerto filling the space of my apartment: "That is, that the things have us, and that it is not we who have the things" (VI 194). As held within the depths of things, one finds one's past in jolts and foldings, weavings and tears, that render time a tufted, chiasmatic implosion and interlacing, as well as an unfolding.

It is in thinking of how radically one is within the field of Being "dotted with lacunae and the imaginary" instead of within a flux of unfolding experiences that Merleau-Ponty takes up Husserl's notion of "rays of time and of the world" (VI 240). He realizes, however, this more radical sense of depth dictates a more radical approach: "The ray of the world does not admit of a noema-noesis analysis" (VI 242). How and what we are towards things can shift and jostle, explode or implode so dehiscently, yet still be fated to burrow into the heart of *what has been* so inexorably, that the radicality of the *sens* of emergent time must be savored in its tufted, reversingly transformative ebbing as well as in its larger progressive flow.

For Merleau-Ponty, there is no present in time, as we have commonly represented it:

> . . . the new present is itself transcendent: one knows that it is not there, that it was just there, one never coincides with it—It is not a

> segment of time with defined contours that would come and set
> itself in place. It is a cycle defined by a central and dominant region
> and with indecisive contours ... (VI 184)

The sense of the present is that there are cycles, circularities turning
towards themselves in their elongations: this is the rhythm of perception, and it is the movement of time. My body is in things, at their
depths. Things do not rend themselves open as unfurling announce-
ments of transparent formulaic significations. They do not transform
themselves as frictionless, weightless, diaphanous meanings. They
hold me, haunt me, hunt me, as the one who may slowly yield parts
of their meaning always heard in echo and endlessly improvising on
their origins. For this reason, Merleau-Ponty must recast Husserl's
sense of the present:

> ... the present, also is ungraspable from close-up, in the forceps of
> attention, it is an encompassing. Study exactly the *Erfullung* of the
> present: the danger of this metaphor: it makes me think that there
> is a *certain void* that has *its own* dimensions and that is filled by a
> defined quantity of the present (VI 195–6).

The present never fills what was somehow "missing" but impending
in time. The past was always there as itself indeterminate, as cyclic.
It dances away from itself in other rhythms that echo and blend,
distend and distort, as what was to come in the next leap of the
improvised jazz line. The present isn't necessarily held to a debt of
time; it is not enslaved to past promises; it renders not the past's due,
but gives the past the present of itself, allowing the past to become
itself, in new depths.

One ongoing metaphor for the reversibility of perception that
runs throughout *The Visible and the Invisible* is the example of two
hands touching. Sartre had also used this metaphor for the impossibility of ever bridging the ontological gap of the for-itself and in-itself,
of the subject confronting an object. For Merleau-Ponty, it is true that
there is a divergence at any one instant between the hand touching
and the hand touched; reversibility does not mean coincidence:

> To begin with, we spoke summarily of a reversibility of the seeing
> and the visible, of the touching and the touched. It is time to em-
> phasize that it is a reversibility always imminent and never real-
> ized in fact. My left hand is always on the verge of touching my
> right hand touching things, but I never reach coincidence (VI 147).

This never quite overlapping is itself the basis for reversibility. There
is always a gap, but one which is shifting, which is almost overcome
at moments, which leaves a vector inscribed, which in its reversals is

slipping now to one side then to another, which, in the becoming of time, becomes itself a "shifting," a "spreading," a "spanning" which itself is the "tissue" of the "flesh of the world." The "almosts," the divergences, the blurrings, the many varieties of the indeterminacies of even such simple instants have themselves a positive significance, a weight, a force, a *sens,* which tokens reversibility within the reversibility of time. What comes back in time to the past as a transforming power itself is a gaping openness, which nevertheless has this transformative power—vortices circling one another. The earlier moments arrived at deeper meaning in that they always had in themselves to be through the later moments which led back to them despite their open shifting. The later instants found themselves rendered in being shifted with the flash of earlier moments now come round to round off these later meanings.

The body is always a "taking back into" no matter how far it reaches out, as is the world as a larger body of which we let ourselves be in this touching-touched. Time and meaning as emerging within the body, time as itself of the body, mean that gaps are the giving to time its play of reversibility in order for there to be manifestation, not as laying out progressively, but as reversing back to continually become. Gaps do not indicate the damning break in a totality: the "hiatus between my right hand touched and my right hand touching . . . is not an ontological void, a non-being: it is spanned by the total being of my body and by that of the world . . ." (VI 148). Within the world as a becoming, there is the movement around vortices of significances, none of which is complete, but rather in its open face of incompleteness has an expressivity taken up into the larger interplay. The crossing and crisscrossing are not between solids in a space that would be removed from time, but are the ebbs and pulsations of passage of an ongoing verticality of time, comprised of circles meeting within the tracking of other circles, meandering about in their windings.

Retrograde Temporality within the Circularity of Becoming

In its reversibility, time circles inside of itself and becomes what it now had to always have been in order to produce this new meaning. In the point of reversibility in which time itself becomes a chiasm, there flares up the sense that "things are the prolongation of my body and my body is the prolongation of the world . . ." (VI 255). This *sens* is always there flooding the body and the world. However, there are moments in which special flarings become emblematic and found a deeper sense of the dimensionalities of reversibility, yet as always

having been there, while still as the new gift of the reversibility of
time.

For a moment, let us enter the flux of a consciousness returning
to such enlaced and impacted moments that have once opened in a
highlighted flare such prolongations and reversibilities, and now are
still coming to do so in a further chiasmatic leap of time sixteen years
later in the small hours of an imagined June 16, 1904 in a bedroom
on Eccles street in Dublin, Ireland. Molly Bloom, the character who
enters Joyce's *Ulysses* in its last chapter in such a way as to make the
reader reexperience the sense of all the preceding chapters in light of
this final, rich internal monologue, lies in bed and also within the
landscape of her childhood environs of Gibraltar:

> . . . and O that awful deepdown torrent O and the sea crimson
> sometimes like fire and the glorious sunsets and the figtrees in the
> Alameda gardens yes and all the queer little streets and the pink
> and blue and yellow houses and the rosegardens and the jessamine
> and geraniums and cactuses and Gibraltar as a girl where I was
> Flower of the mountain yes when I put the rose in my hair like the
> Andalusian girls used or shall I wear a red yes and how he kissed
> me under the Moorish wall and I thought well as well him as
> another and I asked him with my eyes to ask again yes and then he
> asked me would I yes to say yes my mountain flower . . .[5]

As Molly Bloom lies sleepless, she is the landscape of Gibraltar, its
flowers, hills, streets and houses as she is caressed by them as she
caressed them, with her hands, with her eyes, and with her body
rolling on a hill later with Leopold Bloom, for both these times and
others have wound into *a time* for Molly, a time in which the yes goes
back and forth, shuttlelike from Molly to landscape, from Bloom to
Molly, from now to Gibraltar, to another time on a hill, and further
into other interlacings of things and Molly, within a time itself a
chiasm. Here is a fever pitch of the manifestation of reversibility, but
that is Molly's genius. Here, after more than ten years of estrange-
ment from Poldy in their grief over their dead son, today in going to
bed with Blazes Boylan, and in the new developments with Leopold,
most notably his demand that in reversing their decade's custom she
should *bring him* breakfast, that might further develop, Molly has
been led back to a time or rather ahead to a time that was the time of
Gibraltar. The time of Gibraltar of her youth has been made to become again what it was to be in this night of crisis and promise.

Merleau-Ponty's richer description of time allows us to understand how some phenomena might not be simply unfolding and gradu-
ally receding in the passage of time. Many aspects of the world so

appear and take their place within the background of the world and our personal lives. However, there are also quantum leaps in time's passage: rendings, riftings, that are also radical shiftings, birthing transformations. They are not upsurges of creation *ex nihilo*. Time doesn't only "move ahead" in its flow. It circles back. This flow is a risk of time, its play with itself that is a gamble as well as a gambol. In going back, time will surely lose itself and become something else. The present not only transforms, but the past enters the circle of becoming. Molly is a woman able to give voice to haltings, discontinuities, to circularities, to the urgings and openings of the body alive to the world and itself. At least on this night, when the reader gets to know her thoughts, Molly is able to enter and articulate what Merleau-Ponty called in *Eye and Mind* the "deflagration of Being" [*deflagration d l'Etre*] (PrP 180). Time burns itself up in the phoenix fire of its renewal and becoming. Its kindling is the bodily enmeshment in things, in the landscape, in the life lived with others as gestural, embodied beings. Molly, the renowned singer, on this night of June 16, 1904, takes up language to exercise its power to sing the world's being, as Merleau-Ponty had put it.[6] In her fine attunement to her body and the body of her *mater* country she is able to sing time's rondeau: its circular chorus that always returns to begin later refrains, as new but always found in the old and as old echoes but always transformed.

Molly's time of the past which in crisis has become her future promise, which she has already started to become on this eventful day is lodged within Gibraltar, but only what Gibraltar comes to be. Gibraltar ever unfolds the rich overripeness of its caressing offer to Molly in her then young body, which she now comes to be after many years of dormant waiting. This Gibraltar is not in Cartesian space as a collection of objects which could be totalized. Gibraltar for Molly has always been a region of pain and abandonment, by an absent mother, a distant father, and a place of soft, enveloping smells and colors that race with promise and sensuality and beauty and the spirit of resurgence, and the longing regard for which Molly has been a magnet in her lush body and powerful voice and overflowing thought patterns, her way of savoring the nuance. These lush qualities of Molly, in their meaning and style, are the meaning and style of a Gibraltar in its soft night air and scent, its figtree-ed, flowered, winding, sunset-bathed, interlaced streets that insinuate the body's textured affirmation of flowering, of Molly, the flower, and Bloom, the flower, and their coming together, Yes. The time of nos has now become a later path fated to return to the earliest time of Yes, of yes flickering, beckoned, gone, but always possible as where she goes, Yes.

Notes

1. The "common sense" reading often espoused that Heidegger was interested in articulating phenomena from the perspective of time and Merleau-Ponty from that of space. However, this is a misreading of Merleau-Ponty's project.

2. From the introductory paragraph on the section about the nature of the chiasm: "Seeing, speaking, even thinking (with certain reservations, for as soon as we distinguish thought from speaking absolutely we are already in the order of reflection), are experiences of this kind, both irrecusable and enigmatic. They have a name in all languages, but a name which conveys signification in tufts, thickets of proper meanings and figurative meanings, so that, unlike those of science, not one of these names clarifies by attributing to what is named a circumscribed signification. Rather, they are a repeated index, the insistent reminder of a mystery as familiar as it is unexplained, of a light which, illuminating the rest, remains at its source in obscurity" (VI 130).

3. The quoted passage lies in the "working notes" right after the enunciation of the "barbaric principle" of time within the flesh of the world, and right before Merleau-Ponty speaks of understanding "time as chiasm."

4. Margaret Atwood, *Surfacing* (New York: Popular Library, 1976), pp. 166–8. Further references within this essay to this text will be indicated by the page number placed within parentheses.

5. James Joyce, *Ulysses* (New York: Random House, 1986), pp. 643–4.

6. ". . . if we took up the emotional content of the word, which we have called above its 'gestural' sense, which is all-important in poetry, for example, It would then be found that the words, vowels and phonemes are so many ways of 'singing' the world . . ." (PhP 187).

6

Language and Imperfect Consensus: Merleau-Ponty's Contribution to the Habermas-Gadamer Debate

 За За

Shaun Gallagher

A variety of attempts have been made to reconcile, resolve, or further the famous debate between Jürgen Habermas and Hans-Georg Gadamer concerning the universality of hermeneutics.[1] The debate itself takes place on many levels and addresses a plurality of interconnected topics, including the nature of authority and tradition, scientific methodology, the distinction between theory and practice, the nature of historical experience, education, and reflection. Clearly, however, one of the fundamental issues concerns the question of language. It is not simply the case that a consensus about the nature of language would facilitate a more general consensus with regard to other issues of the debate, but, as both Habermas and Gadamer would agree, the very nature of consensus, and thus the kind of consensus one might reach within philosophical debate, depend on language and how language operates.

In this paper my intention is to show how, with respect to the question of language, Merleau-Ponty can act as mediator between Habermas and Gadamer. To the extent that in their debate Gadamer relied on Martin Heidegger's thinking concerning language, while Habermas turned to Jean Piaget to find support for his view, a mediation on this issue can be cast in terms of a mediation between Heidegger and Piaget. Two things are thus required: (1) to show how Merleau-Ponty mediates between Heidegger and Piaget with respect to language; and (2) to indicate some of the implications of this mediation for the Habermas-Gadamer debate. I begin by summarizing

some of the important aspects of this debate, with a special focus on
the question of language.

I

All interpretation is linguistic. This is a central principle of
Gadamer's hermeneutics: language conditions all understanding. "The
phenomenon of understanding . . . shows the universality of human
linguisticality as a limitless medium which carries *everything* within
it—not only the 'culture' which has been handed down to us through
language, but absolutely everything—because everything (in the world
and out of it) is included in the realm of 'understandings' and under-
standability in which we move."[2]

Gadamer has followed Heidegger in recognizing the hermeneutical
significance of language. Language is so much a part of human ability and possibility that it operates as a condition of all human behavior. It shapes our encounters with others; it shades our perceptions of
the world; it makes possible work, play, self-understanding, the development of culture, and the communication of knowledge. Heidegger,
in referring to language as "the house of Being" conceived of language
as something "larger" than that which could be relegated to instrumental use. "Man acts as though *he* were the shaper and master of
language, while in fact *language* remains the master of man."[3] Language is not something that we have complete control over; language
in some real sense has control over us. "If we may talk here of playing
games at all, it is not we who play with words; rather, the essence of
language plays with us . . ."[4]

There is general agreement between Heidegger and Gadamer
that a "definite articulation of the world," built into language, conditions practical and political consciousness, as well as scientific interpretation. Language has a hermeneutical priority which, even if it
does not rule out a prelinguistic dimension, implies that such a dimension can only have its effect through linguistic mediation. Any
attempt to transcend linguistically constrained understanding can
only find expression in the form of language. "Hence," Gadamer contends, "language always forestalls any objection to its jurisdiction. Its
universality keeps pace with the universality of reason" (TM 363).
There is an "intimate unity of language and thought" and in this
sense there can be no extra-linguistic cognition (TM 364).

For Gadamer language is the vehicle which carries the process of
tradition forward into our interpretations. Gadamer suggests that
the model of dialogue or conversation captures our relationship to

traditions through language. "[T]radition is not simply a process that we learn to know and be in command of through experience; it is language [*Sprache*], i.e., it expresses itself like a 'Thou.' A 'Thou' is not an object, but stands in a relationship with us" (TM 321). Language speaks traditions through us. We, as interpreters, are involved in a dialogical relationship with a variety of traditions through the medium of language. This is universally the case; language conditions all of our interpretations, and in so doing introduces the constraints, the prejudgments, of the traditions in which we find ourselves enmeshed. There is no point of view that escapes the domain that is constituted by language. Language is not a possession at the disposal of the interpreter; rather the disposition of the interpreter is to be caught up within language.

In contrast to Gadamer, Habermas requires the possibility of maintaining a critical distance from both language and the process of tradition. His critique of ideology is intended as a critique of the hegemony of traditions and an unmasking of the deceptions and distortions that normally characterize language use. Indeed, his critical hermeneutics aims to establish a communicative relation which escapes the constraints of tradition. Furthermore, Habermas insists, the usual distortions of communication are not all the result of the tradition-context of language; there are extra-linguistic forces, the power relations of political domination and economic exploitation, that no amount of dialogue with traditions will overcome. Habermas cites Albrecht Wellmer to summarize his own objections to Gadamer:

> The Enlightenment knew what a philosophical hermeneutic forgets—that the 'dialogue' which we, according to Gadamer, 'are,' is also a context of domination and as such precisely no dialogue. . . . The universal claim of the hermeneutic approach [can only] be maintained if it is realized at the outset that the context of tradition as a locus of possible truth and factual agreement is, at the same time, the locus of factual untruth and continued force.[5]

From Habermas' perspective, the model of conversation proposed by Gadamer is too trusting since it fails to take into account extra-linguistic factors and the objective and hegemonic force of traditions. Gadamer's model can only work within "the walls of the traditional framework."[6] What the critique of ideology requires, and what Gadamer rules out, is an escape from the constraints of the tradition process—a methodological, scientific distanciation which would allow for an adequate critical reflection that would recognize and thereby escape the distortions introduced by traditions and extra-linguistic forces. The task of Habermas' critical philosophy is precisely to undo the domination of tradition and to promote liberation through self-reflection.

For critical reflection to be possible Habermas requires a view of language different from the one proposed by Gadamer. While hermeneutics is appropriated by Habermas to play a role in critical theory, Gadamer's philosophical hermeneutics does not, on its own, thematize everything that needs to be thematized. In Habermas' view, there is no universality to hermeneutics, because there is no universality to language. Language is not the only "metainstitution" or medium of force that constrains social action; indeed, language itself is constrained by extra-linguistic forces. The "metainstitution of language as tradition is evidently dependent in turn on social processes that are not reducible to normative relations. Language is *also* a medium of domination and social power; it serves to legitimate relations of organized force."[7]

For the development of a concept of critical reflection Habermas finds a more appropriate theory of language explicated in Piaget's genetic epistemology. Habermas specifically cites Piaget's conception of the "non-linguistic roots of operative thought."[8] In this view, cognitive categories such as space, time, causality, and substance, as well as "rules for the formal-logical combination of symbols," are pre-linguistic. Language, according to Piaget, "sits upon" such pre-linguistic cognitive schemes which form the basis of operative thought. Our use of language is thereby determined by extra-linguistic conditions. While Habermas admits that this issue is not yet completely clarified, he suggests that "if it is the case that operative intelligence goes back to pre-linguistic, cognitive schemes, and is therefore able to use language in an instrumental way, then the hermeneutical claim to universality would find its limit in the linguistic systems of science and the theories of rational choice."[9]

Gadamer, while reiterating the universality and inclusiveness of language, clarifies his position in his response to Habermas. "There is no societal reality, with all its concrete forces, that does not bring itself to representation in a consciousness which is linguistically articulated."[10] This does not mean that everything *is* language: "every linguistic experience of the world is experience of the world, not experience of language" (TM 495). Human existence does involve extra-linguistic experience: "our experience of the world is not accomplished only in the apprenticeship and use of language. There is a pre-linguistic experience of the world, as Habermas, drawing on Piaget's researches, reminds us."[11] Nonetheless, our interpretive access to pre-linguistic experience, our possibility of understanding it, and the possibility of it having an effect upon our understanding, are through and through conditioned by language. Language remains "the medium of hermeneutic experience."

The impasse between Gadamer and Habermas concerning language constitutes a central *aporia* within contemporary hermeneutical theory. To explore this *aporia* we need to look deeper into the contrasting theories of language operative in the debate.

II

The work of Piaget and his followers counts against the view of language proposed by Heidegger and Gadamer. Piaget argued that interpretive intelligence precedes language acquisition. Language is one among a number of semiotic or symbolic or representational functions, including imitation, symbolic play, drawing, and mental images, which are acquired only after some ability to interpret has already developed in the child. Language, defined by Piaget is a symbol or sign system of "differentiated signifiers" which the child learns only after she already commands a system of prelinguistic "undifferentiated signifiers." Prior to linguistic representation

> the baby forms and uses significations, since every sensorimotor assimilation (including perceptual assimilations) already implies the attribution of signification, of a meaning. Significations and consequently also a duality between 'signified' . . . and 'signifiers' are already present. However, these 'signifiers' remain perceptual and are not differentiated from the 'signified.' An undifferentiated signifier is, in fact, as yet neither a 'symbol' nor a 'sign' (in the sense of verbal signs). It is by definition an 'indicator' (including the 'signals' occurring in conditioning, like the sound of the bell that announces food).[12]

An indicator or signal is undifferentiated in the sense that it is identical to the signified. Differentiated signs emerge around the second year of childhood when "certain behavior patterns appear which imply the representative evocation of an object or event not present."[13] According to Piaget, there is already a certain logic built into the undifferentiated signifiers of pre-linguistic action which helps to structure linguistic behavior. He concluded that "language does not constitute the source of logic but is, on the contrary, structured by it. The roots of logic are to be sought in the general coordination of actions (including verbal behavior), beginning with the sensorimotor level, whose schemes are of fundamental importance."[14] Language, therefore, does not guide thought, but vice versa, language itself would not develop without thought.

It is clear that in Piaget's view, the acquisition of the child's initial linguistic skill presupposes the ability to understand a sign as representing something 'signified.' On this view, the learning of language would depend on one's ability to interpret. Hans Furth has noted this in the following way: "In other types of symbol behavior [e.g., imitation or mental images] we speak freely of the production or formation of symbols; with language it appears to be first a problem of comprehension, followed only afterwards by expression or production."[15] The infant needs to understand the symbol in a way that is similar to understanding the referent.[16] In this view language has no power of its own; it receives its power from the speaker who, out of his intellectual experience, decides how to employ signs proper to a situation.

The debate between Gadamer and Habermas can be clarified, and perhaps moved towards resolution, only if we can decide which view of language (the one offered by Heidegger and Gadamer, or the one offered by Piaget and Habermas) is correct. One way to sort this out would be to recognize that two different definitions of language are operating here. For Piaget, language is the system of differentiated signifiers acquired when the child learns to speak at around the age of two years. For Heidegger and Gadamer, language is a *way of being* which involves not only Piaget's system of differentiated signifiers but also the system of undifferentiated signifiers which can be traced back to the earliest experiences of the child. From the viewpoint of philosophical hermeneutics, what Piaget called 'pre-linguistic' experience is linguistic in a different sense. In this view the acquisition of language is not the acquiring of language by the two-year old, but the acquisition of the infant by language.

Merleau-Ponty's thinking on language is extremely useful for clarifying the larger sense of language that Heidegger had proposed, and for translating this view into the Piagetian context. Merleau-Ponty, who was trained in both philosophy and psychology, attempted to set the Heideggerian view of language into the context of developmental psychology. He described the child's experience with language in the following way: "During the first months of life, the child cries; he makes expressive movements; and then he begins to babble. . . . This babbling is . . . a polymorphic language, which is spontaneous with respect to its environment. (It exists in deaf-mute children, even though it is not as well developed.). . . . Speech emerges from the 'total language' as constituted by gestures, mimicries, etc" (CAL 11–12).

Merleau-Ponty pointed to the importance of the fact that from birth (and today we know that even *in utero*) the infant receives linguistic stimulation from the environment. Obviously parents do not wait for the child to speak before speaking to it; rather,

> from his first waking moments the child hears someone speaking. Most of the time, language is addressed to him directly, and this acoustic sensation provokes the stimulation, first of his limbs, and then of the phonatory organs. . . . The child receives the 'sense' of language from his environment. . . . The child's relationship with his environment is what points him toward language. It is a development toward an end defined by the environment and not preestablished in the organism. (CAL 14)

Merleau-Ponty cited the work of Karl Bühler who had shown that as early as four months the child's intonation takes on the accent of his native language.[17] The point is that intelligence does not develop in a linguistic vacuum; even if the child has not yet acquired the ability to speak, language is structuring his experience.

If the concept of language as presented by Merleau-Ponty remains obscure in regard to the kind of psychological mechanisms that Piaget would require, still, his view has been reinforced by a more recently developed consensus in the scientific community. George Dennison, for example, writes that "the infant . . . is born into an already existing continuum [of sounds—speech—language]."[18] In more precise terms, Merleau-Ponty's claims have been confirmed in recent systematic research on language development in infants. In their exhaustive summary of this research, Bates, O'Connell, and Shore state:

> Language development is a process that begins early in infancy. . . .
>
> Babbling does seem to indicate that children are "tuned in" to language in a new and very explicit way.
>
> Infants in the first few weeks of life can hear most and perhaps all of the phonological contrasts that are used by human language.
>
> In the first 2–3 weeks of life, infant sounds are restricted primarily to crying and a familiar set of "vegetative noises." Laughing and cooing begin at 2–3 months of age, and systematic play with speech sounds . . . [at 3 months] (when infants also begin to play games of reciprocal imitation or "vocal tennis" with their caretakers).[19]

Again, reinforcing Merleau-Ponty's contention that the equivalent of babbling exists even in deaf-mute children, recent studies show that games of babbling become more and more geared into the imitation of the surrounding language, and in a corresponding way, in deaf children, gestural signs are imitated as early as 5 months.[20]

Merleau-Ponty's course of lectures on the acquisition of language contains an extended discussion of Piaget's views. His basic criticism concerns Piaget's understanding of the difference between the child's language and the language of the adult (CAL 55ff). Adult language is a matter of logic and communication, and, in Piaget's view, the child's language is deficient in these respects. Merleau-Ponty suggested that "logical language has the relative advantage of being exact. But one loses sight of the fact that this is only one element, a dead element, of the total language" (CAL 62). Language *in toto,* whether belonging to the adult or to the child, is not simply logical or communicative. It involves self-expression and an appeal to others.[21] Moreover, language involves an act of transcendence (CAL 63)—an important point to which we return shortly.

Piaget may not have been wrong in his characterization of the infant's prelinguistic experience as an ambiguous system of undifferentiated signifiers where the rule is one of identity rather than differentiation. Merleau-Ponty agreed, for example, that in the infant's experience the mother's voice does not *represent* the mother; it is identical with the mother (see PrP 109). Precisely in this regard, however, language cannot be just one other object in the infant's environment, as Piaget argued. Furthermore, it seems clear that language, in the more general, hermeneutical sense, plays a role in the infant's development long before it comes to the point of speaking. Intelligence can be given a priority over language only if language is understood in an objective and narrow fashion.

Merleau-Ponty demonstrated the adequacy of Heidegger's view of language in contrast to Piaget, and he did so on Piaget's home ground of developmental psychology. In line with Heidegger, Merleau-Ponty asserted that from the very beginning and before we know it we find ourselves caught up in a "whirlwind of language" (S 40). In an ambiguous way our intelligence, our thinking, our interpretations are developed within and through language in its most basic and general sense. Language is a more basic experience than Piaget would allow. It appropriates the child, sweeps the child up into a linguistic "whirlwind," immerses the child in a linguistic world from the very beginning.

Despite these contrasts, the two views of language do not have to be understood as contradictory to one another. The narrow definition of language given by Piaget can fit within and add specification to the wider definition offered by Heidegger. If, in this way, it is possible to reach a consensus, albeit an uneasy consensus, between Heidegger and Piaget—and on my view Merleau-Ponty was working towards that consensus—then it may also be possible to reach a consensus between Gadamer and Habermas. We turn now to see whether Merleau-Ponty can act as mediator in working toward this latter consensus.

III

For philosophical hermeneutics the implication of Merleau-Ponty's analysis of language, and the most recent scientific evidence that reaffirms it, is clear. No partial, methodological suspension of the hermeneutical circle is possible;[22] we are on the inside of language, and language keeps us on the inside of the process of tradition. The tradition-context of language places constraints on any attempt at critical reflection. But this does not mean that critical reflection is impossible, or if possible that it is condemned to reproduce ideologies or traditional social evils (see TM 495). If language keeps us on the inside, that doesn't mean that it keeps us imprisoned within the forces of specific interests or power relations. Merleau-Ponty emphasized the very aspect of language that Gadamer came to recognize, and that Habermas requires as the *sine qua non* of critique—namely, the aspect of freedom or transcendence involved in language.

Language, as Gadamer indicates, operates as a constraint, but also as an enabling condition; it implies "at once both constraint and freedom for the individual."[23] Emancipation will not be accomplished in a total escape from the process of tradition. It will involve an incomplete transformation or partial transcendence within language. Only through language is it possible to transcend a tradition, which means that one must work within a tradition to transform it, or to produce a new one. Gadamer is right, nothing is exempt from the community of dialogue: "neither the specialization of modern science. . . . nor natural labor . . . nor political institutions of domination and administration . . . exist outside the universal medium of practical reason (and unreason)"[24] Political and economic forces, as well as class relations, are mediated by language; but precisely for that reason, they can be modified only through language. As Habermas himself realized, only by discourse, communication, education, or enlightenment can emancipation be effected.[25] But, Gadamer adds, and Merleau-Ponty would have agreed, communication, education, and enlightenment within the bounds of language and the process of tradition, and not by the accomplishment of an impossible, ideal communication which would amount to something like an ahistorical conversation between gods. What Habermas calls an "unlimited interpretive community," a consensus "achieved under the idealized conditions of unlimited and control-free communication," not only cannot be "permanently maintained," but, given the nature of language and interpretation, is impossible to attain.[26] Even if this ideal is conceived of as a formal, regulative measure for truth, it cannot be conceived of outside of a discourse, or exterior to a hermeneutical situation constrained by the particular traditions in which we always already exist. In this regard Habermas' more recent appeal to speech-act theory does not save him from criticism on this score, since his theory of communicative action still requires an "unbound," ideal speech act of standard form. Gadamer and Merleau-Ponty would not be alone in objecting to the very possibility of an "unbound" (context-free) speech act.[27]

Language places real constraints upon our communication. Language, however, not only transmits traditions; through language we gain the power to transform traditions. Transformation does not mean that we step outside of a particular tradition, but that we reform it by reformulating it. Through such reformulation, which is always, at least, a linguistic act, it is possible to transform the power structures of domination and exploitation. Critique is possible, but only from within the "walls" of the language-tradition framework. It cannot be based on an absolute and external reflection, but must operate within the hermeneutical bounds of interpretive understanding. The critique of ideology must be continuous, a constant process, because it cannot in principle be exhaustive. As Ricoeur contends, and he attributes this insight to Gadamer, a critique of ideology is not something that can ever be finished.[28]

Here Merleau-Ponty, beyond his considerations about language, would have something to add to the debate: he developed a philosophy of history that sees in historical existence no easy transformations, nor total revolutions; no unambiguous appropriations of traditions, nor complete escapes from them. History is, as Merleau-Ponty insisted, an open dialectic which calls for something beyond a liberalism which "reduces the history of a society to speculative conflicts of opinion, political struggle to exchanges of views on clearly posed problems . . ." (AD 225). Praxis cannot be reduced to either trouble-free conversation or context-free speech acts, because there will always be contestation within history. There will always be what Ricoeur calls "irreducible perspectives."[29] Not only because of the nature of language, but also because of the nature of history, there is no possibility for perfect consensus.

Certainly from Merleau-Ponty we learn to reverse Wellmer's emphasis, or at least to set it in balance, without disputing the appropriateness of Habermas' intentions. The tradition-context of language is not exclusively a locus of factual untruth and force of domination; it is also, and at the same time, a locus of possible but incomplete truth, and factual but limited cooperation. Due to the inescapable ambiguity of historical existence, consensus will never be perfect, since, as Merleau-Ponty indicated, historical reality is the excess of the signified over the signification, "the excess of what we live over what has already been said" (S 83). However, even imperfect consensus may improve a situation and may reduce the degree of domination or exploitation to a level that, even if not absolutely emancipatory, must be somewhat acceptable. Nothing, not even emancipation, is exempt from this ambiguity.

If we include Merleau-Ponty in the debate between the proponents of hermeneutics and the critical theorists, then the debate itself may be the most immediate evidence that consensus, but only imperfect consensus, is possible. By calling attention to the ambiguous nature of language and of history, we do not resolve the debate, we arrive at an imperfect consensus which recognizes that these problems do not have definitive solutions but are open-ended.

Notes

1. The debate itself can be followed through a series of essays, including: Habermas: "Zur Logik der Sozialwissenschaften," *Philosophische Rundschau* 14 (1967), 149–180, partially translated as "A Review of Gadamer's *Truth and Method*," in F. Dallmayr and T. McCarthy (eds.), *Understanding and Social Inquiry* (Notre Dame: University of Notre Dame Press, 1977); "The Hermeneutic Claim to Universality," in Josef Bleicher, *Contemporary Hermeneutics* (London: Routledge and Kegan Paul, 1980); and "Summation and Response," *Continuum* 8 (1970), 123–133. Gadamer: "Rhetoric, Hermeneutics, and the Critique of Ideology: Metacritical Comments on *Truth and Method*" [1967], trans. Jerry Dibble, in *The Hermeneutics Reader*, ed. Kurt Mueller-Vollmer (New York: Continuum, 1988), 274–292; "Replik," in K–O. Apel, et al., (eds.) *Hermeneutik und Ideologiekritik* (Frankfurt: Suhrkamp, 1971); "Hermeneutics and Social Science," *Cultural Hermeneutics* 2 (1975) 307–316; "On the Scope and Function of Hermeneutical Reflection," and "The Universality of the Hermeneutical Problem," in *Philosophical Hermeneutics*, trans. David E. Linge (Berkeley: University of California Press, 1976).

For various perspectives on this debate, see, e.g., Alan R. How, "A Case of Creative Misreading: Habermas's Evaluation of Gadamer's Hermeneutics,"

Journal of the British Society for Phenomenology 16 (1985), 132–144; David J. Depew, "The Habermas-Gadamer Debate in Hegelian Perspective," *Philosophy and Social Criticism* 8 (1981) 425–446; Dieter Misgeld, "Discourse and Conversation: The Theory of Communicative Competence and Hermeneutics in the Light of the Debate between Habermas and Gadamer," *Cultural Hermeneutics* 4 (1977), 321–344; Rüdiger Bubner, "Theory and Practice in the Light of the Hermeneutic-Criticist Controversy," *Cultural Hermeneutics* 2 (1975), 337–352.

2. Hans-Georg Gadamer, "On the Scope and Function of Hermeneutical Reflection," *Continuum* 8 (1970), p. 83; also see *Truth and Method* (New York: Seabury Press, 1975), p. 350; hereafter cited as 'TM.'

3. Martin Heidegger, "Building, Dwelling, Thinking," in *Basic Writings,* ed. David Krell (New York: Harper and Row, 1977), p. 324.

4. Heidegger, "What Calls for Thinking," in *Basic Writings,* p. 365; also see Heidegger, *On the Way to Language,* trans. Peter D. Hertz and Joan Stambaugh (New York: Harper and Row, 1971).

5. Habermas, "The Hermeneutic Claim to Universality," pp. 204–205; also "Summation and Response," p. 125.

6. Habermas, "A Review of Gadamer's *Truth and Method,*" p. 360.

7. Ibid.

8. Habermas, "The Hermeneutic Claim to Universality," pp. 188–189.

9. Ibid., p. 189.

10. Gadamer, "On the Scope and Function of Hermeneutical Reflection," p. 90.

11. TM 496. Also see Gadamer, "Summation," *Cultural Hermeneutics* 2 (1975), p. 330.

12. Jean Piaget and Barbel Inhelder, *The Psychology of the Child,* trans. Helen Weaver (New York: Basic Books, 1969), reprinted in *The Essential Piaget,* eds. Howard E. Gruber and J. Jacques Voneche (New York: Basic Books, 1977), p. 489.

13. Ibid., p. 490.

14. Ibid., p. 507.

15. Hans Furth, *Piaget and Knowledge: Theoretical Foundations* (Englewood Cliffs, New Jersey: Prentice-Hall, 1969), p. 108.

16. See ibid., p. 111.

17. Karl Bühler, *Sprachtheorie: Die Darstellungsfunktion der Sprache* (Jena: Fischer, 1934), cited by Merleau-Ponty, CAL 15. Habermas also relies on Bühler's work. See below, note 21.

18. George Dennison, *The Lives of Children* (New York: Random House, 1970), p. 90.

19. E. Bates, B. O'Connell, and C. Shore, "Language and Communication in Infancy," in *Handbook for Infant Development*, 2nd ed., ed. J. D. Osofsky (New York: John Wiley and Sons, 1987), pp. 150, 151, 157, and 156. Also see I. Uzgiris and J. McV. Hund, *Assessment in Infancy: Ordinal Scales of Psychological Development* (Urbana, Ill: University of Illinois Press, 1975).

20. See, Bates, O'Connell, and Shore, p. 165. This is in clear contrast to the work of Hans Furth, a follower of Piaget who specializes in the study of deaf children, and who is also cited by Habermas.

21. CAL 30–31. The basis of this claim can be found in Bühler's functional semiotics which distinguishes three functions common to all signs: cognitive, apellative, and expressive. Habermas also builds on Bühler's analysis in his distinction between representational, performative, and expressive functions. See Habermas, *The Theory of Communicative Action, Vol. I: Reason and the Rationalization of Society*, trans. Thomas McCarthy (Boston: Beacon Press, 1984), pp. 275ff.

22. For reference to the partial suspension of hermeneutic communication, see Karl-Otto Apel, "Szientistik, Hermeneutik, Ideologiekritik: Entwurf einer Wissenschaftslehre in erkenntnisanthropologischer Sicht," in *Hermeneutik und Ideologiekritik*, eds. K.-O. Apel et al. (Frankfurt: Suhrkamp, 1971), p. 39.

23. Gadamer, "The Problem of Language in Schleiermacher's Hermeneutic," trans. David E. Linge, *Journal for Theology and the Church* 7 (1970), p. 70.

24. Gadamer, "Replik," in Apel, et al. (eds.), *Hermeneutik und Ideologiekritik*, p. 289; cited and translated in Bleicher, *Contemporary Hermeneutics*, p. 157.

25. See, e.g., Habermas, "Summation and Response," pp. 130, 133.

26. Ibid., p. 126.

27. See Habermas, *Theory of Communicative Action, I*, pp. 293–297, 440n40). John Searle's conception of the relativity or context dependency of literal meaning would speak against any such context-free illocution (see, *Expression and Meaning: Studies in the Theory of Speech Acts* [Cambridge: Cambridge University Press, 1979], p. 117ff; and Habermas, *Theory of Communicative Action, I*, pp. 335ff.). To the extent that Habermas emphasizes "the contextual independence of illocutionary and locutionary meanings in order to differentiate them from perlocutionary effects," David Ingram objects: "speech acts seldom occur in standard form; many are institutionally bound (nongeneralizable); actual conversations often combine strategic and communicative types . . ." Habermas must admit "that actual instances of

82 *Shaun Gallagher*

speech are 'impure' " (*Habermas and the Dialectic of Reason* [New Haven: Yale University Press, 1987], pp. 40 & 202n.36; also, Habermas, *Theory of Communicative Action, I* pp. 328ff). For a critical discussion of the ideal speech situation, see John B. Thompson, *Critical Hermeneutics: A Study in the Thought of Paul Ricoeur and Jürgen Habermas* (Cambridge: Cambridge University Press, 1981), pp. 169, 209ff.

28. Paul Ricoeur, "Phenomenology and Hermeneutics," in *Hermeneutics and the Human Sciences,* trans. John B. Thompson (Cambridge: Cambridge University Press, 1981), p. 111.

29. Paul Ricoeur, "Ethics and Culture: Habermas and Gadamer in Dialogue," *Philosophy Today* 17 (1973), p. 163.

7

Did Merleau-Ponty Have a Theory of Perception?

ૐ ૐ

G. B. Madison

1.

Is there a theory of perception in Merleau-Ponty? Does the notion of perception play a significant role in Merleau-Ponty's philosophy? Rather unusual questions, no doubt. After all, his major work was entitled *Phenomenology of Perception,* and it dealt extensively with the issue of perception as discussed by philosophers and scientists. Since my question has all the appearances of being somewhat *insolite,* I might as well present my answer at the outset, since it is equally rather unheard of and is probably not very likely to secure immediate adhesion on the part of my audience. My answer is quite simple: No, the notion of perception was not one of Merleau-Ponty's guiding concepts. What traditionally has been referred to as "perception" no longer figures in Merleau-Ponty's postfoundationalist mode of thinking. While my answer is simple, attempting to justify it will likely prove to be a more difficult matter. Let me at least give it a try.

To start off, a provocative quote from a successor to Merleau-Ponty on the Paris scene is perhaps in order:

> Now I don't know what perception is and I don't believe that anything like perception exists. Perception is precisely a concept, a concept of an intuition or of a given originating from the thing itself, present itself in its meaning, independently from language from the system of reference. And I believe that perception is interdependent with the concept of origin and of center and consequently whatever strikes at the metaphysics [of presence] of which I have spoken strikes also at the very concept of perception. I don't believe that there is any perception.[1]

Along with Derrida, I too don't believe that there is any perception. Nor do I believe that Merleau-Ponty believed there is any perception either. My reason for saying this is two-fold: (1) Perception, as
Derrida so aptly remarks, is precisely a *concept* (one which, like most
other concepts, is normally taken to "refer" to something which is not
a concept, such as, in this case, "perception"), and (2) there is no place
for this concept in the particular conceptual arrangement that constitutes Merleau-Ponty's "philosophy." Before arguing for (2), let me say
a word about (1).

Like all of the other "things" philosophy has always talked about—
forms, atoms, entelechies, the soul, Being, and so on—"perception" is
a concept, a theoretical construct, or, as James might say, *une entité
métaphysique*. It is not, that is, something that is directly experienced; it is, rather, like all other philosophical concepts, a semantic or
metaphorical innovation whose purpose is to make our lived-through
experience intelligible to ourselves, to *explain* it. However, as Merleau-
Ponty has pointed out, it seems to be a peculiar characteristic of
human understanding that it has a kind of natural or built-in tendency to misunderstand itself—by, in particular, taking its imaginative creations for actual, lived realities.[2] This has certainly been the
case with regard to "perception." Today, as a result of several centu-
ries of philosophical speculation, we readily imagine that we are constantly (at least while we are awake) "having perceptions" (in much
the same way that we imagine that we "have" a body). But before the
modern period, before, that is, the subject-object split that Heidegger
talks about in his essay "The Age of the World Picture," no one "perceived" anything—in the same way as before Saint Augustine worked
out the notion of free will no one "willed" anything or, for that matter,
before the Greek philosophers had worked out the concept of mind
anybody "thought" anything.[3]

"Perception" is a metaphysical construct, a creation of that particular form of the metaphysics of presence known as "modern philosophy." "Perception," as the term is generally used today by philosophers (analytic ones in particular), psychologists, cognitive scientists,
AI people, and other such theorizers, refers to an activity which, it is
supposed, goes on *inside* a "cognizing subject" and by means of which
this epistemological subject (which is directly conscious only of its
own inner states) is somehow able to form a mental picture or *representation* of what exists *outside* itself, in the so-called "external world."
The notions of *perception* and of the *empirical* (i.e., a reality which is
fully defined in itself and which, as it were, simply waits around for a
cognizing mind to come along and form a mental copy of it) are

indissolubly linked. They are the key notions of modern objectivistic naturalism, which it was the life-goal of Merleau-Ponty's philosophizing to overcome or, as we might be tempted to say today, deconstruct. In the light of all the current talk about deconstruction and the "end of metaphysics"—with which, as a Merleau-Pontyean, hermeneutical phenomenologist I find myself in great sympathy—it might not be inappropriate to take note of how, in regard to the specific question of perception, Merleau-Ponty's philosophical project already accomplishes a decisive overcoming of the objectivistic metaphysics of presence. To argue my case, I shall not try to make things easy by turning directly to *The Visible and the Invisible*—whose postmetaphysical character should be obvious to anyone—but shall first attempt to show how the modern notion of "perception" plays no role whatsoever in Merleau-Ponty's early work, the *Phenomenology of Perception,* which so many poststructuralist anti-phenomenologists seem to regard, curiously enough, as a kind of last hangover of the old metaphysics of presence.

2.

In order fully to appreciate how the notion of perception is *absent* from the *Phenomenology of Perception,* it is important, I think, to call to mind the exact nature of this text. The *Phenomenology* is a rather peculiar kind of text in terms of the genre "philosophical work." It is in fact a kind of anti-text, philosophically speaking. That is, it contrasts with what could be called the "standard" philosophical treatise wherein an author presents a positive thesis to such and such an effect and musters a variety of arguments in defense of this thesis. In the *Phenomenology* there are, strictly speaking, no positive theses; the work as a whole is essentially "negative." That is, the position Merleau-Ponty seeks to present here is inseparable from the positions he is arguing against and, in fact, exists, and can exist, only in dialectical *opposition* to these other positions. Merleau-Ponty's own position can be characterized only negatively, as anti-empiricist or anti-intellectualist. It exists only as *other* than the positions he criticizes. Thus, as readers of Merleau-Ponty we must not allow ourselves to be misled by the grammatical form of many of his sentences. Merleau-Ponty does at times make what to all appearances are propositional utterances (such and such is the case, the nature of X is Y), but this is simply his way of saying that the body or some other thing or state of affairs is *not* to be understood in the way empiricism or intellectualism understands it but in an altogether different way. As to what, say, the body *really* is, what it is "in itself," Merleau-Ponty does not say, nor could he. The philosophy to be found in the *Phenomenology* is in the last analysis a philosophy of ambiguity or indeterminacy.[4] Merleau-Ponty's ultimate, bottomline thesis in this book is that the "essence" of existence is ambiguity. This amounts of course to saying that, strictly speaking, existence has no essence (a position Merleau-Ponty shares with Sartre; the definition of man, Merleau-Ponty says, is that he is that being which has no definition). In terms of traditional philosophy (metaphysics), which has always sought to determine unequivocally the essence of what is, a philosophy of ambiguity or indeterminacy is a very peculiar kind of philosophy, if indeed it can still be called "philosophy" at all; it is, we should perhaps say, an anti-philosophy. It is in any event a philosophy which is devoid of positive doctrinal content. "Perception" in the *Phenomenology* is the name for a non-concept.

Let me attempt to make my position more precise. The two main positions in opposition to which Merleau-Ponty seeks to elaborate his "own" position are, as I indicated, empiricism and intellectualism. Empiricism and intellectualism are in turn instances of what Merleau-Ponty calls "*la pensée objective*," objectivism. Both intellectualism and empiricism share the same fundamental prejudice; this is the prejudice of what Merleau-Ponty calls "a universe perfectly explicit in itself" (PhP 41). For empiricism, perception is an objective event in nature. It is the causal action of a physical thing on an organ; sensation is the internal registering of this action. Strictly speaking, there is no *subject* who perceives; perception is a natural or third person process, an objective event occurring within empirical reality itself (which is why, nowadays, AI people seek to provide a purely naturalistic account of perception and to devise robots which can duplicate within their subjectless selves the "external world").

For intellectualism, in contrast, perception is essentially a subjective activity, an activity of the transcendental ego itself which actively takes cognizance of the world or, more particularly, of certain objective processes occurring in the objective body (itself part of the world) to which it is somehow attached. The only difference between intellectualism and empiricism is that for the former the objective world exists as such and in the final analysis only for a consciousness which upholds it. As Merleau-Ponty remarks: "We started off from a world in itself which acted upon our eyes so as to cause us to see it, and we now have consciousness of or thought about the world, but the nature of this world remains unchanged; it is still defined by the absolute mutual exteriority of its parts, and is merely duplicated throughout its extent by a thought which sustains it" (PhP 39). For both intellectualism and empiricism, therefore, perception is, at least in part (as in the case of intellectualism), an *external, causal, physical* relation between an epistemological subject (whose existential status is totally undefined in empiricism) and "empirical" reality.

For Merleau-Ponty, however, "perception" is none of these things. In fact, perception so conceived is for Merleau-Ponty a logical (or phenomenological) absurdity, as he seeks to show in great detail in the *Phenomenology.* In a way similar to Husserl, Merleau-Ponty maintains that one lands oneself in philosophical absurdities if one conceives of perception as an external relation between two different, separate *things,* thinking things and empirical things. What Husserl referred to as "transcendental psychologism" or "transcendental realism" is shot through with a vicious circularity in that it attempts to give an account of objects, the perceived world, in terms of conscious acts and operations which are themselves conceived of in mundane terms, as mundane events occurring alongside other mundane events, "in" a mundane organism occupying its place "in" the spatio-temporal order of the "real" world. For both Husserl and Merleau-Ponty the dual notions of "an encapsuled . . . self-enclosed world of bodies,"[5] on the one hand, and of an independent psychic substance standing over against and mirroring this self-contained reality, on the other hand, are theoretical constructions of philosophical modernity which must be deconstructed or reduced, in the phenomenological sense of the term, if we are to have any hope of rediscovering what Merleau-Ponty referred to as "the phenomenal field," the world as we actually experience it, as it exists before it is theorized in metaphysical or scientific speculation. "To return to the things themselves," Merleau-Ponty says, "is to return to that world which precedes knowledge, of which knowledge always *speaks,* and in relation to which every scientific schematization is an abstract and derivative sign-language, as is geography in relation to the country-side in which we have learnt beforehand what a forest, a prairie or a river is" (PhP ix). Both the epistemological subject or, as Foucault so aptly called it, the empirico-transcendental doublet, and so-called empirical reality are to be "reduced," placed in abeyance, if what traditionally has been referred to as *man* and *world* are to be understood in a less metaphysical fashion than has hitherto been the case.

How then does Merleau-Ponty seek to conceive, or reconceive, what traditionally has been referred to as "perception?" The important thing to note in this regard is that the various characteristics of perception (as he portrays them phenomenologically) are essentially "negative" in that, even when couched in positive terms, they are

simply ways of saying that perception is *not* to be conceived in this
way or in that way or in some other way again. If Merleau-Ponty's
argumentative strategy in the *Phenomenology* is, as I have said, to
show how the traditional, objectivistic way of conceiving of the perceptual relation of the subject and the world leads into philosophical
absurdities, then it is only to be expected that the alternate terms he
latches onto in order to characterize perception in a seemingly positive way should derive whatever semantic value they may possess for
his readers from the fact that these terms are essentially *different
from* and *opposed to* the usual, traditional terms. Thus, for example,
if objectivism views perception as an *external, one-way* relation between two *separate* or disjunct things (cognizing subject, physical
object), then it is only natural that Merleau-Ponty should maintain,
in opposition to this, that the relation between perceiving subject and
perceived object is an *internal,* two-way or *circular* relation in which,
accordingly, each term of the relation exists only through its *dialectical* relation to the other. It is quite natural that he should say: "Inside
and outside are inseparable. The world is wholly inside and I am
wholly outside myself" (PhP 407). The philosophical "justification" for
remarks such as these (which are typical of Merleau-Ponty's "positive" theses) is, as I have indicated, that they are pretty much the
only things one can say *if* one's overriding goal is the deconstruction
of objectivism. In other words, it must not be thought that Merleau-
Ponty's own theoretical position "admits of empirical corroboration."[6]
Let us, accordingly, consider in a bit more detail a few of the principal
ways in which Merleau-Ponty actively describes the perceptual relation.

   In the first instance, the perceiving subject is itself defined dialectically as being *neither* (pure) consciousness *nor* (physical, in-itself)
body. Consciousness, perceptual or other, is not a pure self-presence;
the subject is present to and knows itself only through the mediation
of the body, which is to say that this presence is always *mediated,* i.e.,
is indirect and incomplete and thus is never (as Derrida might say) a
"full presence." Or, as Merleau-Ponty says, "I can never say 'I' absolutely" (PhP 208). The perceiving subject or the lived body (two different ways of saying the same thing) is a philosophically bizarre mix-
ture of being-in-itself and being-for-itself. It falls outside all the
traditional philosophical categories. Throughout the *Phenomenology,*
Merleau-Ponty is at pains to break with what he sees as the dominant conception of modern philosophy, namely that there are "two
senses, and two only, of the word 'exist': one exists as a thing or else

one exists as a consciousness" (PhP 198).[7] The perceiving subject, however, does neither; its mode of existence is, therefore, essentially *ambiguous.*[8] Existence is ambiguous because it calls into question the traditional distinction of subject and object and, in so doing, one of the central, foundational principles of philosophy, the so-called law of excluded middle (a thing must be *either* this *or* that). The only way in which the perceiving subject could be described positively is in a way which is not positive at all, namely as a union of opposites, a *coincidentio oppositorum.*

The relation between the perceiving subject, thus "defined," and the perceived world is, in its turn, defined dialectically. It is in terms of (or within) the perceptual, intentional relationship itself that Merleau-Ponty seeks to define *both* the subject *and* the world. If the subject is essentially not what it is, that is, if it is not a pure coincidence of itself with itself in the intimacy of consciousness but is rather, in its very "essence," a *relation* to what it is not, i.e., the world, then it follows that the world is essentially nothing other than a relation to the subject. As Merleau-Ponty writes: "The world is inseparable from the subject, but from a subject which is nothing but a project of the world, and the subject is inseparable from the world, but from a world which it projects itself" (PhP 430).[9] Another way of expressing the matter would be to say that the lived body (*corps propre*) and the perceived world are, for Merleau-Ponty, *correlative, correlates* of one another.[10] Neither exists apart from the other; each exists only in terms of the other. The body and the world form as it were a circuit and co-exist *internally.* As Merleau-Ponty says:

> The relations between things or aspects of things having always our body as their vehicle, the whole of nature is the setting of our own life, or our interlocutor in a sort of dialogue. . . . The thing is inseparable from a person perceiving it, and can never be actually *in itself* because it stands at the other end of our gaze or at the terminus of a sensory exploration which invests it with humanity (PhP 320).

If, as he goes on to say, this was not realized earlier, it is because "any coming to awareness of the perceptual world was hampered by the prejudices arising from objective thinking." The latter, he says, "severs the links which unite the thing and the embodied subject, leaving only sensible qualities to make up our world." Of course, for Merleau-Ponty, as for French phenomenology in general, there are, in our actual experience of the world, no "sensible qualities," no pure sensations, no brute sense (or, as Husserl would say, hyletic) data. Quoting from Scheler, Merleau-Ponty says that " 'the world is not given and things are not accessible to the person to whom "sensations" are the world's data' " (PhP 321).[11]

It should be noted in passing how, in characterizing perception as he does, Merleau-Ponty effectively abandons the kind of language which philosophy, like science, has officially claimed for itself: a supposedly literal mode of discourse backed up with univocal concepts. Already in the *Phenomenology* Merleau-Ponty's counter-philosophical discourse is basically figurative or *metaphorical*. One has only to open the book to almost any page to encounter a whole host of metaphors. On the page from which I just quoted for instance, Merleau-Ponty speaks of nature as our *interlocutor* in a sort of *dialogue;* he describes perception as a *communication* or *communion,* a *coition* [*accouplement*] of our body with things. Consider, finally, the following text in which Merleau-Ponty sums up—metaphorically—the perceptual relation: "The lived body [*corps propre*] is in the world as the heart is in the organism: it keeps the visible spectacle constantly alive, it breathes life into it and sustains it inwardly, and with it forms a system" (PhP 203).

Now it is important to remember that metaphorical description is, in regard to the usual, literal, philosophically acceptable modes of predication, a very peculiar way of saying something about something. To describe something metaphorically is to describe that thing in terms, precisely, of what it is *not* (e.g., man is a wolf, my loved one, a rose). A metaphor tells us what something is in its ownmost proper self by comparing that thing to something which is essentially (in terms of its own constitutive "essence") *other* than what it is. A metaphor communicates its own proper meaning to us only if we realize that the utterer of the metaphor does not really mean what he or she is apparently saying (they don't "really" mean that man is a wolf). Unlike literal discourse, metaphorical discourse achieves its proper effect only if, so to speak, the utterance cancels itself out, self-destructs, undercuts its own semantic positivity.[12] Thus, here once again, in regard Merleau-Ponty's very style of writing, is a salient instance of how, as I have been saying, the theses put forward in the *Phenomenology* are essentially "negative."

So in the *Phenomenology* Merleau-Ponty is not saying much more than that perception is *not* this and that it is *not* that. He defines perception in much the same way as the Hindu defines Brahman: *Neti neti.* What, it could perhaps be said, perception above all is not for Merleau-Ponty is what it is for the naturalist: a purely *causal* relation. The relation between subject and object is not, as he sees it, a linear, *partes extra partes* or external relation of *causality,* the physical action of one thing (the object) on another, separate thing (the sense organ), where the first thing is supposed to exist on its own and to be just exactly *what* it is apart from or before its acting on the second.[13] The relation between the two terms is, instead, an *internal* relation, a relation not of causality but of *significance*.[14] It is a relation of significance or meaning since, just as in the case of linguistic terms, each term of the relation is *what* it is, is defined in terms of its own proper "essence," only by reason of the relation itself.

This relation of significance is also, let it be noted, a relation of *expressivity*. Even before the advent of language in the proper sense of the term, the bodily subject and the perceived world, through their mutual reference, lead one another to expression, articulate themselves in what they are.

Let it further be noted that not only is the being of the subject a relation to the object, and vice versa, but the being of things themselves is, so to speak, a matter of expressive inter-referentiality. The Great Book of Nature, as early moderns called it, is one huge body of intertextuality. Nothing is what it is in itself but only in its many possible relations to things "other" than it—which amounts to saying that everything is, in itself, a possible something other. This is one lesson that Merleau-Ponty drew from Gestalt psychology. Not only is a thing a certain "significance" for the perceiving body, but the "significance-thing" is itself a function of the figure-background dialectic. The positive significance that a thing has at any given moment is a function of the way that that "thing" profiles itself against an indeterminate, but determinable, background. When the relations of determinate and indeterminate are altered, as they always can be, everything becomes something other than what it was: The duck becomes a rabbit, the vase becomes two faces confronting one another. Merleau-Ponty expresses the matter in another way when he says that a thing is not some kind of dense, rigid, unchanging "substance" but is, rather, a certain *style*—as indeed the subject is itself a certain style, a certain way of inhabiting the world.[15] The unity or self-identity of a thing is, not, therefore, a function of some "unknown X," some kind of interior "substance" underlying and upholding the thing's "properties" or "accidents." Rather, what constitutes the self-identity of a thing is a certain "*symbolism* . . . which links each sensible quality to the rest" (PhP 319; emphasis added). In short, "The thing is an entity of a kind such that the complete definition of one of its attributes demands that of the subject in its entirety" (PhP 323).

Things, therefore, are not mere "things," *blose Sachen,* as Husserl might say. By reason of their inter-referentiality, things are in fact *signs,* signs which signify or symbolize one another. Each single thing is, as Peirce might say, the interpretant of some other thing. Or as Merleau-Ponty says, "There is a symbolism in the thing which links each sensible quality to the rest" (PhP 319). It could thus be said that, through the intermediary of the body, things *converse* among themselves ("The perceived world is . . . a system of symbols of each sense in terms of the other senses . . ." [PhP 319, n. 1]) and that it is through this process of *semiosis* that they achieve whatever positive meaning or significance they have. The *existence* of things is in fact, Merleau-Ponty says, their *significance:* "The miracle of the real world ...is that in it significance and existence are one" (PhP 323). One last thing to note in this regard is that it is this inter-referentiality which accounts for the fact that, contrary to what traditional philosophy has preached, the normal way in which we describe things is by means of *metaphor,* as, for instance, when we describe a sound as sharp or a color as warm.[16]

All of what I've said so far could be summed up by saying that the perceiving subject and the perceived object are *diacritical* entities and that perception, like language, is a matter of pure *diacriticality.* Indeed, it could be said that for Merleau-Ponty the relation, in the perceiving subject, between body and consciousness is like the relation between signifier and signified. I am even tempted to say that it is not just a matter of a "likeness" here but that the relation of body and consciousness *is* that of signifier and signified (metaphorically speaking, naturally).[17] Recalling one of the things Derrida said in the quote with which I started out, it could be said that perception is not independent of language, or from a diacritical system of inter-referentiality. Although it may seem to go against the grain of philosophical common sense, *le bon sens* as Descartes called it, I don't think there is anything particularly extravagant or outrageous about saying this. It is really the only thing one can say if, like Merleau-Ponty, one rejects the idea that there is anything like brute, "value-free" sense data which need subsequently to be interpreted in order to become perceptions. There is really no such thing as pure sensation for Merleau-Ponty; sensation is always already *interpretation.* The essence of perception is hermeneutical; to see something is always to see it *as* something (the hermeneutical "as").[18] But if this is the case, then one really has no other choice but to say that perception is linguistic through and through. Just as, as Nietzsche observed, there are no pure facts, no facts "in themselves," just as all experience is, as we say nowadays, theory-laden, so it could likewise be said in all propriety that all perception is language-laden.

I freely admit that I am pushing Merleau-Ponty a bit here to get him to come out and say what I would like to hear him say. But it must also be admitted that in the *Phenomenology* he did not really think through the relation between perception and language and that this is one of the structural faults of the work. As he himself later remarked in a critical note: "There remains the problem of the passage from perceptual meaning to language meaning . . ." (VI 176) One of the criticisms that can be made of the *Phenomenology* is that in this early work Merleau-Ponty is not always fully consistent and that, indeed, he tends to waffle on a number of key points. It should therefore not be surprising if some texts can be found which seem to speak for a non-linguistic character of perception.[19] These fade in significance, however, when placed alongside other texts and when, above all, one takes into account the general drift of the work and when one rereads this work in the light of the later work. I thus find myself in agreement with my friend Tom Busch when, after quoting Merleau-Ponty's line to the effect that "sexuality is co-extensive with life," he goes on to say:

> If for "sexual" are substituted terms such as the linguistic, cultural, or moral, one can see that, as ambiguity spreads out over existence, it would be impossible to preserve something called "the perceptual" from interfusion with the others. Language and culture would not be derived from perception but would, at the start, be defining elements of perception. . . . With the breakdown of the nature-culture bifurcation perception would become a hermeneutical problem, for, as Merleau-Ponty said in the spirit of holism, "everything we live or think always has several meanings."[20]

Finally, let me quote one particularly revealing remark of Merleau-Ponty in the *Phenomenology:* "There is no experience without speech, as the purely lived-through has no part in the discursive life of man" (PhP 337). Thus, to conclude this discussion of Merleau-Ponty's early work, it could be said, by way of a paraphrase of Merleau-Ponty's friend, Jacques Lacan: *la perception est structurée comme un langage.* Lacan's own original line (*"l'inconscient est structuré comme un langage"*) is one which appeals to the hermeneuticist Gadamer, and I could equally well sum up the hermeneutical point I have been trying to make by paraphrasing the latter: *Being that can be perceived is language.*[21]

Thus, if "perception" is understood in its traditional sense, as referring to some kind of reproductive, mirroring process, whereby what is "outside" is duplicated "inside," the concept "perception" does

not figure in the *Phenomenology,* since, as Merleau-Ponty uses the
term, it refers to something which is thoroughly linguistic in structure, and language is *never* the mere representation of *anything,* of
either Thoughts or Things (to use Frege's terminology). How, we might
now ask, do matters stand in Merleau-Ponty's later work?[22]

3.

Given the way Merleau-Ponty effectively characterizes perception in the *Phenomenology,* as a system of differential or diacritical
relations wherein each term of the relation (subject, object) is what it
is only in terms of the other, it is not at all surprising that in his
subsequent work he should increasingly focus his attention on language itself, since diacriticality and language are pretty well synony-
mous. In his later writings Merleau-Ponty explicitly builds on the
Saussurian or structuralist conception of language. Thus in his key
1952 article, "Indirect Language and the Voices of Silence," he writes:

> What we have learned from Saussure is that, taken singly, signs do
> not signify anything, and that each one of them does not so much
> express a meaning as mark a divergence of meaning between itself
> and other signs (S 39).

Whence he concludes: "Language is made of differences without terms;
or more exactly, . . . the terms of language are engendered only by the
differences which appear among them." This, he admits, "is a difficult
idea." It is in fact, in regard to traditional philosophy (the philosophy
of identity), an impossible idea, and, in pursuing its ramifications,
Merleau-Ponty will progressively be led to draw a number of "extravagant consequences" (VI 140) and to abandon all residual traces
of the metaphysics of presence.

In order fully to appreciate this development, it might be worth
our while to pause for a moment to take note of some of the extravagant consequences that, a half decade or so after Merleau-Ponty's
death, Jacques Derrida was to draw from Saussure's legacy and which
he expounded under the heading *différance.* Given Derrida's belief
"that all of the great philosophical texts. . . . are still *before* us"[23] and
given also the fact that Derrida has indeed still to *read* Merleau-
Ponty, I shall, in what follows, focus on those aspects of Derrida's
notion of *différance* as expressed in his article of the same name,
"traces" of which he would likely discover in Merleau-Ponty's earlier
work were he to give it a serious reading.[24]

In order to express the dual character of linguistic sign systems
highlighted by Saussure—the arbitrariness of signs and the differen-

tial character of signs—Derrida coins the word *différance*. Since this word recalls Saussure's radically counterintuitive thesis that in language "There is nothing but differences,"[25] it is, as Derrida says, and not without reason, "neither a word nor a concept."[26] It refers, rather, to that which is the productive "origin" of all words and concepts, i.e., the pure play of semiological difference. Since *différance* is "what makes the presentation of being-present possible, it never presents itself as such" (SP 134). It is therefore not a *phenomenon* which could be described positively. Derrida attempts to say something about *différance* in the same way that in *The Visible and the Invisible* Merleau-Ponty tried to say something about what at times he called "Being" but which he also said has no name: by means of an approach resembling that of a negative theology. Let us note a few of the characteristics of *différance*.

Différance designates a kind of primordial productivity, "the process of scission and division whose differings and differences would be the constituted products or effects" (SP 137). The semiological differences which are at the origin of all positive meanings (words, concepts) are not *caused* by "a subject or substance, a thing in general, or a being that is somewhere present and itself escapes the play of difference" (SP 141). Since "There is no presence before the semiological difference or outside it," *différance* could, accordingly, be said to designate a kind of originary *absence*. Or as Derrida says: "If the diverted presentation continues to be somehow definitively and irreducibly withheld, this is not because a particular present remains hidden or absent, but because difference holds us in a relation with what exceeds (though we necessarily fail to recognize this) the alternative of presence or absence" (SP 151). *Différance*, it could be said, escapes all of the traditional alternatives or oppositions. Since *différance* points to a kind of "radical alterity, removed from every possible mode of presence" (SP 152), Derrida compares it to the Freudian unconscious, just as Merleau-Ponty so compared "Being" in his last unfinished work. What, in the last analysis, *différance* signifies is that which has and can have no name, that which must forever remain unnameable (see SP 159).

It is time now to backtrack, tracing back to their "origin" some of these elements of *différance*. In *The Visible and the Invisible* Merleau-Ponty sought to, as he said, take up again, deepen, and rectify (see VI 168) his earlier phenomenological analyses. Indeed, in this unfinished work he recognized the need to "recommence everything" (VI 130). What he began here was in effect a thoroughgoing philosophical house-cleaning, a discarding of all the "psychologistic" notions, all the mentalistic "*bric-à-brac*" of modern philosophy. Thus, as he says: "We must, at the beginning, eschew notions such as 'acts of consciousness,' 'states of consciousness,' 'matter,' 'form,' and even 'image' and [*nota bene*] 'perception' " (VI 157–58). If "perception," even in the *Phenomenology,* is, as I have maintained, a non-concept, in *The Visible and the Invisible* it becomes, quite simply, a non-term. In this last, unfinished, non-book of his, Merleau-Ponty undertook a pitiless critique of all forms of the metaphysics of presence—of mentalism, psychologism, and, as Rorty might say, epistemologism. "The whole architecture of the notions of psycho-logy," he wrote, ". . . all this bric-a-brac, is suddenly clarified when one ceases to think all these terms as *positive* . . . in order to think them . . . as *differentiations* of one sole and *massive* adhesion to Being which is the flesh" (VI 270).[27] Under the term "flesh," Merleau-Ponty sought to think differentiality or diacriticality *as such.* What exactly is the "flesh?" Could this perhaps be another name for the unnameable, for *différance?* Let us, in any event, take heed of some of the things Merleau-Ponty has to say on the subject.

Reminding us that "there is no name in traditional philosophy to designate" (VI 139)[28] that which the term "flesh" seeks to designate, Merleau-Ponty proceeds, in an exercise in negative philosophy, to say that "The flesh is not matter, is not mind, is not substance." It is indeed nothing factual but is, rather, "the possibility and exigency for the fact . . . what makes the fact be a fact" (VI 140). Like Derrida's *différance,* the flesh is a kind of primordial productivity, the "origin" of both the visible and the invisible, the sensible and the sentient, "the formative medium of the object and the subject" (VI 147). "It is that the thickness of the flesh between the seer and the thing is constitutive for the thing of its visibility as for the seer of his corporeity" (VI 135). If Derrida speaks of a "process of scission and division whose differings and differences would be the constituted products or effects," Merleau-Ponty for his part spoke of a process of "segregation," "fission," "deflagration," "differentiation," or "dehescience" of which the seer and the seen are the constituted effects. The flesh is the tissue, or the *texture,* as Merleau-Ponty might say,[29] of this active difference. It is inner divergence, scission, non-coincidence—*écart.* It is "a unique space which separates and reunites, which sustains every cohesion" (PrP 187).[30] The flesh, it could be said in Derridean fashion, is a kind of "spacing." The flesh or "Being" is "a *universal dimensionality*" (VI 265).

What the term "flesh" signifies, then, is the constitutive difference or, as Merleau-Ponty would say, the chiasmic reversibility and intertwining—or, as he says on one occasion, the "invagination" (VI 152)—of subject and object, the "coiling over of the visible upon the

visible" (VI 140), "the return of the visible upon itself, a carnal adher-
ence of the sentient to the sensed and of the sensed to the sentient"
(VI 142): "The chiasm binds as obverse and reverse ensembles unified
in advance in process of differentiation" (VI 262). This ontogenetic
process, what Merleau-Ponty often refers to as "Being," the active
source of all phenomenal positivities, is not, however, to be thought of
as some kind of positive or causal process.[31] "Being" is not something
positive in itself, some kind of ultimate "reality"; it is nothing other
than differentiation and dehescience and thus, as Merleau-Ponty says,
"never fully *is*" (PrP 190). "Being," as Merleau-Ponty uses the term,
should always be written crossed-out-wise, *barré*. The "origin" of all
presence, the flesh or wild being is, it could be said, the "originating
presentation of the unpresentable" (VI 203; see also VI 254). As origin, it is thus a certain kind of originary absence. It is that which, in
its self-presentation, remains always and irremediably dissimulated.
Being is "the untouchable of the touch, the invisible of vision, the
unconscious of consciousness (its central *punctum caecum,* that blindness that makes it consciousness)" (VI 254).[32] One could say of the
flesh what Derrida says of arche-writing as spacing, that it "cannot
occur *as such* within the phenomenological experience of a *presence.*"[33]
This is why Merleau-Ponty speaks of the need for an indirect ontology and a negative philosophy, on the model of negative theology.[34]

And yet Merleau-Ponty's *mode of procedure* in *The Visible and
the Invisible* is still phenomenological in that it is, as he says "to our
experience that we address ourselves" (VI 159). This, however, he is
careful to point out, need not commit one to any kind of phenomenological "positivism" or idealism for, as he goes on to say: "This does
not even exclude the possibility that we find in our experience a
movement toward what could not in any event be present to us in the
original and whose irremediable absence would thus count among
our originating experiences."[35] *The Visible and the Invisible* was nothing other than an abortive attempt on his part "to discern these
references," "to see these margins of presence." It was his last attempt to say the unsayable and to name the unnameable. One of
Merleau-Ponty's remarks about "the philosopher" fits Merleau-Ponty
himself perfectly: "His entire 'work' is this absurd effort. He wrote in
order to state his contact with Being; he did not state it, and could not
state it, since it is silence. Then he recommences. . . . " (VI 125)

4.

After all this I hope that my original thesis—that, for Merleau-
Ponty, there is no "perception"—will have gained in plausibility. There
is no more "perception" in Merleau-Ponty than there is in Derrida.

And yet, between these two different ways of thinking/writing about difference, there remains an important difference, one which, in conclusion, I would like to comment on. If I may speak anachronistically—and why not? hermeneutically speaking, it is entirely fitting to do so, given the fact that although, as Kierkegaard said, we live forwards, we nevertheless understand backwards, the consequence of which being that the past is always the future of subsequent presents—Merleau-Ponty's position strikes me as being a decided "advance" over Derrida's.

In his later work (and by means of his notion of the "flesh") Merleau-Ponty abandoned not only what he called "phenomenological positivism" but, as Derrida sought to do subsequently, all philosophical positivities. Unlike his poststructuralist successors, however, Merleau-Ponty did not seek to abandon philosophy itself, even though in his later work he reflected seriously on the "end of philosophy" theme which so much dominates our time.[36] The reason he did not do so is because he staunchly refused to jump on the anti-humanism bandwagon, even though he sought strenuously to rid his thinking of all "anthropocentrism." Merleau-Ponty remained a philosopher precisely because he did not believe in the "death of man," i.e., the human *subject*. Indeed, for him the philosopher is none other than "the man who wakes up and speaks."[37] Merleau-Ponty's philosophizing was, nonetheless, fully post-metaphysical in that for him the task of philosophy was not to provide definitive answers to the riddles of life. The most that philosophy can do is to raise to the level of reflective awareness the ultimate, and thus unsurpassable, questions of existence. " 'From time to time,' " Merleau-Ponty writes, quoting Claudel:

> 'a man lifts his head, sniffs, listens, considers, recognizes his position: he thinks, he sighs, and, drawing his watch from the pocket lodged against his chest, looks at the time. *Where am I?* and, *What time is it?* such is the inexhaustible question turning from us to the world . . .' (VI 103)

And he writes under his own signature:

> If we are ourselves in question in the very unfolding of our life, . . . it is because we ourselves are one sole continued question, a perpetual enterprise of taking our bearings on the constellations of the world, and of taking the bearings of the things on our dimensions.[38] The very questions of curiosity or those of science are interiorly animated by the fundamental interrogation which appears naked in philosophy.

For Merleau-Ponty philosophy was nothing other, and nothing more, than the stubborn pursuit of "the central question that is ourselves, of that appeal for totality to which no objective being answers" (VI 104).[39]

In the end, the proper name for philosophy that Merleau-Ponty settled on was "*interrogation*," self-interrogation, we might add. Philosophy is the self-reflection (i.e., the turning back and intertwining of itself on itself; "reversibility") of the speaking/perceiving subject who persistently asks, to paraphrase a line from the linguist Emile Benveniste: Who exactly is the *I* who, in its speech, is always refering to itself as "I?"[40] A question which is as inescapable and irreducible as it is inexhaustible.

Notes

1. Jacques Derrida, "Structure, Sign, and Play in the Human Discourses" in *The Structuralist Controversy,* ed. R. Macksey and E. Donato (Baltimore: Johns Hopkins University Press, 1972), p. 272. In the *Phenomenology of Perception,* Merleau-Ponty had already written: "In the natural attitude, I do not have *perceptions*" (p. 281).

2. In regard to the natural tendency on the part of human understanding to misunderstand itself, see, for instance, PhP 37, 57, 58, 67, 70–1, 82, 327. Merleau-Ponty's observations on this score are neatly summed up in the following line in *The Visible and the Invisible:* "The temptation to construct perception out of the perceived, to construct our contact with the world out of what it has taught us about the world, is quasi-irresistible" (VI 156).

3. In regard to "mind" or "thinking," see Bruno Snell, *The Discovery of the Mind* (New York: Harper and Row, 1960). It could be said that for "prephilosophical man" thinking was not something that a "subject" "did." Rather, as in the case of Homeric man, thoughts, like dreams and other such mental going-ons, were things that "happened" to a human being, the voice of the god or goddess speaking in him, inclining him in this direction or that. Homeric man neither "thought" nor "acted," in our sense of the terms. Referring to Snell, Paul Feyerabend remarks: "There is no spiritual centre, no 'soul' that might initiate or 'create' special causal chains, and even the body does not possess the coherence and the marvelous articulation given it in later Greek sculpture." (*Farewell to Reason* [London: Verso, 1987], p. 139) Contrast this with the portrait of the human being that emerges from Descartes' *Regulae ad directionem ingenuii,* that of a subject which is not only fully conscious of itself but which also seeks, by means of the appropriate, consciously manipulated *method,* to be the absolute master of its own thoughts.

4. See in this regard G. B. Madison, "Merleau-Ponty's Deconstruction of Logocentrism," in M. C. Dillon, ed., *Merleau-Ponty Vivant* (Albany: State University of New York Press, 1991), pp. 117–152.

5. Edmund Husserl, *The Crisis of European Sciences and Transcendental Phenomenology,* trans. David Carr (Evanston, Ill.: Northwestern University Press, 1970), §10.

6. As M. C. Dillon nonetheless maintains. See his article "Apriority in Kant and Merleau-Ponty," *Kant-Studien,* 4 (1987), p. 421.

7. See also PhP 37: "Everything that exists exists as a thing or as a consciousness, and there is no half-way house."

8. "The experience of our own body . . . reveals to us an ambiguous mode of existing" (PhP 198).

9. See G. B. Madison, *The Phenomenology of Merleau-Ponty* (Athens: Ohio University Press, 1981), p. 34.

10. See Madison, *The Phenomenology of Merleau-Ponty,* p. 27ff. Cf. PhP 320: "Thus the thing is correlative to my body and, in more general terms, to my existence, of which my body is merely the stabilized structure. It is constituted in the hold which my body takes upon it."

11. "The sensible quality, far from being co-extensive with perception, is the peculiar product of an attitude of curiosity or observation" (PhP 226).

12. For a detailed discussion of metaphorical predication, see G. B. Madison, *Understanding: A Phenomenological-Pragmatic Analysis* (Westport, Conn.: Greenwood Press, 1982).

13. "The sentiment and the sensible, do not stand in relation to each other as two mutually external terms, and sensation is not an invasion of the sentient by the sensible. . . . in this transaction between the subject of sensation and the sensible it cannot be held that one acts while the other suffers the action . . ." (PhP 214; also see p. 207).

14. See in this regard PhP 212–13.

15. In regard to "style," see PhP 327. In *The Visible and the Invisible* Merleau-Ponty writes (p. 132): ". . . a visible is not a chunk of absolutely hard, indivisible being . . . but is rather . . . a certain differentiation, an ephemeral modulation of this world—less a color or a thing, therefore than a difference between things and colors, a momentary crystallization of colored being or of visibility."

16. At roughly the same time that Merleau-Ponty was composing the *Phenomenology of Perception,* Friedrich A. Hayek, in a totally different intellectual environment (i.e., England), was working on his own study of perception, *The Sensory Order* (Chicago: The University of Chicago Press, 1976 [1952]). The affinities between these two texts are in many ways quite striking. Like Merleau-Ponty's, Hayek's work is an attack on what he calls

the "objectivist attitude." In regard to perceptual synaesthesia (which Merleau-Ponty for his part discusses in the chapter of the *Phenomenology* entitled "Sense Experience"), Hayek says:

> ... when we try to describe the differences between different qualities belonging to the same modality, such as different colours, we find that in order to do so we usually resort to expressions borrowed from other modalities. One colour may be warmer or heavier or louder than another, one tone brighter or rougher or thicker than another.... There exist apparently certain intermodal or intersensory attributes, and with regard to some of the terms which we use for them, such as strong or weak, mild or mellow, tingling or sharp, we are often not immediately aware to which sense modality they originally belong....

> We may become aware of their existence only when we attempt to describe a particular sensory quality and in doing so find ourselves driven to describe a colour as soft or sweet, a tone as thick or dark, a taste as hot or sharp, or a smell as dry and sweet. There can be little doubt that these seemingly metaphorical expressions refer to truly intersensory attributes ... In this way certain groups of qualities tend to 'belong' together, and particular qualities come to 'mean' to us certain other qualities.... directly or indirectly, all mental qualities are so related to each other that any attempt to give an exhaustive description of any one of them would make it necessary to describe the relations existing between all (pp. 20–3).

As for Merleau-Ponty, so for Hayek too meaning is a matter of *difference:*

> All that can be communicated are the differences between sensory qualities.... It seems thus impossible that any question about the nature or character of particular sensory qualities should ever arise which is not a question about the differences from (or the relations to) other sensory qualities.... all the attributes of sensory qualities (and of other mental qualities) are relations to other such qualities, and ... the totality of all these relations between mental qualities exhausts all there is to be said about the mental order ... (pp. 31, 35)

Compare these remarks with PhP 229, 234.

17. Merleau-Ponty was fond of saying that the body is to the mind as language is to thought. This is what is known as an analogy of proper proportionality. In *The Visible and the Invisible* the body-language analogy is strengthened. Not only are body and language analogous, they intertwine and are *reversible.*

18. The point that Merleau-Ponty wishes to make has been stated by Gadamer in the following way:

. . . interpretation is not an isolated activity of human beings but the basic structure of our experience of life. We are always taking something *as* something. That is the primordial givenness of our world orientation, and we cannot reduce it to anything simpler or more immediate. . . . Is sense perception something given or is it an abstraction that thematizes an abstract constant of the given? Scheler, aided by his contacts with psychologists and physiologists of his epoch as with American pragmatism and Heidegger, demonstrated with vigor that sense perception is never given. It is rather an aspect of the pragmatic approach to the world. We are always hearing-listening *to* something and extracting [sic] *from* other things. We are *interpreting* in seeing, hearing, receiving. In seeking, we are looking *for* something; we are just not like photographs that reflect everything visible. ("The Hermeneutics of Suspicion" in *Hermeneutics: Questions and Prospects,* ed. Gary Shapiro and Alan Sica (Amherst: University of Massachusetts Press, 1984), pp. 58–60.

Gadamer goes on to refer to Merleau-Ponty by name. See also Heidegger's earlier remark: ". . . our simplest perceptions and constitutive states are already *expressed* [*ausgedruckt*], even more, are *interpreted* in a certain way.... To put it more precisely: we do not say what we see, but rather the reverse, we see what *one* says about the matter [*die Sache*]." Martin Heidegger, *History of the Concept of Time,* trans. T. Kisiel (Bloomington: Indiana University Press, 1985), p. 56.

19. For an argument to the effect that Merleau-Ponty does indeed propose a non-linguistic perception see M. C. Dillon, " 'Eye and Mind': The Intertwining of Vision and Thought," *Man and World,* 13 (1980), pp. 155–171.

20. Thomas Busch, "Perception, Perspectivism, and Interpretation: Another Look at *Phenomenology of Perception,*" paper presented to the Merleau-Ponty Circle in 1986.

21. For an attempt to argue, in a like fashion, that being that can be *imagined* is language (i.e., not sense data), see G. B. Madison, "The Philosophic Centrality of the Imagination: A Postmodern Approach" in *The Hermeneutics of Postmodernity: Figures and Themes* (Bloomington: Indiana University Press, 1988).

22. In regard to the relation between perception and language, Merleau-Ponty says in *The Visible and the Invisible:* ". . . what is lived is lived-spoken . . . . vision itself, thought itself, are, as has been said, 'structured as a language,' are *articulation* before the letter. . . . [one's native language] is the folding over within him of the visible and lived experience upon language, and of language upon the visible and lived experience" (VI 126).

23. See Richard Kearney, *Dialogues with Contemporary Continental Thinkers: The Phenomenological Heritage, Paul Ricoeur, Emmanual Lévinas, Herbert Marcuse, Stansilas Breton, Jacques Derrida* (Manchester: Manchester University Press, 1984), p. 113.

24. I do not of course mean that Derrida hasn't read Merleau-Ponty, in the ordinary sense of the term. I mean that he hasn't *read* him in the Derridean sense of the word, i.e., hasn't *written* about him (except, apart from an instance or two, by way of indirect and anonymous allusions), hasn't devoted a specific text to him.

Subsequent to the writing of the present essay, my attention was drawn to the very interesting article by Nancy J. Holland, "Merleau-Ponty on Presence: A Derridian Reading," *Research in Phenomenology,* 16 (1986), 111–120. Holland notes that in the course of a visit by Derrida to a class on Merleau-Ponty she was attending, Derrida remarked that Merleau-Ponty's work falls within the metaphysics of presence. Pressed to defend himself, Derrida was forced to admit that "the case was not quite so clear-cut, given the breadth and complexity of Merleau-Ponty's work"; "he left us with an interesting thought," Holland writes, "—if one might argue that the *Phenomenology of Perception* falls within the metaphysics of presence, with *The Visible and the Invisible* 'it is even harder to say' " (p. 111).

In this article Holland shows convincingly how, as I myself have tried to show in this essay, the *Phenomenology* itself already breaks the bounds of the metaphysics of presence: "What interests me . . . is the way in which much of what Merleau-Ponty says, even in the *Phenomenology of Perception,* denies any primacy to, or often even any possibility of presence. In this respect Merleau-Ponty's work often seems to foreshadow some of the criticisms Derrida himself makes of traditional phenomenology [see in this regard the text of Merleau-Ponty quoted in note 34 of the present essay]. . . . Merleau-Ponty can be seen to exceed the tradition, often in words that echo Derrida's own before their time" (pp. 111–12).

Another noteworthy article dealing with Merleau-Ponty and Derrida that subsequent research on my part has turned up is: Bernard Charles Flynn, "Textuality and the Flesh: Derrida and Merleau-Ponty, *Journal of the British Society for Phenomenology,* 15 (1984), pp. 164–179.

25. Ferdinand de Saussure, *Course in General Linguistics,* trans. W. Barkin (New York: Philosophical Library, 1959), p. 120.

26. Jacques Derrida, "Difference" in *Speech and Phenomena,* trans. David Allison (Evanston, Ill.: Northwestern University Press, 1973), p. 131. Hereafter cited as SP.

27. In regard to Merleau-Ponty's rejection of mentalistic "bric-a-brac" see also VI 235: "All the positivist bric-a-brac of 'concepts,' 'judgments,' 'rela-

tions' is eliminated, and the mind quiet as water in the fissure of Being"; VI 253: "The meaning of being to be disclosed: it is a question of showing that the ontic, the 'Erlebnisse,' 'sensation,' 'judgments'—(the ob-jects, the 'represented,' in short all idealizations of the Psyche and of Nature) all the bric-a-brac of those *positive* psychic so-called 'realities' . . . is in reality abstractly carved out from the ontological tissue, from the 'body of the mind.'"

28. See also VI 147: "What we are calling flesh . . . has no name in any philosophy."

29. See PrP 187. Merleau-Ponty is speaking in a quasi-Derridian way when he says: "As the nervure bears the leaf from within, from the depths of its flesh, ideas are the texture of experience, its style, first mute, then uttered. Like every style, they are elaborated within the thickness of being and, not only in fact but also by right, could not be detached from it, to be spread out on display under the gaze" (VI 119).

30. Merleau-Ponty immediately goes on to say: "Every visual something, as individual as it is, functions also as a dimension, because it gives itself as the result of a dehiscence of Being. What this ultimately means is that the proper essence [*le propre*] of the visible is to have a layer [*doublure*] of invisibility in the strict sense, which it makes present as a certain absence."

And in a working note dated November 6, 1960, he writes: "Position, negation, negation of negation: this side, the other, the other than the other. What do I bring to the problem of the same and the other? This: that the same be the other than the other, and identity difference of difference—this 1) does not realize a surpassing, a dialectic in the Hegelian sense; 2) is realized on the spot, by encroachment, thickness, *spatiality*—(VI 264).

31. ". . . there is dehiscence, and not positive production . . . " VI 265.

32. Thought cannot think Being except as that which withdraws from consciousness, since it is that which makes consciousness (the intentional, subject-object relation) be consciousness and which is the possibility or the latency of all presence: "if Being is hidden, this is itself a characteristic of Being, and no disclosure will make us comprehend it" (VI 122).

33. Jacques Derrida, *Of Grammatology,* trans. G. C. Spivak (Baltimore: The Johns Hopkins University Press, 1976), p. 68.

34. In the course of his lengthy critique of Husserlian phenomenology in *The Visible and the Invisible,* which he viewed as being still a "philosophy of consciousness," Merleau-Ponty remarked that a philosophy of wild being or the flesh "is *not* compatible with 'phenomenology,' that is, with an ontology that obliges whatever is not nothing to *present* itself to *consciousness* across *Abschattungen* and as deriving from an originating donation which is an *act,* i.e. one *Erlebnis* among others" (VI 298). This is why the discovery of the flesh calls for nothing less than a "complete reconstruction of philosophy" (VI 193).

In regard to "negative philosophy" see VI 179: *"One cannot make a direct ontology. My 'indirect' method (being in beings) is alone conformed with being—'negative philosophy' like 'negative theology.'"*

35. It is as if Merleau-Ponty were responding in advance to Derrida when he writes: "Negatively, as a disclosure of the 'unknown' language, this attitude is profoundly philosophical, it is constitutive of the attitude of reflection at its best. This reflection is not, and cannot be, a limitation to the phenomenology of the *Erlebnisse*. The mistrust with regard to lived experience is philosophical—one postulates that consciousness deceives us about ourselves and about language and one is right: this is the only way to see them. Philosophy has nothing to do with the privilege of the *Erlebnisse*, with the psychology of lived experience, etc." (VI 181–82).

And it is as if he were admonishing Derrida when he writes: "lived experience is not flat, without depth, without dimension, it is not an opaque stratum with which we would have to merge" (VI 124). The following remark of Merleau-Ponty I take to be a criticism of structuralism and thus, in effect, of Derrida: "It is the error of the semantic philosophies to close up language as if it spoke only of itself: language lives only from silence; everything we cast to others has germinated in this great mute land which we never leave" (VI 126).

36. See, in particular, Maurice Merleau-Ponty, *Themes from the Lectures at the Collège de France, 1952–1960,* course summary for the year 1958–59. Translated in English as "Philosophy as Interrogation," the title given this section in French is *"Possibilité de la philosophie."*

37. Maurice Merleau-Ponty, *Eloge de la philosophie* (Paris: Gallimard, 1953), p. 100 (last sentence).

38. This, let it be noted, is the very essense of the metaphorical process.

39. Further on in the text, on pages 128–29, Merleau-Ponty writes, speaking about what the philosophical questioning is *not:* "Not the *an sit* and the doubt, where Being is tacitly understood, and not the 'I know that I know nothing,' where already the absolute certitude of the ideas breaks through, but a true 'what do I know?' ['*que sais-je?*'] which is not quite that of Montaigne. For the 'what do I know?' could be a simple appeal for the elucidation of the things that we know, without any examination of the idea of knowing. In that case it would be one of those questions of cognition [epistemology!] (as can also be the 'where am I?') where we are hesitating only about what to call entities—space, knowledge—which are taken as evident in themselves. But already when I say 'what do I know?' in the course of a phrase, another sort of question arises: for it extends to the idea of knowing itself; it invokes some intelligible place where the facts, examples, ideas I lack, should be found; it intimates that the interrogative is not a mode derived by inversion or by reversal of the indicative and of the positive, but an original manner of aiming at something, as it were a *ques-*

tion-knowing, which by principle no statement or 'answer' can go beyond and which perhaps therefore is the proper mode of our relationship to Being, as though it were the mute or reticent interlocutor of our questions."

40. Benveniste maintained that the personal pronoun "I" "... refers to the act of individual discourse in which it is pronounced, and by this it designates the speaker.... The reality to which it refers is the reality of discourse. It is in the instance of discourse in which *I* designates the speaker that the speaker proclaims himself as the 'subject.' And so it is literally true that the basis of subjectivity is in the exercise of language. If one really thinks about it, one will see that there is no other objective testimony to the identity of the subject except that which he himself thus gives about himself." "Subjectivity in Language" in *Problems in General Linguistics,* trans. M. Meck (Coral Gables, Fla.: University of Miami Press, 1971), p. 226.

One way of locating the key difference between Merleau-Ponty and Derrida would be with regard to the notion of *experience.* This is easily the central notion of phenomenology. Merleau-Ponty was fond of quoting Husserl's line: "It is the experience ... still mute which we are concerned with leading to the pure expression of its own meaning" (see, for instance, VI 129). For Derrida, however, the very notion of experience is still part and parcel of the metaphysics of presence. Merleau-Ponty would have strenuously disagreed. Or, more precisely, he would have admitted that the notion of experience *could* be, and indeed has generally been, interpreted idealistically. Merleau-Ponty's overriding goal in *The Visible and the Invisible* was precisely that of, so to speak, de-idealizing the notion of experience.

Moreover, he would have maintained that a "denial" of experience is impossible, philosophical nonsense. He says, for instance: "The resolution to confine ourselves to the experience of what is in the originating or fundamental or inaugural sense presupposes nothing more than an encounter between 'us' and 'what is'.... *The encounter is indubitable,* since without it we would ask no question." As if in response to Derrida he goes on to write: "Is not the resolution to ask of experience itself its secret already an idealist commitment? We would have made ourselves badly understood if that were the conclusion drawn" (VI 159; emphasis added).

To turn the tables on Derrida, it should be noted that deconstruction does not just happen by itself, as it were, anymore than books (contrary to what some poststructuralists would have us believe) simply write themselves. It is always a thinking, experiencing subject *who* engages in the deconstruction of metaphysics. And what, one might well ask, is the point of deconstruction anyway? What worthwhile purpose does it serve, can it serve, to deconstruct metaphysics, if this be not, ultimately, the hermeneutical one of arriving at a better, less speculative or mythical *self-understanding.* Merleau-Ponty understood this perfectly (see, in this regard, Madison, "Merleau-Ponty and Postmodernity" in *The Hermeneutics of Postmodernity*). Derrida does not yet appear to do so. If Derrida himself is anything to go by, he may actually not be all that wrong when he dismisses the notion of *progress* in philosophy.

Part Two

Postmodernism

8

Introduction:
"…. Being … which is Staggered Out in Depth …"

૱ ૱

Thomas W. Busch

At the center of *Phenomenology of Perception* is a repetitious critique of attempts to found reason in either some sort of Absolute Mind or realist version of the world. Merleau-Ponty argues that truth is factical and produced. "Philosophy is not," he writes, "the reflection of a pre-existing truth" (PhP xx). *The Visible and the Invisible* reiterates the earlier critique of reason, focusing especially on versions of a possible "coincidence" of mind with essence or existence.

> What we propose here, and oppose to the search for the essence, is not the return to the immediate, the coincidence, the effective fusion with the existent, the search for an original integrity, for a secret lost and to be rediscovered, which would nullify our questions and even reapprehend our language. If coincidence is lost, this is no accident; if Being is hidden, this is itself a characteristic of Being, and no disclosure will make us comprehend it. (VI 121–122)

Merleau-Ponty's ontology, in rejecting coincidence, involves itself with the question of distance, differentiation, and separation, an issue that he had previously debated with Sartre, but to which he now returns with intensity. He agrees with Sartre that distance or differentiation is the very condition of possibility of experience: "But if I express this experience by saying that the things are in their place and that we fuse with them, I immediately make the experience itself impossible …" (VI 122). Differentiation is not an alienation of experience and its overcoming would not result in achieving absolute knowledge. Merleau-Ponty disagrees, however, with Sartre's depiction of difference as *néant,* a nothingness beyond being, which would have the effect of desituating experience. On this point Merleau-Ponty reiterates the centrality of bodily experience from his earlier work, now holding that the body is the "prototype of Being." In the body's touching of itself is found a differentiation (*ecart*) and an encroachment which is neither sheer identity nor non-identity. He then moves from the prototype to Being: "The negations, the perspective deformations, the possibilities, which I have learned to consider as extrinsic denominations, I must now reintegrate into Being—which therefore is staggered out in depth, conceals itself at the same time as it discloses itself, is abyss and not plenitude" (VI 77). The *ecart,* unlike Sartre's *néant,* is not brought about by consciousness. It is, instead, "a *natural* negativity, a first institution, always already there. ..." (VI 216). The inspiration for this "natural" negativity and for the reference to Being as "abyss and not plenitude" is the diacritical logic of structural linguistics. Merleau-Ponty's rejection of coincidence, his claim that the "originating breaks up" (VI 124), his preoccupation with *ecart,* offer common ground for comparison with the temporal distantiation of hermeneutics and the "differance" of postmodernism. Despite the fact that his unexpectedly early death left his work incomplete, its richness, originality, and suggestiveness afford a valuable opportunity for a dialogue with hermeneutics and postmodernism that can only benefit those interested in the contemporary philosophical scene.

Our consideration of Merleau-Ponty and postmodernism begins with a discussion on that topic among Gary Madison, Martin Dillon, and Hugh Silverman. Madison cordons off "postmodern" elements in Merleau-Ponty's thought, such as his anti-foundationalism, anti-essentialism, anti-dualism, from certain elements present in the works of Foucault, Deleuze, and Derrida, such as anti-humanism, anti-truth, and anti-philosophy. Merleau-Ponty, according to Madison, is able to rightfully avoid these rejections with his own reconstructed versions of humanism, truth, and philosophy. Thus, in Madison's estimation, Merleau-Ponty presaged the best in postmodernism without lapsing into its excesses. Martin Dillon takes language as his point of comparison between Merleau-Ponty and postmodernism. While he views Merleau-Ponty and postmodernism to share a common critique of transcendental foundations, as well as a common appropriation of elements from structural linguistics, he sees a major break between them over the referentiality of language. He claims that Merleau-Ponty's appreciation of language allows him to seek "grounds" in the world, whereas postmodernists, such as Derrida, opt for the "abyss." Merleau-Ponty, according to Dillon, establishes the language/world relation through his notion of "reversibility." Reversibility, says Dillon, can be infra-linguistic, as is the case when signifiers systematically implicate one another diacritically, and extra-linguistic, when perception and language implicate one another. The entertwining of perception and language brings language out of itself. Dillon accuses Derrida of holding only to an infra-linguistic view of language, wherein language closes about itself. The "between" of critical opposition of signifiers becomes for Dillon an "abyss" of a nihilistic sort, since it cuts off reference to a world outside of language. Hugh Silverman approaches comparison between Merleau-Ponty and postmodernism with caution. He first discriminates certain notions which, while entangled, are often mistakenly conflated, such as postmodern, post-hermeneutic, and post-structuralist. Armed with his own elaboration of these various classifications, Silverman takes issue with what he perceives to be reductionistic readings of postmodernism by Madison and Dillon. He is especially concerned with Dillon's interpretation of the "between" in Derrida as nihilistic, claiming that Derrida's oft referred to remark about there being nothing "outside of the text" in no way constitutes an enclosing of language within itself. In Silverman's reading, Derrida is simply holding that language is the only access to the world, so that "text" becomes the way we must encounter the world. This is not unlike Merleau-Ponty's own position according to Silverman, and not to recognize this is to undermine the radicality of Merleau-Ponty's work. He suggests that the understanding of the "between" in Merleau-Ponty and Derrida may not at all be different, but that Merleau-Ponty's insistence that differences are somehow gathered (in the Flesh) marks his path off from Derrida's.

The theme of postmodern politics is the pivot of the discussion among Derek Taylor, Eleanor Godway, and Geraldine Finn. Taylor explores the differences between Deleuze's postmodern politics, an anti-phenomenological politics based on the free play of signifiers, and Merleau-Ponty's politics, based on a phenomenology of perception. In Deleuze's case structuralism is appropriated to uproot, in a theory of difference, all presence and to preclude any hinge for the collection and sedimentation of meaning which could be used for absolutistic purposes. In Merleau-Ponty's case structuralism is appropriated in terms of a phenomenology of perception and of contingent meaning, which, while avoiding metaphysical absolutes, offers a situational politics. Taylor places the crucial difference between Merleau-Ponty and Deleuze in their respective appropriations of the critical notion of difference. According to Taylor, Deleuze translates difference into a rootless becoming, whereas Merleau-Ponty translates difference (as divergence) into the perceptual discourse of figure/background. While the relation between figure and background is always contingent (since neither is defined as such in itself), the relationship al ways entails a situational meaning, including a perceptual attention, which, as a point of view, is always implicated. Since Taylor reads Deleuze's critique of absolutism as a refusal of any position or identity (and thus of responsibility), including its own, he accuses it of being an "escapism," and a consequent devaluation of the political, while Merleau-Ponty's position of situational meaning exacts from human beings a continual account of their social and historical lives. Eleanor Godway takes up the figure/background theme as it relates to Merleau-Ponty's distinction between originary and sedimented speech. In her project of sketching out what a politics beyond empiricism and intellectualism might be, she first locates some political positions she find compatible with each. With the empiricist she places the tradition from Hobbes to Foucault, and with the intellectualist the tradition from Kant to Habermas. She, as with Merleau-Ponty before her, faults these traditions from the perspective of an embodied rationality. In their place she suggests a politics "originaire," in the spirit of Merleau-Ponty's speech "originaire," his alternative view of meaning to the empiricist and intellectualist traditions. This sort of politics, she argues, is both situational and creative. Its point is to equilibrate needs, tensions arising within a previously contingently balanced situation. Using a personal experience from her university days, she provides a lived experience of her own discovery of such a politics. In "The Politics of Contingency and the Contingency of Politics," Geraldine Finn appreciates, in opposition to many commentators, a political dimension to Merleau-Ponty's ontology, and sees it as a deepening of engagement with the political. She shows how the notions of contingency, flesh, and reversibility can be used to subvert what one might call the "all or nothing" dilemma posed to political thinking by modern and postmodern approaches. Modern thought, aspiring to necessity and universality, absorbs the political, ultimately legitimating hierarchies and violence. Finn thinks that Merleau-Ponty himself was victim of this sort of attitude prior to his later ontology when he spoke of an "inevitability" of violence. Postmodern thinkers reject the "all" horn of the dilemma and end up embracing the "nothing," rejecting the notions of reason, subjectivity, and responsibility, ʼnd thus the relevance of philosophical thinking itself to the political. ʼn draws out the assumptions of certain sexist and racist politics ʼıses them as a contrast with the assumptions she thinks are ʼ by Merleau-Ponty's ontology. A politics of contingency, flesh, ʼty, would be sensitive to locality, particularity, alterity, re-ʼch a politics would look to the contingent formation of ʼems, would reject unambiguous polarities, and would ʼtions, fixed programs. Much in the spirit of Godway's politics "originaire," Finn's reading of Merleau-Ponty leads her to reject overarching theory in favor of situational practice.

Following these discussions are several in-depth essays on various facets of Merleau-Ponty's work in relation to postmodernism. Martin Dillon offers a close analysis of Merleau-Ponty and Derrida on temporality. He examines Derrida's critique of Husserl in *Speech and Phenomena,* noting the steps by which Derrida comes to the conclusion that presence is an effect of repetition, and how phenomena come to be replaced by signs. Phenomena and transcendental subjectivity itself are deconstructed and replaced by signs. Dillon offers a formula for Derrida's moves: identity is reduced to ideality, ideality to non-identity. There is a problem, according to Dillon, in the heart of Derrida's strategy when he assumes that retention (in Husserl's temporal analysis) is the equivalent of representation (and, thus, of repetition). In a broader criticism, he views Derrida's project to fall within Merleau-Ponty's critique of intellectualism (as worked out in *Phenomenology of Perception*), wherein the intellectualist uses signs or concepts to remedy what the intellectualist judges to be deficiencies in perception. Dillon holds that Derrida subscribes to the view that sensory perception is a flux having no stability, with the result that signs must be brought in to supply stability by means of offering a basis of repetition. Merleau-Ponty had, Dillon points out, through his notion of an autochthonous significance in perception, responded to the intellectualists by recognizing a type of stability in the perceived world. Dillon concludes by calling for recognition of a phenomenal temporality of natural segments in opposition to Derrida's notion of an "insufficient" temporality.

Mark Yount initiates a dialogue between Merleau-Ponty and Derrida on the issue of "reversibility." He sees their projects as going in different directions, but crossing at this juncture. Yount carefully explores the development of reversibility in Merleau-Ponty's works from *Phenomenology of Perception* to *The Visible and the Invisible,* from its inception as the touching/touched in the body's "self-reflection" to its application ontologically to all levels and dimensions in the notion of Flesh. Where Merleau-Ponty's thought crosses that of Derrida is in their common appropriation of the oppositional logic of structuralism. Merleau-Ponty had always resisted the notion of a meaning transcendent to its expression and inscription. He found in the diacritical relation of signs a congenial view and a new way of resisting the transcendental. In the ontology of *The Visible and the Invisible* the reversibility of signifier and signified also become a possible avenue for relating perception and language, a persistent problem for him.

Yount briefly traces out the development of Derrida's view of meaning from his critique of Husserl to his later work. At the heart of his view is a resistance to detaching meaning from signs. With his appropriation of structuralism, Derrida develops his view of textualism and the function of signs as "pirouettes." This sort of reversibility of signs weds the Derridian deconstruction of presence and the undecidability of meaning.

In comparing Merleau-Ponty and Derrida, Yount points out how a reading of each leads to an illumination of the other's texts. He thinks that Derrida has been too harsh on Merleau-Ponty, that it is unfair to convict the latter of holding to a metaphysics of presence, and that Derrida should be open to much of what Merleau-Ponty was offering in his ontology. The major difference between them, according to Yount, is that Merleau-Ponty finds diacriticity, contingency of meaning, ambiguity, reversibility, in phenomena and expresses this in an ontology of Flesh, whereas Derrida follows the path of Husserl's reduction, along the course of withdrawing from experience to seek an underlying logic. Yount claims that Merleau-Ponty has shown how a phenomenology of experience can be kept vital, avoiding the pitfalls of traditional metaphysics.

Alphonso Lingis reexamines Merleau-Ponty's notion of the primacy of perception as it relates to the primary or founding role of natural or worldly space. The subject/natural world relation of the *Phenomenology of Perception* is viewed by Lingis as a privileging or normalizing of the practical. The body-subject is "competent," "laborious," "occupied," with the world as a set of manipulanda. Its space is a working space. This is the space, according to Lingis, upon which Merleau-Ponty founds other, derivitive worlds and spaces, mythic, primitive, phantasmic, erotic. The latter are derivitive formulations of the former, built up with elements borrowed from it. While Lingis ·elcomes Merleau-Ponty's work on perception as an appropriate cri-
ιe of the Enlightenment's fixation on the rational subject and its
ᴵ of ideas, he is uneasy with Merleau-Ponty's own normalizing of
ᵢn experience of the world. For Lingis things have a dimension
ᵉndence of which the practical is only one possible manifes-
ᵢngs engender their own images, ghostly reflections, and
ᵉ opening of consciousness to these "other" worlds does
ᵢctory of subjective creation for, as any artist knows,
ᵗives other than those imposed by the practical world.
ce reveals *its own* structure and demands. Our per-
ᵉing normalized by disciplinary practices, by a regi-
ᵧ and seeing. In contrast are the nomadic spaces of

the "walkabout" practices of some non-Western peoples. Such practices, expansive of the sense of reality of things and of self, are liberating, and their analogues in Western society are becoming most rare. Yet, Lingis advises, we all must continually be open to those moments in our lives when certain transformative perceptions suggest themselves.

Our final essay, Joseph Margolis's "Merleau-Ponty and Postmodernism," brings a further perspective to some of the issues raised by Madison, Dillon, and Silverman in their discussion of the same topic. In assessing Merleau-Ponty's relation to postmodernism Margolis employs three representative texts from Merleau-Ponty's works and measures them on a scale at the extremes of which are, on the one hand, Husserl and Habermas, and, on the other, Heidegger and Lyotard. Citing Merleau-Ponty's rejection of Husserl's anti-historicism, his chiasmic epistemology ("My thought is indeed only the other side of my times."), and his continuous stress on the preconceptual, Margolis judges that Merleau-Ponty "subverts" the philosophical canon, while, for example, Habermas "restores the canon with only minor adjustments." Identification between Habermas's project and Merleau-Ponty's only serves, according to Margolis, to compromise Merleau-Ponty's originality and disguise the "full improvisational possibilities of his work." Instead of placing Merleau-Ponty's work in the tradition of Enlightenment reason, Margolis sees a more pragmatic reason at work, one which "hints of the infinity of open possibilities of alternative conceptual idioms that may prove fruitful."

As the reader engages the following essays, perhaps no more appropriate admonition could be taken to heart than the one that Merleau-Ponty himself offered about approaching the work of a philosopher in his study of Husserl:

> Just as the perceived world endures only through the reflections, shadows, levels, and horizons between things (which are not things and are not nothing, but on the contrary mark out by themselves the fields of possible variation in the same thing and the same world), so the works and thought of a philosopher are also made of certain articulations between things said. There is no dilemma of objective interpretation or arbitrariness with respect to these articulations, since they are not objects of thought, since (like shadow and reflection) they would be destroyed by being subjected to analytic observation or taken out of context, and since we can be faithful to and find them only by thinking again. (S 160)

9

Between Phenomenology and (Post)Structuralism:
Rereading Merleau-Ponty

ᵶ᪻ ᵶ᪻

G. B. Madison

That quintessential Californian, Alan Watts, renowned expert on Zen Buddhism and author of innumerable books, including one entitled simply *The Book* (which contains a number of phenomenologically noteworthy points), made a hermeneutically noteworthy point when he said: "Once you've got the message, hang up the phone." I suggest that this is a good maxim to apply to most of the things one reads in the course of one's everyday (*alltäglich*) existence. It certainly applies to all those texts which conform to scientistic theories as to what communication is or ought to be all about, namely, those texts whose sole purpose is to communicate what is nowadays called "information." You shouldn't waste too much time on them, and once you've got the message, go on to something else. Some texts, however, refuse to be treated in this way and continue to maintain a hold on our attention—precisely because their primary function is not the communication of "information" at all. Great works of literature— what Gadamer calls "eminent texts"—are of this sort. And so also are the great works of philosophy from the past—even though most of them would have us believe that their sole aim was to communicate true, propositional information about "the real world" (however that be defined). Of course, if this were all they did—if their "truths" were all they had to offer us—we would never bother reading or rereading them—any more than scientists continue to read old scientific writings.

Those works which one cannot simply hang up on, which indeed one finds oneself coming back to time and again, are what Merleau-Ponty called "classics," of which he said:

These do not endure because there is some miraculous adequation or correspondence between them and an invariable 'reality'—such an exact and fleshless truth is neither sufficient nor necessary for the greatness of a doctrine—but because, as obligatory steps for those who want to to go further, they retain an expressive power which exceeds their statements and propositions. These doctrines are the *classics*. They are recognizable by the fact that no one takes them literally, and yet new facts are never absolutely outside their province but call forth new echoes from them and reveal new lustres in them. (S 10–11)

If today we find ourselves together talking about Merleau-Ponty, it is because, I submit, his work has itself become a classic. Of course, what that means is that if we are *still* talking about him, it is because we *no longer* take him "literally," as some of us did when we first encountered his work a quarter of a century ago. We no longer read his work for "the answer" or "the truth," as we did then, since the precise questions Merleau-Ponty was dealing with no longer agitate us today. This is because the central problematic to which his work was a response is one which arose at a specific moment in the working out of the phenomenological project initiated by Husserl and thus, by definition, as it were, is context specific. No longer is it one which confronts us today, after a couple decades or so of structuralism and poststructualism which, like it or not, have effectively altered the parameters within which our problems get posed. *Tempora mutantur, nos et mutamur in illis;* Times change, and we change along with them. Even with regard to the problematic which was its own, Merleau-Ponty's work, qua response to this problematic, was not exactly what you could call a total success (which does not in any way diminish the value of it). If Merleau-Ponty continues to have something to say to us, if his work continues to have a "truth-value," it can only be what he himself called a "secondary truth," *"une vérité seconde"* (S 11).

Even though Martin Dillon believes that Merleau-Ponty's work "provides the closest approximation to philosophical truth in the history of Western thought"[1] (no small claim, you've got to admit), and even though he appears to regard subsequent developments in philosophical thinking as something of an unmitigated disaster (or, at least, a regrettable falling away from the truth), even he, I should think, would have to admit that the truth of Merleau-Ponty's work is a "secondary truth." (If he didn't, why did he spend so much time and effort working out his own original interpretation of Merleau-Ponty rather than simply letting the texts "speak for themselves?")

The fact of the matter is that Dillon, Silverman, and I (in my recent work on Merleau-Ponty) are all reading—or rereading as

Silverman appropriately puts it—Merleau-Ponty's texts not in the light in which his contemporaries read them (or in which Merleau-Ponty himself, qua first reader of his writing, read them) but in the light of those writings which have appeared since his death. As interpreters we cannot do otherwise, since, as hermeneutics tells us, this is the way human understanding works. As I said in my essay "Merleau-Ponty and Postmodernity"[2] (which, besides being a paper I once gave at the Sorbonne was also, in another guise, a paper presented to the Merleau-Ponty Circle in 1982 at Binghamton, at the invitation, precisely, of Martin Dillon): "Since human understanding is always retrospective . . ., the way we understand what was is by situating it in relation to what then did not yet exist, in relation to what in fact followed it in time and now is." And, of course, what now is is hermeneutics, deconstruction, and all other kinds of postmodern things. This is why, improvising on the title of Hugh Silverman's book,[3] I have entitled these remarks "Between Phenomenology and (Post)structuralism." To read Merleau-Ponty today entails taking a position on the significance and relevance of his work, given what has been said and written since his time. The positions that the three of us take in this regard, the ways in which, so to speak, we inscribe Merleau-Ponty between phenomenology and (post)structuralism, are each somewhat different from the other, and this difference (with-an-"e") is basically what I would like to talk about. Were I pressed to give a summary statement at the outset as to how we differ, I would be tempted to say that while Silverman's interpretation appears to be what could be called a left-leaning one, and while Dillon takes a philosophically right-wing approach to Merleau-Ponty's *oeuvre,* I find myself, as usual, occupying the liberal middle ground. What all that means should become clearer as we proceed.

If there is one common element in that otherwise extremely heteroclite body of writings customarily grouped together under headings such as "structuralist," "poststructualist," "deconstructionist," and what-have-you—which for the sake of convenience might be best referred to simply as "post-Merleau-Pontyean"—it is the quasi-universal rejection on the part of their authors of what they tend, often with barely concealed disdain, to refer to as "phenomenology." After the grandly proclaimed demise of the subject, of the author, of "man," or humanism, and of you-name-it, phenomenology, which is supposed to represent the last gasp of the modernist philosophy of consciousness, has, it seems widely to be presumed, been relegated to the ash-heap of history (which, it is said, has also passed away). Merleau-Ponty was of course a self-proclaimed phenomenologist, and thus it follows, according to current wisdom, that he remained bogged down in the "metaphysics of presence" and therefore no longer has anything to say to us postmodernists.

This is not the way I read, or reread, Merleau-Ponty. Quite to the contrary. To be sure, I do not believe, as I indicated above, that Merleau-Ponty's work can today be taken "literally." But I do believe, to allude to the passage of his I quoted, that what Merleau-Ponty had to say retains an expressive power which exceeds his statements and propositions. I believe that the new, post-Merleau-Pontyean issues which currently occupy the attention of the philosophical community are not "outside their province but call forth new echoes from them and reveal new lustres in them." There is a great deal that we postmodernists could still learn from Merleau-Ponty.

One aspect of his work that retains the utmost relevance is the role played in his thinking by the notion of *ambiguity*. We have been accustomed for a long time now to hearing his philosophy be referred to as a "philosophy of ambiguity," but, as I mentioned in the paper I presented to this Circle at the Rhode Island meeting hosted by Galen Johnson the year before last: "What it means to characterize Merleau-Ponty's philosophy as a philosophy of ambiguity is something the (counter-traditional) significance of which I do not believe we fully appreciate even today, some forty years after the publication of his major work." I entitled that paper "Merleau-Ponty's Deconstruction of Logocentrism" precisely in order to suggest that, as I said, "phenomenology, in Merleau-Ponty's hands, already accomplishes a decisive break with metaphysical logocentrism." It does so because it takes seriously the notion of ambiguity, something that the mainline tradition in philosophy never did. And when one does take ambiguity seriously, everything changes. Capital-P Philosophy, the "metaphysics of presence," finds itself being *ébranlée*, deconstructed.

Silverman is quite right, therefore, to single out the issue of ambiguity for detailed treatment in his book. "Ambiguity" is most definitely not, as Henri Lebevre would have had it (as Silverman reports), the mark of an "eclectic" philosophy. It is something altogether different. Rather than being an attempt to combine into a conceptual hodgepodge (as metaphysicians are wont to do) various oppositional terms such as mind and body, soul and body, for-itself and in-itself, mental and physical, transcendental and empirical (to use Silverman's list of terms), the emphasis Merleau-Ponty places on "ambiguity" is the mark of a thought which is resolutely seeking to overcome oppositional thinking itself. This is to say that it is a systematic attempt at "overcoming metaphysics," since the characteristic mark of "metaphysics" is, as Nietzsche pointed out, that it always thinks in terms of "opposites," which it seeks to play off against one another, in one way or another.

Thus, I'd be rather hesitant to use the (very traditionalist) term "dualism" when speaking of Merleau-Ponty, as Hugh nevertheless does. As for instance when he says: "Merleau-Ponty's *ambiguité*, therefore, continues to bear a trace of dualism" (85). Maybe just the very slightest of traces. Certainly his thought does not, to use Hugh's own words, "restrict itself to traditional philosophical dilemmas." Indeed not. The most remarkable thing about this thought is precisely the way in which it is, as Hugh says, a "continued struggle against a tradition that allows for the separation between nature and reality, objectivity and subjectivity, appearance and truth" (122).

In this struggle against the Tradition, Merleau-Ponty the Counter-Traditionalist, as I once referred to him,[4] more than anticipates many of the anti-essentialist, anti-foundationalist, and deconstructivist themes one encounters today. One even finds him musing over "the possibility of philosophy today," (T 99) i.e., the currently ubiquitous "end of philosophy" theme. Have we, Merleau-Ponty asks, entered into "an age of non-philosophy?" The non-philosophy issue is one which runs through much of Silverman's book, but I'm not quite sure what the import of it all is. I am wondering what he means when he speaks of philosophy becoming non-philosophy. Does it mean that for Merleau-Ponty philosophy becomes, or ought to become, experience, life (as Silverman says of Heidegger and Sartre)? There is no doubt that the later Heidegger, in his attempt to achieve a direct experience of Being itself, abandoned philosophy altogether—as have many of his epigones. I would very much hesitate saying that of Merleau-Ponty. Unlike a number of disillusioned postmodernists, Merleau-Ponty was not inclined to respond to the possibility-of-philosophy question in the negative, or the end-of-philosophy question in the affirmative. He said that the negation of metaphysics in Marx or Nietzsche "cannot take the place of philosophy" (T 102). And he said of his inquiry into the "ontology of Nature" that it sought to maintain "the same attention to what is fundamental [*le fondamental*] that remains the privilege and the task of philosophy" (T 112). I do not think that Merleau-Ponty ever seriously questioned the validity of philosophy's claim to a unique cultural vocation, however much he may have recognized the need for a "complete reconstruction of philosophy" (VI 193). For Merleau-Ponty philosophy was not, as it is for our contemporary advocates of anti-philosophy and anti-theory, something to be dissolved into life (*qui devrait se confondre avec la vie*), into the particularities of a multitude of differing ways-of-life ("local

knowledge"); it was for him, as it was for Socrates, a means for living
better. Consider, for instance, the following two texts:

> Assuredly a life is not a philosophy. I thought I had indicated . . . that
> description is not the return to immediate experience; one never
> returns to immediate experience. It is only a question of whether
> we are to try to understand it. I believe that to attempt to express
> immediate experience is not to betray reason but, on the contrary,
> to work toward its aggrandizement. (PhP 30)

> Far from thinking that philosophy is a useless repetition of life I
> think, on the contrary, that without reflection life would probably
> dissipate itself in ignorance of itself or in chaos. (PhP 19).

Thus, while Hugh and I are in agreement, I believe, on the degree to
which Merleau-Ponty's thought remains alive and, as Gadamer might
say, "effective" even in those postmodernist authors who officially
discount his work, we very likely differ on the degree to which there
exists, or persists, between these authors and Merleau-Ponty a common orientation or accord, a basic *continuité,* so to speak. I call
Silverman's rereading of Merleau-Ponty "left-leaning" since it tends
to merge Merleau-Ponty's thought with the "radical" ruminations of
today's poststructuralist crowd. I get the impression on reading Hugh
that people like Foucault, Barthes, Althusser, Lacan, Derrida, Lyotard,
Deleuze, and perhaps others, are to be looked upon as part of Merleau-
Ponty's "legacy," as he refers to it (146ff). He says for instance: "Difference, repetition, dissemination—these are the indices of Merleau-
Ponty's legacy. His unspoken presence permeates these formulations
of current thought" (150). While I am in full agreement with Silverman when he says that there is a "path of thinking leading from
Merleau-Ponty to Derrida"[5] and that "Merleau-Ponty's unspoken
presence . . . permeates post-structuralist activity" (149), I do not for
all that believe that poststructuralism is simply a further, and more
refined, development of Merleau-Ponty's philosophical project. As I
argued in "Merleau-Ponty and Postmodernity," Merleau-Ponty ought
not to be regarded as a mere "proto-poststructuralist," simply a
poststructuralist *avant la lettre.* Indeed, in my paper which was presented to this Circle last year, "Did Merleau-Ponty Have a Theory of
Perception?," I suggested that while Merleau-Ponty was in many ways
as much a deconstructionist as Derrida, there is a thing or two that
Derrida could still learn from Merleau-Ponty and that, to speak
anachronistically, Merleau-Ponty's position is in fact an "advance"
over Derrida's. Thus, whoever it was who objected to my paper by
asking, "Has Derrida now become the benchmark by which we're

supposed to read Merleau-Ponty" (or something to that effect)—that person got my point all wrong. I certainly do not think that Derrida or any other poststructuralist fully embodies Merleau-Ponty's "legacy." While there is much in common between him and them, there is also much in him that they have ignored—at their own loss. The latter part of this last remark is surely one with which Martin Dillon might actually be prepared to agree. For he says that Merleau-Ponty's true successors "have yet to appear" (101). Thus, to recall once again Merleau-Ponty's words, while I believe that much of what the poststructuralists have to say calls forth new echoes from Merleau-Ponty's writings and reveals new lustres in them I don't think that they necessarily "go further" than Merleau-Ponty himself did—which is perhaps fitting enough for people who, unlike Merleau-Ponty, have given up on the Western, liberal belief in "progress."

If Merleau-Ponty's philosophy is rightly referred to as a "philosophy of ambiguity," it is because the central thrust of his thinking, from beginning to end, lay in his attempt to overcome the discrete, oppositional categories of modern philosophy and, indeed, of the entire metaphysical tradition. This is something that Dillon, too, recognizes. If he sees Merleau-Ponty's work as providing "the closest approximation to philosophical truth in the history of Western thought," it is because for him Merleau-Ponty comes closer than any other thinker to overcoming in a decisive way all forms of traditional *dualism*. Dillon's entire book is a sustained attempt to show precisely how Merleau-Ponty does so.

Dillon rather appropriately groups all the various dualisms that Merleau-Ponty deals with—mind/body, thought/language, self/world, inside/outside, myself/others, and so on—under the general heading: immanence/transcendence. The "paradox of immanence and transcendence," Dillon says, "defines the nexus of ontological dualism that Merleau-Ponty spent his philosophical life trying to overcome" (35–6). I fully agree. I also agree that "Our culture is mired in the polarized thinking that produces the dualisms of mind and body, form and matter, activity and passivity, invisible and visible, etc." (37) I agree likewise that "The next step for our culture is the step that will take us out of the mire of dualist ontology onto another ground." That other ground is precisely what I would call "postmodern" or "postmetaphysical," about which I am now writing a book. And I also can't help but agree with Dillon when he says that "Merleau-Ponty has taken this step." I don't want to agree with Dillon on everything, however, since if I did there'd be nothing left for us to talk about. So, as a contribution to the furthering of the "conversation of mankind,"

I'd like to express a reservation or two as to Dillon's handling of this issue.

The task Dillon has set himself is "to bring others to see his [Merleau-Ponty's] footprint—and the direction in which it points." He's done a very good job on this, I'd say. My only critique is that he may at times, and inadvertently, no doubt, be pointing us in somewhat the wrong direction. To cram my remarks into as small a nutshell as possible, I would say that at times Dillon, in his way of phrasing issues, appears to fall back into a (mild) form of pre-phenomenological objectivism (coming from someone who still views himself as a phenomenologist, this is a serious objection, make no mistake about it).

Dillon recognizes that any genuine overcoming of the immancence/ transcendence dualism requires "reconceiving immanence and transcendence in such a way that they no longer exclude each other" (36). What this means is that if we are to overcome the either/or of immanence versus transcendence we must find a way of conceiving the world as *neither* immanent *nor* transcendent or, as Dillon says, "as both immanent and transcendent." What this obviously requires (what is required if we are to overcome the law of excluded middle which dominates logocentric thinking) is, as Dillon also recognizes, some kind of middle term or *tertium quid*. This middle term is what, in a discussion some time ago between Theodore Geraets and myself, Geraets referred to as "experience."[6] It is also what Merleau-Ponty referred to as the "perceived world" or, later on, the "flesh."

Now, my criticism of Dillon is that he does not always treat Merleau-Ponty's "perceived world" or "flesh" with all the respect it deserves as a genuine "middle term," by which I mean that in his eagerness to rescue Merleau-Ponty from the snares of phenomenological immanentism (Husserl's transcendental idealism) he has a tendency to conflate Merleau-Ponty's "perceived world" with the so-called "real world" of pre-phenomenological, objectivist, empiricistic thinking. Merleau-Ponty was certainly struggling as hard as he could to overcome the "transcendentalism" (the transcendental immanentism) he inherited from Husserl, but it would be doing him a great disservice to imply that in his attempt to do so he reverted to some kind of pre-phenomenological realism. On this matter I refer you to my Merleau-Ponty book.

To furnish an example of what I mean, consider the way in which Dillon deals with the notion of "reference." At times Martin gets carried away with his critique of what he perceives to be contemporary reincarnations of intellectualism, which he labels "posthermeneutic skepticism" and "semeiological reductionism" (it's perhaps hard to blame him for this when you read some of the poststructuralist literature), and, in so doing, he tends to go to the other extreme and too uncritically equates "truth" with "reference." I would advise Dillon to be more cautious when making use of this latter notion. The notion of reference is one that Ricoeur had recourse to in his book on metaphor where, in opposition to scientistic positivism, he attempted to argue that metaphors have truth-value in that they, too, have "reference," albeit of a higher-order, non-empirical sort. I think, however, that the notion of reference cannot really be extricated from the objectivistic context of its Fregean origin and that it can only cause trouble for anyone who, like Ricoeur or Dillon, wants to overcome traditional dualism. At a conference several years ago in Santa Barbara in which Ricoeur was also a participant, I argued in the paper I gave that Ricoeur would do best to stop fiddling around trying to rehabilitate the notion of reference and simply drop it altogether.[7] I'm happy to announce that at the meeting of the Society for Phenomenology and Existential Philosophy last year he said that he subsequently took my advice to heart. Now I wish Dillon would do so as well. I think that if he did he would find his *Denkweg* a bit smoother going.

Another, related example of an overreaction which gets Dillon into some trouble has to do with the issue of language, which of course is central to most poststructuralist thinking. I think it was central to Merleau-Ponty's thinking as well, as I tried to indicate in my paper "Did Merleau-Ponty Have a Theory of Perception?" and not simply an "afterthought," as Silverman says.[8] To be sure, Merleau-Ponty did not play up the language issue to the degree that our poststructuralists have. What upsets Dillon about the latter is what he perceives to be a tendency on their part to *reduce* everything to language (e.g.: *Il n'y a pas de hors-texte*). In reaction to this "semeiological reductionism" Dillon tries to detour around the "linguistic turn" so as to be able to speak directly of an extralinguistic or prelinguistic reality which, qua "transcendent ground" (178), would allow us to escape from "immanentism" and furnish us with a sure-fired measure for truth. Apart from the fact that *arguing* for the existence of a prelinguistic reality or experience seems to me to be self-refuting enterprise (if there is such a thing, it surely wouldn't require language in order for us to be made aware of it), and apart from the fact that I don't see Merleau-Ponty doing anything like this, it seems to me that, from Dillon's own point of view, this tactic is a very risky one, in that an emphasis on the extra- or the prelinguistic—

an emphasis on the "transcendence" side of the immanence/transcendence duality—can easily land us back in the old dualism. I hear an echo of the old either/or mentality of metaphysical dualism when Dillon says: "either language is founded on something prior to it which serves as its ground origin, measure, and referent—or language refers only to itself and any appeal to a foundation which would serve as its ground, origin, or measure is an appeal to onto-theology" (177).

All in all, I don't think Dillon is sufficiently appreciative of the snares of empiricistic thinking, of the ease with which one can forget what the phenomenological reduction teaches and lapse back into the "natural attitude." I call Martin's rereading of Merleau-Ponty "right-wing" because, although he is indeed one of us, i.e., a phenomenologist, he seems to harbor some sympathy for the "reactionary" concepts of pre-phenomenological naturalism, for the *ancien régime* of transcendent realities and referential languages.

With Dillon's great fear of linguistic reductionism in mind, I am tempted to say of language what Husserl said of subjectivity:

> For children in philosophy, this may be the dark corner of solipsism and, perhaps, of psychologism, of relativism. The true philosopher, instead of running away, will prefer to fill the dark corner with light.[9]

To illuminate the darkness, you need language. Language, I would say, is something we need have no fear of—though, to be sure, we should handle it with great care, lest we allow ourselves to get all tangled up in it.

Dillon ends the last chapter of his book, which is on language, with what looks like a quote from St. John: "In the beginning, there was the world" (223). In all the versions of the text I have, I read something different, namely: "In the beginning was the *word.*" What a world of difference the insertion of one small letter can make when one sets out to tamper with a text: w-o-r-d, w-o-r-l-d. Not only does the word precede the world, in the unadulterated version of the text, in it is also written: *"In ipso vita erat et vita erat lux hominum;* In it (i.e., the word) was life, and this life was the light of men." Language is, as Merleau-Ponty might have said, *lumière naturelle (lumen naturale), the light or the truth of the world itself.* Language therefore does not "refer" to the world, it *is* the world, insofar as the world has been lit up, has become *meaning.* Meaning is what results when the darkness of our prereflective lives is illuminated by language: *Verbum erat lux, et lux in tenebris lucet.* Can Dillon disagree, when he himself quotes Merleau-Ponty as saying that language is "our life and the life of things?"

Finally, to throw out a hermeneutical question to whomever would like to catch it, what does it mean that Dillon, Silverman, and I are able to reread Merleau-Ponty in the differing ways we do? Does this fact about text-interpretation perhaps have something to tell us about the meaning of Merleau-Ponty's own text? Surely, one thing it does is to confirm the fact that his work has indeed become a "classic," that is, something that can no longer be taken "literally," that can properly be read in a number of quite different ways, precisely because there is more to the work than what the author himself thought he was putting in to it and because a text, to be a text, needs readers who can always see more in it. It is this *Mehrmeinung*, this "meaning-more" of the world that we are both confirming and celebrating in our conversation today.

Notes

1. M. C. Dillon, *Merleau-Ponty's Ontology* (Bloomington: Indiana University Press, 1988). Dust jacket.

2. In Madison, *The Hermeneutics of Postmodernity: Figures and Themes* (Bloomington: Indiana University Press, 1988).

3. Hugh J. Silverman, *Inscriptions: Between Phenomenology and Structuralism* (New York: Routledge and Kegan Paul, 1987).

4. In an essay entitled "Merleau-Ponty et la contre-tradition," *Dialogue*, XVII, 3 (1978). Reprinted in an English translation as an appendix to my book, *The Phenomenology of Merleau-Ponty* (Athens: Ohio University Press, 1981).

5. *Inscriptions*, dust jacket.

6. See Th. Geraets and G. B. Madison, "Autour de Merleau-Ponty: Deux lectures de son oeuvre," *Philosophiques*, II, 1 (Avril 1975). Reprinted in an English translation as an appendix to my *The Phenomenology of Merleau-Ponty*.

7. The paper was entitled "Ricoeur's Philosophy of Metaphor" and is reprinted in part in my *The Hermeneutics of Postmodernity*.

8. See *Inscriptions*, p. 7: "Phenomenology—as elaborated by Husserl, Heidegger, Sartre, and Merleau-Ponty—offers a full-scale attempt to understand the self-world relation. To the extent that language is inserted within this self-would relation, it is almost as an afterthought. The fundamental

relation is epistemological: how the world can be experienced, known, under-stood—intentionality, consciousness, interpretation, and perception are the principal modes according to which the self-world relation is elaborated."

I don't think it fair to say that, in the case of Merleau-Ponty, language is merely "inserted" into the self-world relation, nor would I at all want to characterize his major concern as "epistemological."

9. *Formal and Transcendental Logic,* § 95.

10

Merleau-Ponty and Postmodernism

ॐ ॐ

M. C. Dillon

I think I share with Gary Madison and Hugh Silverman the belief that the postmodern critique of the phenomenological tradition has had the effect of dismissing Merleau-Ponty on the basis of arguments directed primarily against Husserl and secondarily against Heidegger and Sartre. Whether those arguments find their primary and secondary targets is only of tangential interest to me here. The concern I share with Madison and Silverman is that Merleau-Ponty has been side-tracked, shunted into obscure regions, on the basis of a critique that has largely failed to address his thought.

As all who have studied Merleau-Ponty know well, he offers his own critique of the phenomenological tradition which differs significantly in focus and portent from the postmodern critique. The postmodern critique is the one that has claimed popular attention. But the initial enthusiasm for the postmodern revolution has begun to wane in some quarters as veterans of other revolutions begin to query the direction in which this one seems to be headed, and ask whether the overwhelming negativity of the postmodern critique, in seeking to bring the great philosophical debates to an end, has failed to provide a new beginning. Or even left conceptual space in which it is possible to think of a fresh start. Perhaps something of value has been abandoned in the wholesale deconstruction.

In common with the postmodern critique, Merleau-Ponty challenges the conception of transcendental subjectivity as the foundation of traditional phenomenology, and finds it inextricably bound up with the ontological bifurcations that establish the matrix of modern or Cartesian thought. But here their ways part. Where the postmodern critique follows Husserl in bracketing the transcendent world on the basis of a presumed inaccessibility. Merleau-Ponty opens his eyes to the world in hopes of finding in it a ground for changing the ways we think about it and comport ourselves within it.

I have read what Madison and Silverman have written in their recent books to bring Merleau-Ponty's thought to bear on the problems generated by the postmodern critique. And I was gratified to find a Merleau-Ponty I recognized. Gratified as well to have revealed to me faces of Merleau-Ponty which were new to me but consonant with the ones I knew. But I was troubled that I could not find anything of real significance with which to take issue. So: in an attempt to provoke a debate that might be enlightening to us all, I will develop some of their thoughts with which I am in solid agreement into a thesis with which I suspect they may be in solid disagreement: the thesis of the transcendent world as philosophical foundation.

Madison

Madison argues that Merleau-Ponty is a postmodern thinker without being postmodernistic.[1] If one assigns the term 'modern' to the conception of reason which guarantees a strict correlation between words and things [HP 70], then, in displacing that conception, Merleau-Ponty is indeed postmodern. But he is not "postmodernistic" because he does not reject reason as a positive value or call for a transcendence of rationality.

As interpreted by Madison, Merleau-Ponty adopts a criterion of reason based on universalization: "what makes a thought rational is that it can be universalized" [HP 70].

> For Merleau-Ponty . . . , human beings are rational, not because what they say and do has a transcendent guarantee in things, but simply because of the fact that, despite all the differences which set them apart, they can still, if they make the effort, communicate with and understand one another. Rationality has no other foundation than the uncertain communication among people whereby they succeed in working out mutual agreements . . . [HP 70–71].

I am in essential agreement with this elegantly simple formulation of the position Merleau-Ponty occupied in his middle period.[2] But I want to extent the interrogation a step further by asking how it is that people can communicate and succeed from time to time in working out mutual agreements.

Let us assume an initial controversy with two people or groups of people committed to conflicting points of view on some pressing issue, e.g., whether or not nature allows the existence of a vacuum, whether or not space is filled with some light-transmitting substance or luminiferous ether. I want to suggest that, absent some compelling reason, the controversies would persist—as they have on the pressing issue of the existence or nonexistence of gods—and that mutual agreement would remain indefinitely elusive. What might that reason be?

Although consensus among postmodernist thinkers is hard to find, it might not be far afield to ascribe to them the position that language is the arbiter. I have some difficulty setting forth the structure of the supporting argument (because the thesis at stake is usually presupposed rather than thematically developed), but the general idea seems to stem from Heidegger's assertion that language masters humanity rather than the other way round. In any case, this thesis—which might be termed the thesis of the normative autonomy of language—maintains that it is language, itself, that generates accord among humans by establishing the norms of thought presupposed by communication.

Not all postmodern thinkers espouse the thesis of the normative autonomy of language as I have just described it. Foucault, for example, maintains that language is either responsive to locally emergent structures of power or is the prime medium through which power transforms history. Thus, Foucault contends that the normative function of language does not operate autonomously but is itself codetermined by other cultural forces subsumed under the general heading of power.

In contrast, Derrida and those others who maintain that all differentiation is ultimately attributable to the play of *différance*[3] are committed to the thesis that language exerts its normative force autonomously. *Différance* drives the distinctions of language (which determine how we see things),[4] but is itself driven by nothing. It is the origin, but, since it is not a possible presence, "the name 'origin' no longer suits it."[5]

Merleau-Ponty is among those who ascribe to language an intrinsic movement of unification:[6] "the continued attempt at expression founds one single history. . . ." (S 70). But he does not regard this normative force of unification as a function of the autonomy of language. .

> . . . Each partial act of expression, as an act common to the whole of the given language, is not limited to expending an expressive power accumulated in the language, but recreates both the power and the language by making us verify in the obviousness of given and received meaning the power that speaking subjects have of going beyond signs toward their meaning. (S 81)

> Language is not meaning's servant, and yet it does not govern
> meaning. (S 83)

What, then, is the relationship between language and meaning?

> ... If my words have a meaning, it is not because they present the
> systematic organization the linguist will disclose, it is because that
> organization ... refers back to itself. ... As there is a reversibility of
> the seeing and the visible, and as at the point where the two meta-
> morphoses cross what we call perception is born, so also there is a
> reversibility of the speech and what it signifies. ... [VI 154]

There is a reversibility of language and meaning, of words and
what they signify. This reversibility, this relation of signs to their
organization or syntax, is a relationship of infra-referentiality: the
meaning or significance or organization is the whole that makes the
words cohere, but that unity is dependent upon the parts that com-
pose it.

Here we have a thought beyond *différance,* the thought that
différance tacitly presupposes, the thought of the organized whole
that is the necessary correlate of the thought of differentiation. This
is the thought that the diacritical understanding of signs which Derrida
appropriated from Saussure fails to acknowledge: the thought that
differentiation presupposes a continuum to be differentiated. To this
must be added the thought that, unless the process of differentiation
is totally arbitrary, the continuum to be differentiated must be organized or structured in such a way as to delimit the play of differentiating signifiers.

Now, within the range of historical time it is true that this continuum has always already been differentiated by signifiers. It is an
extrapolation from the idea of evolution (which I am willing to make)
that leads one to speculate about original acts of differentiation and
the organization that they presuppose. If we confine ourselves to
historical time, however, it is nonetheless true that the play of differentiation is constrained. Were this not the case, we could never be
mistaken in what we say. Were this not the case, people could never
convince each other to change their ways of speaking or writing: that
is, there could be no accounting for the reconciliation of discord among
dissenting humans.

How are we to understand this organized continuum presupposed by both differentiation and reconciliation? Here is what Merleau-
Ponty says.

> When ... silent vision falls into speech, and when the speech in
> turn, opening up a field of the nameable and the sayable, inscribes

itself in that field, in its place, according to its truth—in short, when [speech][7] metamorphoses the structures of the visible world and makes itself a gaze of the mind. . . . this is always in virtue of the same fundamental phenomenon of reversibility which sustains both the mute perception and the speech. . . . (VI 154–155)

"When speech metamorphoses the structures of the visible world . . .:"—here Merleau-Ponty writes of another reversibility in addition to the infrareferentiality that relates words and syntax. This is the reversibility of extra-referentiality, the relation between language and the visible world. The idea here is that authentically expressive speech refers[8] to the world, that it is "speech about the world," that "the possibilities of speech" are delimited by "the structure of its mute world" [VI 155].

This reference to the world is not to be understood as confined to the traditional paradigm of representation, although it includes this model among others. The fact is that there are several models of referentiality operative in Merleau-Ponty's writing about language. These include, but are not limited to, the ostensive (*zeigen*), the pragmatic (*greifen* and the other use models), the constitutive, the descriptive, etc.

If any model tends to dominate his discourse, it would be the model of allusion: in allusion, the play of language allows the world to show itself in a way hitherto unremarked but demanding revelation. Allusion is the linguistic correlate of the bodily gesture.[9] "Look out!" I shout as you step off the curb, and you jump back as your eyes follow my glance and see the approaching car. Your world immediately reconfigures itself: threat displaces safety; you see according to my vision, and we are brought into accord. What accounts for this accord is not history, not power, not culture—although all of these are presupposed—it is the car to which I have alluded. "Nothing," Merleau-Ponty says, "equals the ductility of speech," and "the reason is that statements claim to unveil the thing itself, [because] language goes beyond itself toward what it signifies" (S 81).

It would take pages to describe all that takes place in the instant of my warning shout: the alarm on my face, the movement of my hand to stop your forward motion, the transfer of body schema by means of which your body instantly apprehends the world in identification with mine, the context in which this ensemble occurs, and so on. But one or two points should be stressed. Without the ductility of speech, you would have been injured. Without the car, the worldly apparition, you would have been angry, displeased at being the butt of a demeaning joke—anything but in grateful accord.

Expressive allusion is but one moment of the reversibility that takes place in extra-referentiality; the other moment is sedimentation. Henceforth, this street corner will have a new meaning, and street crossings in general may acquire a different intensity of significance. This articulation of the world may abide.

Postmodernism knows about infra-referentiality, but has ignored extra-referentiality (or tried to reduce the latter to an aspect of the former: for Derrida and company, the reference of language is always only to language). Language thus becomes the only ground of communication and human accord. My point is that, unless language refers beyond itself, there is no accounting for the accommodation of one language system to another, especially if there is initial conflict—as there always is, given the diversity of individual and cultural perspectives.

So far as I know, there is nothing in Madison's writings that directly challenges the notion of extra-referentiality. But I think that it is unlikely that we are in full agreement on this subject. In a forthcoming essay, Madison remarks in a footnote that "Dillon emphasizes the, so to speak, non- or prelinguistic character of perception [conceived of as the extra-linguistic 'ground' or 'origin' of language] more than I (Madison) would care to."[10] Since I (Dillon) do not shy away from the assertion that the car alluded to above appears to such pre-linguistic forms of life as dogs and that its worldly being is not dependent on language, there may be grounds for significant discourse between us here.

Silverman

Silverman's treatment of Merleau-Ponty begins with ambiguity and ends with interrogation. The point of departure anticipates the conclusion because both ambiguity and interrogation install themselves in a non-spatial place that Silverman designates as "the between." From ambiguity to interrogation, Silverman reads Merleau-Ponty's philosophy as a progressive articulation of the between.

> Interrogation situates questioning in the between, at the juncture, on the hinge. Interrogation opens up and makes what is philosophical in language (or whatever is to be interrogated) speak for itself. When interrogating philosophy itself Merleau-Ponty sought to indicate how philosophy becomes non-philosophy in the present age. In this respect philosophy interrogates its own meaning and possibility—that is, it situates itself in the system of differences which are marked by significations. Philosophy interrogates the *Ineinander* of

Being in its difference from beings.[11]

It is significant that Silverman finds the between informing the philosophical inscriptions of the major figures in the three traditions he takes up: phenomenology, structuralism, and postmodernism. It is significant to Silverman because it provides the basis of his own interpretations of these figures, and it is significant to me because it tacitly asserts a continuity in twentieth century Continental thought. If Silverman's interpretation can be sustained—and I am convinced that it can—then there is a unity of problematic that arrays postmodernism alongside its competitors instead of placing it in a domain apart. And that, in turn, means that the value or validity of the postmodernist response to the problematic of the between can be assessed relative to its competitors by means of a common measure.

Taking Derrida as representative of the postmodern thinkers, let us compare his treatment of the between with that of Merleau-Ponty. Silverman provides a context for this comparison.

> Deconstruction . . . operates at the juncture which Merleau-Ponty described as the chiasm or intertwining between the visible and the invisible, between philosophy and non-philosophy; it fills out the Heideggerian "in-between" as indicated by the crossing out of Being in the *Seinsfrage*. In its own right, it determines the literal meaning of writing as metaphoricity itself. The citing of writing as literally metaphorical places Derrida's texts at the interface between the closure of metaphysics which Nietzsche, Heidegger, and Merleau-Ponty inaugurate and the post-closure which remains pure *différance*. [*Inscriptions* 183.]

Différance and metaphor: how do these terms operate in Derridean texts? Let me oversimplify for the sake of brevity. *Différance* is differentiation. It names, I think, what Heidegger called appropriation or *Ereignis*. With this difference: that appropriation delimits the range of language appropriate to what claims us, whereas *différance* opens a free space where the differentia are so plastic as to accommodate a multiplicity of conflicting but interchangeable metaphors. For Derrida, the metaphor, in setting the limit, is responsible to no antecedent limit. Silverman may or may not find this interpretation compatible with his own thinking, but I would say that, for Derrida, in the nonspatial place of the between one finds only the abyss: emptiness, nothing. Or, in other words, the difference between the differentia (what is to be differentiated) and the differentiating metaphor collapses. As Derrida says, there is only the free play of signifiers; the play of signifiers is absolutely free, constrained by nothing.

What about Merleau-Ponty?

For Merleau-Ponty, as I have argued, the play of signifiers is bound by the world. Language is allusive and how it alludes to the world is delimited by the emergent sense (*sens,* meaning) of the world. One cannot say anything about anything and make as much sense every time. The condition of extra-referentiality requires, minimally, that reference refers to something, and that it refers in a meaningful way. The measure of meaning is the reversible flow of appropriation: the world appropriates metaphors to the extent that metaphors are appropriate to the world.

Let me conclude by citing a text whose appropriateness to this context may not be immediately apparent. The text is the opening paragraph of the first chapter of *The Visible and the Invisible* which is entitled "Reflection and Interrogation."

> We see the things themselves, the world is what we see: formulae of this kind express a faith common to the natural man and the philosopher—the moment he opens his eyes; they refer to a deep-seated set of mute "opinions" implicated in our lives. But what is strange about this faith is that if we seek to articulate it into theses or statements, if we ask ourselves what is this *we,* what *seeing* is, and what *thing* or *world* is, we enter into a labyrinth of difficulties and contradictions. [VI 3]

Between perceptual faith and its articulation there is a gap, a fissure, which Merleau-Ponty calls dehiscence or *écart,* but this is not the abyss of emptiness. The gap of the between for Merleau-Ponty is not nothing because it holds perception and language apart and keeps them together. The apartness is the ultimate failure of language to displace the things that always outstrip it, the inadequacy apparent in the labyrinth of difficulties cited in the text just quoted. But the gap also keeps language in relation to the world; as noted earlier in these comments, this relation is one of reference: allusion, *zeigen, greifen,* constitution, description, etc. This gap of reference might simply be designated the transcendence of the world, as long as that transcendence is conceived—not in binary opposition to immanence—but as a necessary correlate to the revelation of the world in language.

The between as it emerges in Merleau-Ponty accounts for ambiguity (insofar as it allows things to be described, grasped, referred to, etc. in different ways), but it also accounts for interrogation or the attunement to the world which allows us to measure, assess, and adjudicate among competing descriptions and references.

In Derrida, the collapse of the between results in the displacement of the thing by the sign through the process of philosophical inversion I have called semeiological reduction. The world remains as transcendence, but as absolute transcendence which can no longer function as a measure of reference. That absolute transcendence is an effective immanence which is just as absolute: that is, it denies to signs any reference beyond themselves, thus engulfing extra-referentiality within infra-referentiality, and volatizing truth.

As it was with Madison, so it is with Silverman, I see nothing in his text to contradict what I have argued here, but I suspect he will have something significant to say about my elaboration of his between.

Notes

1. "... This properly postmodern conception of reason has nothing postmodernistic about it ... it in no way involves a rejection of reason. ... Merleau-Ponty never suggested that 'reason' is nothing more than the idea-product of one particular historical tradition, merely a cultural bias of Western man." G. B. Madison, *The Hermeneutics of Postmodernity: Figures and Themes* (Bloomington, In.: Indiana University Press, 1988), p. 71. [Hereafter referred to as HP.]

2. Madison quotes excerpts from "The Metaphysical in Man" which was published in 1947. I divide Merleau-Ponty's thinking into three periods, early, middle, and late, which correspond roughly to the periods during which he published *The Structure of Behavior,* the *Phenomenology of Perception,* and *The Visible and the Invisible.*

3. I refer here to the American writers who rally under the banner of deconstruction and, perhaps, to European thinkers like Lyotard who seem to have adopted the notion of *différance* without significant alteration.

4. "Essentially and lawfully, every concept is inscribed in a chain or in a system within which it refers to the other, to other concepts, by means of the systematic play of differences, such a play, *différance,* is thus no longer simply a concept, but rather the possibility of conceptuality. ..." Later on the same page Derrida writes: "*Différance* is the ... differentiating origin of differences." Jacques Derrida, "Différance," in *Margins of Philosophy,* trans. Alan Bass (Chicago: University of Chicago Press, 1982), p. 11.

5. "Différance," p. 11.

6. "... The fact that each expression is closely connected within one single order to every other expression brings about the junction of the individual and the universal. The central fact ... is that we do not have to choose between the *pour soi* and the *pour autrui,* between thought according to us and according to others, but that at the moment of expression the other

to whom I address myself and I who express my self are incontestably linked together." Maurice Merleau-Ponty, "Indirect Language and the Voices of Silence," in *Signs,* trans. Richard C. McCleary (Evanston, Ill.: Northwestern University Press, 1964), p. 73.

7. "Quand la vision silencieuse tombe dans la parole et quand, en retour, la parole, ouvrant un champ du nommable et du dicible, s'y inscrit, à sa place, selon sa vérité, bref, quand *elle* métamorphose les structures du monde visible et se fait regard de l'esprit, . . . c'est toujours en vertu du même phénomène fondamentale de réversibilité qui soutient et la perception et la parole. . . ." {VI 154–55/202–03] The pronoun underlined above [elle] could refer either to 'vision' [la vision] or 'speech' [la parole], but the context of the sentence leads me to think that its proper antecedent is 'speech.'

8. In the course of advising me to quit insisting on the referential function of language, Madison asserts that I equate 'truth' with 'reference' in an uncritical way. My position is that reference is a condition for truth insofar as truth purports to be truth *about* something.

9. "Speech is comparable to a gesture because what it is charged with expressing will be in the same relation to it as the goal is to the gesture which intends it. . . ." "On the Phenomenology of Language," in *Signs,* trans. Richard C. McCleary (Evanston, Ill.: Northwestern University Press, 1964), p. 89.

10. G. B. Madison, "Merleau-Ponty's Deconstruction of Logocentrism," forthcoming in *Merleau-Ponty Vivant,* ed. Dillon (Albany: SUNY Press, 1991).

11. Hugh J. Silverman, *Inscriptions: Between Phenomenology and Structuralism* (London: Routledge & Kegan Paul, 1987), pp. 168–69. [Hereafter referred to as *Inscriptions.*]

11

Between Merleau-Ponty and Postmodernism

 za za

Hugh J. Silverman

In Merleau-Ponty's day, there would not have been a discourse about the question of Postmodernism.[1] In Merleau-Ponty's day, there would not have been an issue about his relation to Deconstruction. In Merleau-Ponty's day, the issue of a post-hermeneutics or even a post-structuralism would not have occupied any attention at all. When Merleau-Ponty died in 1961, his most significant accomplishment had been to establish a link between phenomenology (as he practiced it) and structuralism (as he understood it). The question to be posed now is not only whether there is a relation between Merleau-Ponty's thought and postmodernism but also what that place should be. While the first part of the question will not be difficult to establish, what remains in dispute is the status of the second. In other words, while the relation between Merleau-Ponty and postmodernism is a compelling question and most distinctly one that cannot be overlooked some three decades after his death, what that relation means is currently undergoing serious debate.

I. The Place Between

To address the first issue, one needs to consider where Merleau-Ponty stood on questions that have been raised about and concerns that preoccupy what goes under the name of "postmodernism." A variety of related terms seem to be current. The idea of a postmodernism, namely an approach, a mode of thinking, an attitude, or a general artistic-cultural-literary-philosophical movement, covers a broad domain that designates a shift in orientation of thought. This shift comes most notably in connection with what is generally called "modernism." Postmodernity (as in the title of Gary Madison's *The Hermeneutics of Postmodernity*[2]) designates the appearance of a new world—something like the age of postmodernity, an age that succeeds modernity, an epoch that has come into its own most definitively at the turn of the 1990s. Further, Madison introduces a third term along with "postmodernity" and "modernity," namely "postmodernistic"—as in "impressionistic"—which he uses in a derogatory way to distinguish it from "postmodernity," and which appears to be an inevitable outcome of our present age. A fourth term "posthermeneutic" is invoked by Martin Dillon in *Merleau-Ponty's Ontology*.[3] Here too the name is introduced to indicate a decline, a degeneration in thought, an attitude that Dillon associates with "skepticism." Poststructuralism has already become *démodé*—though I shall want to say more about its currency. Deconstruction, however, must necessarily be regarded as a specific form of critical thinking that occupies a definitive space in the general orientation now known as postmodernism.

Considering each of these six terms ("postmodernism," "postmodernity," "postmodernistic," "posthermeneutic," "poststructuralist," and "deconstruction") in detail, the place occupied by Merleau-Ponty will become evident.

(1) Postmodernism sets a frame to modernism. It delimits the modernist enterprise, based in the subject which provides an outlook onto the material, objective, empirically elaborated world. In modernism, the subject is given a foundational, inaugurating, grounded, centered, and focal status. Modernist mentality seeks to elaborate an ego-based subjectivity (or self-constitution) from a position that elaborates its own rules, its own formations and then seeks to regard them at the same time as elaborated in the "objective" world. Postmodernism places such a *Westanschauung* in question. Postmodernism seeks to enframe a dualist, subject-object based account of human experience, human enterprises, or human activity. Postmodernism is the critical questioning of the modernist dream.

(2) Postmodernity describes the place to which the contemporary epoch has moved. Postmodernity is the present age: contemporaneity itself. Postmodernity is not an attitude, a philosophy, an outlook, a position, an orientation, or a theory. Postmodernity is a cultural, historical, and epochal description. Modernity has come to an end—whether it is fully recognized as such or not. These are no longer "modern times." Modern times are bygone times, times worthy of nostalgia, times to look back upon as the "good olde days." Postmodernity is the place from which modernity can be viewed, like

viewing a film or a television serial. From postmodernity, pieces of the classical or the modern, the romantic or the real can be looked upon with delight or despair, hope or obliviousness. Postmodernity is something like Foucault's *epistemé* of the human sciences, prophetically described in his 1966 *Les mots et les choses*[4] as the *epistemé* following the age of "man" or the "empirico-transcendental doublet."[5] Foucault did not then know to name it "postmodernity" or what Lyotard calls "the postmodern condition"[6] but it is as good a term as any to describe the epoch that succeeds modernity and the reign of the anthropological age, the Kantian reconciled antinomy of rationalism and empiricism, the hegemony of the subject (characterized by its various forms of *Ich Denke, cogito,* transcendental ego, and id-ego-superego complex), the preoccupation with streams of consciousness delved, explored, and fathomed, and the effective shocks of the new. In postmodernity, the classical might be juxtaposed with the romantic, the modern with the neoclassical, the surrealist with the naturalist (and so forth). There is nothing new in this, and yet the juxtaposition marks off the new, delimits it, and circumscribes it.

(3) Madison's adjective "postmodernistic" has a novel ring to it. Presumably, it is to resonate with "impressionistic," or some similar vagary. "What is interesting from our present-day point of view" writes Madison, "is that this properly *postmodern* conception of reason has nothing *postmodernistic* about it, by which I mean that it in no way involves a rejection of reason or a disavowal of the overriding importance that the Western tradition has always placed on reason" (Madison 71). Madison appeals to the "postmodernistic" in order to show that Merleau-Ponty was not a precursor of this sort of "postmodernistic thinking," that Merleau-Ponty did indeed offer an account of reason that would keep him out of the "ranks of postmodernistic thinkers" (Madison 72). Madison claims that Merleau-Ponty refused "utopianism" and rejected "the possibility of some kind of definitive resolution of the differences and conflicts that separate people" (Madison 72). He therefore suggests that "postmodernistic" thinking is "utopian" offering a resolution to all differences and conflicts. This description is indeed curious and, I submit, has nothing to do with anything that would be called "postmodern" *per se*—either as a feature of postmodernity or as a tenet of postmodernism.[7] This suggests then that what Madison is calling "postmodernistic" is simply his term for all that new theoretical "stuff" that he rejects, while at the same time holding onto the term "postmodernity" for what is good in the present age. This is fine, but then why call it "postmodernistic"—especially since it has nothing to do with the idea of "postmodernism" either.

Indeed, Madison seems to have invented the term "postmodernistic" in order to describe what he thinks he does not like in postmodernism, and from which he wants to be sure to save Merleau-Ponty.

(4) "Posthermeneutic" is employed by Martin Dillon as part of a similar denigratory complex, namely, what he calls "post-hermeneutic skepticism." Dillon weighs heavily on this idea in his otherwise solid account of Merleau-Ponty. Unfortunately, Dillon appeals to "posthermeneutic skepticism" in order to collect together a wide range of contemporary, and, dare I say, "postmodern thinking" that he regards as pernicious. The position goes something like the following: if as Heidegger claims, "language, which grounds our understanding of things, is itself grounded in an abyss, an *Ab-grund,* an absence of ground" (Dillon 180), then there is a grave danger of skepticism and nihilism. However, Heidegger has provided a way out. Heidegger, in his later thought, gives stronger credence to his notion of *Er-eignis.* *Ereignis,* Dillon claims, might provide a ground—a way out of the abyss. Without it, Heidegger remains in skepticism and nihilism. According to Dillon, Heidegger is without grounds or *Ereignis* is without a ground (and while I suspect that this is indeed the case, or at least it is not close enough to what Dillon wants), it means that Heidegger is a skeptic and a nihilist like those who follow in his wake and who, Dillon feels, have also denied a place for ground, logos, reason. In short, post-hermeneutic skepticism is a groundless or foundationless philosophy—something along the order of what one finds in postmodernism broadly and in deconstruction more specifically. Fortunately, according to Dillon, Merleau-Ponty, through his notion of *Fundierung* has escaped the pitfalls of the errant Heidegger and the even more worrisome postmodernists and deconstructionists.

(5) As a kind of companion to "posthermeneutic skepticism" is Dillon's term "semieological reductionism." By this he seems to mean that the reduction to structures is based in a signifier-signified which limits all knowledge to structures and sign systems. As he puts it, "semeiology is the science of signs. Semeiological reductionism is the attempt to reduce all science to semeiology" (Dillon 181). Hence for Dillon the form of semiology that takes its concern as the limits of knowledge is *ipso facto* reductionist. This could well be the case for early forms of semiology, taken in a narrow sense, however de Saussure certainly refused the universality that Dillon describes. There may have been semiologists or even formalists who took the further step that Dillon suggests. However, this is hardly the case with "poststructuralism." Just as what Dillon is calling post-hermeneutics, which presumably follows from Gadamer and Ricoeur and rereads

Heidegger in what he would consider "groundless," poststructuralism follows after de Saussure, Lévi-Strauss, and Lacan and rereads the semiological tradition without affirming anything like a reduction to structures and sign systems. Poststructuralism, which gained momentum after Merleau-Ponty's death in 1961, took hold in the late 1960s with the publications of Barthes, Foucault, Derrida, and others. It reacted against the reductionistic, limited features of structuralism. Until the mid-1970s, poststructuralism was not yet postmodernism, and not even deconstruction in any full-bodied sense. Poststructuralism was still very much a reaction to both structuralism and phenomenology (not so much in Merleau-Ponty's sense, but more as propounded by Husserl, a certain Heidegger, and Sartre). Embedded within poststructuralism was also a postphenomenology (though this name came much later). Poststructuralism then was the transition from structuralism to postmodernism and deconstruction. As a transition, it was still much more of a reaction to that which it sought to reread. But since poststructuralists tended to remain rather silent with respect to their teacher, and perhaps the dominant philosopher in France, namely Merleau-Ponty, their reaction was directed elsewhere. What needs to be understood, however, and what if often simply misunderstood, is that poststructuralism was not an attempt to wipe the slate clean, to reject all that was valuable and effective in structuralism and phenomenology—or psychoanalysis, for that matter. Poststructuralism tended to reread Husserl, Freud, de Saussure, Heidegger, and so on, to examine the dominant features of modernism and to show that they operate sets of limited and limiting binary conditions, that they ultimately present themselves as texts— in spite of themselves. This does not mean that the realities that they describe are thereby reduced to texts, rather the accounts themselves, the philosophical or theoretical narratives circumscribe themselves and concommittantly establish what lies outside their formulations. Poststructuralists read these theoretical elaborations in the context of epistemological frameworks, archives, textual practices, ecritures, and so forth. Poststructuralists did not deny what was at issue in these various formulations. Hence poststructuralism was not at all reductive in the sense that Dillon suggests and Madison intimates.

(6) What deconstruction provides is a set of strategies, a *modus legendi* which is neither reductive nor groundless. Deconstruction does not deny grounds, reasons, intelligibles, or the like. Rather it situates them. Grounds need to be understood in relation to abysses— much as Dillon has attempted to do. Reasons need to be understood in relation to emotions or irrationalities. Intelligibles need to be ex-

plored in relation to sensibles or unintelligibles. In no way does Derrida, for instance, deny that there is anything outside the text. Anyone who has read Heidegger, will know about the *es gibt,* or in French the *il y a.* When Derrida writes: *"il n'y a pas de hors texte,"* he is not denying that there is nothing outside the text, rather he is affirming that what is never *given* is that which is outside the text. Once given, once affirmed as there, once articulated, whatever is under investigation is already a text, already available for a reading, for an enterprise of some sort that will bring out its features, elements, marks, limits, etc. Once it is affirmed as outside the text, affirmation brings it inside. This is not to say that there is no outside any more than there is no inside. Quite the contrary, if one tried to give an account of the inside *qua* inside, it would correspondingly affirm and establish the outside. Missing this point makes it impossible for readers of deconstruction to understand that ultimately, the place between— between the inside and the outside, the text and the context, the intelligible and the sensible, the subjective and the objective, etc.—is what is of interest. But the interest does not reify the between—this was Heidegger's lesson in his account of the onticoontological difference. The Being of beings does not reify the relational difference, it only discloses it, and therein, for Heidegger, lies the truth. Furthermore, as both Dillon and Madison would be quick to admit, reversibility is not coincidence (Madison) and yet reversibility does establishes the place of "flesh," of one's relations to oneself, to Others, and to worldly things, and of the phenomenonal field (as articulated in the *Phenomenology of Perception*). Rather reversibility—the logic of the chiasmatic or intertwining—establishes itself in relation to the very sort of binary, or dualistic pairings that deconstruction re-marks.

II. The Meaning of the Relation

One likely reason for the non-invocation of Merleau-Ponty in poststructuralist, postmodernist, posthermeneutic, and deconstructionist writings is that Merleau-Ponty was too close conceptually and strategically and yet epochally of another time. While a Foucault could claim that Nietzsche and Mallarmé were threshhold figures signalling and marking an epistemological break with the concept of man as an empirico-transcendental doublet, and indeed announcing the death of man before its time, he could not, or would not, dare to give such a status to Merleau-Ponty. Similarly Derrida's explicit citings of Merleau-Ponty are extremely rare. Julia Kristeva has recently admitted to the importance of Merleau-Ponty, but she too has devoted more ink to Husserl, Freud, Frege, and so forth than to any significant invocation of Merleau-Ponty.[8] Indeed for any serious account of the role of Merleau-Ponty in this complex of postmodernist and related theories, one has to look to North American "Continental philosophers" for further elaboration in this direction.

Yet even here, there is disagreement. It should already be evident that neither Dillon nor Madison are willing to admit that Merleau-Ponty was a guiding voice in the background of what has come to be known as postmodernism. Indeed in contrast to my own position, they both want to resist the link, though Madison appears to be more willing than Dillon, yet he too seems to be afraid to recognize the importance of Merleau-Ponty in the writings of Derrida *et al.* He sees more of an affinity between Merleau-Ponty and Gadamer or Ricoeur, even though Gadamer's *Wahrheit und Methode* did not actually appear until the year before Merleau-Ponty's death. While the mainstream of Gadamer's post-*Wahrheit und Methode* writings have appeared almost contemporaneously with and in significant awareness of developments in postmodernism and the like, his track has been significantly other. And although this otherness has not denied dialogue and conversation—the temperament nevertheless remains predominantly within the frame of modernist thought. More needs to be said about this, but not here.[9]

What Merleau-Ponty stressed again and again—and this comes out in both Dillon and Madison as well as in my own writing[10]—is Merleau-Ponty's strong reaction against dualism of many sorts. Merleau-Ponty laboured long and hard to examine the dominant dualisms of the modern age—and he attempted to show their limitations. Dillon effectively chronicles the rejection of both empiricist and intellectualist excesses. And while Dillon offers an account of the reversibility thesis, he does not focus on the role of ambiguity in the response to these divergent positions. Nor does he develop at length, though it is certainly part of his account, the reiteration and revision of his earlier formulation of ambiguity in terms of the chiasm or the intertwining, the respect in which Merleau-Ponty both refuses the binary concepts of body and soul, sensible and intelligible, objectivity and subjectivity, without offering a hegelian synthesis. While Dillon sees in some recent developments, postmodernist, deconstructionist, and in short posthermeneutic writing, the appeal to "language" as a *tertium quid,* what he does not see is that just as language was not a third thing for Merleau-Ponty, so it was also not a third thing for the later Heidegger and certainly not for Foucault, Derrida, Deleuze,

Lyotard, Kristeva, *et al.* Just as Merleau-Ponty carefully developed the in-between (what Heidegger called the *Inzwischen*), so too Derrida marks off the differences between speaking and writing, the intelligible and the sensible, meaning and reference, the literal and the figurative, the text and its context, and shows strategically that neither side has priority, neither side can be rejected totally and conclusively. At the slash or mark, the space or hinge, the deconstructive activity takes place—not as a third thing, but as a strategy that marks the differences. As hinge, edge, of margin, the in-between has no independent status. The marginality itself, the edging, the marking of the between is equally without any independent, separable, self-supporting status.

For Merleau-Ponty, the experience of ambiguity in gesture, touching, seeing, speaking, and acting is not just the co-givenness of many meanings in tension and all at once. The experience of ambiguity is also the marking of a dispersal, a dissemination, a multiplicity. This multiplicity crosses out the univocity that is sought for in a certain scientific thinking. Semiology is not of this order and as Lacan has shown—but not without complexity—the signifying chain of a semiotics is almost never reducible to univocity. Merleau-Ponty was as committed to plurivocity and a polylogos as Deleuze, Derrida, and Kristeva. Later in his life—as in *The Visible and the Invisible* and as in "Eye and Mind"—he transformed this earlier formulation into an account of visibility, of the relation between the visible and the invisible, of the interweaving of seeing and the seen, of touching and the touched, of hearing and the heard, etc. Visibility is multiform and multivalent. Its intertwining opens up into a framed multiplicity of visual, tactile, auditory, but also (and not independently) conceptual complexes.

Postmodernism operates—as Gianni Vattimo has said—with many voices,[11] and those voices all call out in the spaces of difference, in the margins, in the between, in, what Merleau-Ponty called, the "chiasm." Merleau-Ponty's logic of visibility cannot be read now independently of Derrida's logic of supplementarity.[12] The visible and the invisible are no more independent existences than were the older ideas of body and soul. They are interwoven, reversible, intertwined. They mark a place of difference, and that place of difference both brings them together, tears them apart, marginalizes the one in relation to the other, incorporates the one while instantiating the other. There are differences between Merleau-Ponty and postmodernism but the differences lie in the gathering of the differences and in their dispersal or dissemination, their continued sewing and being sewn, their writing and their publication.

Notes

1. In the 1960 interview entitled "The Philosophy of Existence," in *Merleau-Ponty: Texts and Dialogues,* eds. Hugh J. Silverman and James Barry Jr. (Atlantic Highlands, N.J.: Humanities Press, 1991), Merleau-Ponty describes the end of an era, the end of the age of existentialism. While this is not the inauguration of postmodernism *per se,* it is clearly a new beginning.

2. Gary Madison, *The Hermeneutics of Postmodernity* (Bloomington: Indiana University Press, 1989?), pp. 61–71. Henceforth cited in the text as "Madison."

3. M. C. Dillon, *Merleau-Ponty's Ontology* (Bloomington: Indiana University Press, 1988?).

4. Michel Foucault, *The Order of Things,* trans. anon. (New York: Vintage, 1970).

5. For a more detailed account of Foucault's position, see Hugh J. Silverman, *Inscriptions: Between Phenomenology and Structuralism* (London and New York: Routledge, 1987), especially chapters 14 and 18. See also *inter alia* James Bernauer, *Foucault's Force of Flight* (Atlantic Highlands, N.J.: Humanities Press, 1990).

6. Cf. Jean-François Lyotard, *The Postmodern Condition,* trans. Geoff Bennington and Brian Massumi (Minneapolis: University of Minnesota Press, 1984).

7. See, for instance, my own account of postmodernism in "Introduction to the Philosophy of Postmodernism" in *Postmodernism—Philosophy and the Arts* [Continental Philosophy–III] (New York and London: Routledge, 1990), pp. 1–9.

8. See, however, my essay "The Text of the Speaking Subject: Merleau-Ponty/Kristeva" in M. C. Dillon, ed. *Merleau-Ponty Vivant* (Albany: State University of New York Press, 1991).

9. See, for instance, Hugh J. Silverman, ed., *Gadamer and Hermeneutics* [Continental Philosophy–IV] (New York and London: Routledge, 1991).

10. See Hugh J. Silverman, *Inscriptions: Between Phenomenology and Structuralism,* especially chapters 5–9 on Merleau-Ponty.

11. A notion that resonates with Kristeva's and Derrida's idea of the "polylogue." The point appears in many of Vattimo's recent lectures and essays.

12. See Hugh J. Silverman, "Interrogation and Deconstruction," *Phänomenologische Forschungen,* Band 18 "Studien fur neueren französischen Phänomenologie" (Freiburg: Karl Alber Verlag, 1986), pp. 113–127.

12

Phantasmic Genealogy

ፊ ፊ

Derek Taylor

Along with a recent trend among modern theorists to focus our attention upon the body—upon erotics, carnality, the body as metaphor and so on—has come a fresh new attack on phenomenology for its inability to deal with the "new" strategic positions that are being mapped out by postmodernism. Although this attack is, to my knowledge, rarely explicit I believe that it forms a strong undercurrent, particularly in contemporary French thought where the traditions of existentialism and phenomenology form an unspoken backdrop to current, critical research.

I first became aware of this "anti-phenomenology" in the writings of Michel Foucault and then later on more directly in the work of Jacques Derrida, and in the collaborative writings of Felix Guattari and Gilles Deleuze. For the purposes of this paper, however, I should like to concentrate specifically on the work of Deleuze, giving a nod in the direction of Foucault but only in as much as he is supportive of Deleuze's "anti-phenomenology." (Foucault himself puts forth a very complex and sophisticated critique of phenomenology, particularly in *The Order of Things,* but this, of course, warrants a separate treatment not possible here.) I would like to counter this "anti-phenomenology" with a Merleau-Ponty defence, a defence that I believe is warranted in this instance particularly since I believe that Merleau-Ponty is specifically targeted by Deleuze and Foucault. But the ultimate aim of this comparison between Deleuze and Merleau-Ponty is to further develop a relation between ontology and politics and on this basis to suggest a new way of approaching both together.

In an article entitled "Theatrum Philosophicum" Foucault reviews Deleuze's two books, *Différence et Répétition* and *Logique du*

Sens. But this article goes far beyond the usual boundaries of literary review by suggesting that these works herald nothing less than the beginning of a new age: the "Deleuzian century" even.[1] Claiming that it is the only successful anti-Platonic strategy, Foucault goes on to say that Deleuze's innovative approach liberates us from the restrictive confines of the old subject/object debate to finally give us free reign for the "play of surfaces." Deleuze's "anti-phenomenology," according to Foucault, consists precisely of this refusal to seek stable truths beneath these surfaces and thereby place limitations upon the meaning of experience, particularly of the body. What is targeted here, then, is the foundationalism inherent in the phenomenological approach which "reduces" the meaning of experience to an originary presence or origin. In this article Foucault writes:

> It is useless to seek a more substantial truth behind the phantasm, a truth to which it points as a rather confused sign (thus, the futility of "symptomatologizing"); it is also useless to contain it within stable figures and to construct solid cores of convergence where we might include, on the basis of their identical properties, all its angles, flashes, membranes, and vapours (no possibility of "phenomenalization"). Phantasms must be allowed to function at the limit of bodies; against bodies, because they stick to bodies and protrude from them, but also because they touch them, cut them, break them into sections, regionalize them, and multiply their surfaces; and equally, outside of bodies, because they function between bodies according to laws of proximity, torsion, and variable distance—laws of which they remain ignorant. Phantasms do not extend organisms into an imaginary domain; they topologize the materiality of the body. They should consequently be freed from the restrictions we impose upon them, from the dilemmas of truth and falsehood and of being and non-being (the essential difference between simulacrum and copy carried to its logical conclusion); they must be allowed to conduct their dance, to act out their mime, as "extra-beings."[2]

Given what Foucault has to say about the non-possibility of phenomenalization it comes as no surprise when he goes on to remark that Deleuze's works "can be read as the most alien books imaginable from the *Phenomenology of Perception.*" The reason for this incongruity, Foucault argues, is the extent to which Merleau-Ponty (and by implication, other phenomenologists) links primal signification to the body-organism. It is this restrictive effect of the body-organism which, in part, inspires Deleuze to speak of a "body without organs." Not that Deleuze finds the organs themselves objectionable, rather it is the organization of the body according to these organs that is problematic.[3] For Deleuze and Guattari the organization of drives and desires which adhere to the strict delineation of bodily functions and their effects, such as are discernable in the work of Freud, must be replaced with a more flexible concept, such as the "body without organs" which does not presuppose the interpretation of experience according to some guiding narrative.

Foucault's enthusiasm for Deleuze and his anti-phenomenological approach grows out of his own impatience with metaphysics— particularly the Platonic metaphysics of essence and appearance. In Foucault as well as Deleuze this impatience is inherited directly from Nietzsche. The death of God, which is highlighted by Nietzsche, signals the abandonment of any recourse to the Archimedean point of certainty in this philosophical quest for reflective purity. Both Foucault and Deleuze identify a certain antipathy to this metaphysics of essence and appearance and the "phenomenalization" of experience in Nietzsche's uncompromising critique of faith. Nietzsche's critique of faith was not only an attack on religious belief (Judeo-Christian mostly) but was also a condemnation of a certain philosophical attitude which prided itself on its atheistic, intellectual rigour. Not content merely to criticize religious faith Nietzsche also attacks those who attack religious faith (and here I would have to agree with Kaufmann's suggestion that this could be regarded as an auto-critique).[4] In fact Nietzsche believes that these so-called "counteridealists," who still have faith in truth, are worse than those they oppose for "it is precisely in their faith in truth that they are more rigid and unconditional than anyone."[5] It is this (auto) critique that later invokes the displeasure of others such as Habermas who in *Knowledge and Human Interests* mistakenly brands Nietzsche as an anarchic irrationalist. It is one thing to dissolve the unity of the ego but to cast doubt on the sacred quest for truth is to be left with nothing(!).

At its most extreme, Nietzsche's iconoclastic critique of philosophical self-reflection brought him face to face with the fragility of the subject/object distinction which is part and parcel of this metaphysics of essence and appearance. In 1885 Nietzsche wrote: " 'Subject,' 'object,' 'attribute'—these distinctions are fabricated and now imposed as a schematism upon all the apparent facts. The fundamental false observation is that I believe it is *I* who do something, suffer something, 'have' something, 'have' a quality.' "[6] Nietzsche's monumental achievement was not the death of God but the death of certainty which cast the solidity of the Cartesian identity again into irretrievable doubt.

Deleuze, on the other hand, unlike Habermas and others, applauds this terrifying destruction of truth and the subject which seems to open up this yawning chasm under our feet. Through this "transvaluation of all values" Deleuze latches onto the enigmatic Nietzschean concept of the "eternal return" in order to explain the "affirmative" power of Being that is not restricted by the body-organism. But in order to do this Deleuze must come up with a fairly creative interpretation of this concept of the eternal return—one which, I believe, is able to incorporate his own structural-linguistic background yet still remain true to this anti-metaphysical impulse. To do this Deleuze translates Nietzsche's doctrine from the "eternal return of the same" to "the eternal return of difference"—an alteration that, on the face of it, would seem to be too great to be tenable. But naturally, Deleuze maintains that this rendering still remains true to the spirit of Nietzsche's doctrine, if not to the letter. It is this "structuralist" background to Deleuze's interpretation of Nietzsche that bears special scrutiny for it is here that we may discover the roots of Deleuze's anti-phenomenology—in the eternal return of difference.

In order to understand Deleuze's "eternal return of difference" it is necessary to go back to Deleuze's structuralist beginnings. Here, at least, we can identify an affinity between Merleau-Ponty and Deleuze, for while Merleau-Ponty was never a structuralist he *was* heavily influenced by one of its founding fathers, Saussure, as was Deleuze.[7] But the affinity between Merleau-Ponty and Deleuze begins and ends here, for their interpretations of Saussure differ quite significantly. Both Merleau-Ponty and Deleuze extend Saussure's principles of linguistics in order to develop this primal concept of difference. Both agree on the ontological importance of "difference" but disagree on how it is to be thought."

What sets Deleuze apart from the structuralist "orthodoxy" (in other words, what defines him as "post-structuralist") is his translation of this fairly static principle of difference into a more dynamic idea of "becoming." (At a more abstract level, this reflects a move from epistemology to ontology despite the apparent antipathy to ontology.) This movement from "difference" to "becoming" is unintelligible without some recourse to Nietzsche's "eternal return," in which Nietzsche's critique of the "last idealist"—that of the believer in Truth—joins up with the "existentialist" scepticism of essences and identities. The result is a thoroughly anti-identitarian, anti-rationalist concept of Being. In his work on Nietzsche Deleuze writes:

According to Nietzsche the eternal return is in no sense a thought of the identical but rather a thought of synthesis, a thought of the absolutely different which calls for a new principle outside science. This principle is that of the reproduction of diversity as such, of the repetition of difference . . . And indeed, we fail to understand the eternal return if we make it a consequence or an application of identity. *We fail to understand the eternal return if we do not oppose it to identity in a particular way.* The eternal return is not the permanence of the same, the equilibrium state or the resting place of the identical. It is not the 'same' or the 'one' which comes back in the external return but return is itself the one which ought to belong to diversity and to that which differs (emphasis added).[9]

Deleuze's concept of difference could thus be summarized crudely as the fusion of Saussure's first principle ("the arbitrary nature of the sign") with Nietzsche's aversion to the concepts of metaphysical Truth, the subject and the ego. The result is an ontology that does not rely on the stability of the ego or identity but is thoroughly given over to the dynamic repetition of difference as the only guarantee of transcendence. This conception of difference in many respects resembles the Lacanian concept of the phallus which is, as Lacan would say, "always missing in its place." In fact Deleuze himself makes this connection in his important article "How to Recognize Structuralism" in which, like Lacan, he prioritizes the symbolic over the real and imaginary orders. In this article Deleuze compares the "lack," instituted by the Phallus, to the void, or, as Deleuze says, the "empty space" of the non-identitarian subject.

When we compare the concept of difference in the works of Deleuze and Merleau-Ponty what is remarkable is the fact that, initially at least, their use of this concept is so alike. The starting point for both is a rather creative interpretation of Saussure in which difference is ontologized, but the end point, as we can see, is a sharp disagreement about the primacy of the phenomenal subject.

But Merleau-Ponty, like Deleuze after him, is unsatisfied with the inherited immanence/transcendence dilemma. In a sense, Merleau-Ponty's whole career can be read as a battle with this Cartesian dualistic thinking. In fact it is this commitment to breaking down ontological dualism that marks out Merleau-Ponty's very particular reading of Saussure. Unlike others who discovered him at a later date, he was not tempted to overestimate Saussure's first principle: "the arbitrary nature of the sign" at the expense of his second principle: "the linear nature of the signifier." *Like* these others, Merleau-Ponty derives from Saussure the centrality of this relational concept of difference but never confers upon it a "purity" that would lend it any degree of autonomy. By writing difference as "divergence" (*écart*) Merleau-Ponty retains the temporal dimension of language that Saussure strongly affirms in principle II. Merleau-Ponty's "divergence" invokes a temporally contingent relation that is lost in the binary logic of difference as an ideal relation between "X" and "non-X." Like Deleuze's "eternal return of difference," Merleau-Ponty's "divergence" avoids the static, synchronic characteristics of pure difference that is common to semiotics and structuralism in general. But what is most important about this "divergence" is that it does not designate any kind of absolute vector: it is dynamic but not teleological. In this way, through divergence, both meaning and expression are preserved without the sacrifice of history.

Merleau-Ponty's translation of this structuralist "difference" as "divergence" is very much rooted in his existential phenomenology. This existentialism becomes more evident when we see how he combines a phenomenology of perception with a particular understanding of Gestalt psychology. Whereas Lacan situates structure in the unconscious (as an internalized force), Merleau-Ponty uses the gestalt approach to situate structure in our perception of it. This is precisely where Deleuze and Merleau-Ponty part company; while both Deleuze and Merleau-Ponty effect a vitalization of structure by throwing it into motion (more or less existentially in both cases), Merleau-Ponty places limits and values on this "motion" by "situating" it (in the Heideggerian sense) in perception and therefore giving it a "corporeal intention." As Merleau-Ponty says, "these limits and values exist; quite simply, they are of a perceptual order: there is a *Gestalt* of language, in the living present there is something of the expressed and non-expressed" (PW 37f).

Later, in his posthumously published work *The Visible and the Invisible,* Merleau-Ponty drops these terms "limits and values" since even they are overburdened with the negative connotations of a Platonic conception of language (which conceives of both the body and language as a "prison"). The body does not place "limits" on language, which is essentially what both Foucault and Deleuze object to in phenomenology; on the contrary, the contingency of the spatio-temporal body is the fundamental source of language's infinite variability and expression.

Although Merleau-Ponty can be quite critical of gestalt psychology (particularly its attempts to provide itself with a coherent theory of knowledge)[10] what he finds useful is its description of the emergence of meaning along the lines of a figure/background relation. Using perception in its broadest sense, Merleau-Ponty describes the process of cognition as the perception of a figure which suddenly separates itself from the previously undifferentiated background. Merleau-Ponty uses the example in *The Phenomenology of Perception* of a walk along the beach towards a ship that has run aground (PhP

17). In this example, as one walks toward the ship there is first a point at which the ship is part of the background and then there is a point at which features of the ship thrust themselves into the foreground in an irrevocable way. In this ontological fusion of Saussurian "difference" and Gestalt psychology, speech becomes perception, the background becomes what is variously called "sedimented" or "spoken language" (*parole, parlée*), and the object becomes meaning. In this way difference is not reduced to the alternating poles of a binary opposition between "X" and "non-X." But the most important aspect of this divergence is that it is always contingent, in the sense of being contingent *upon* particular circumstances, both social and historical. The background (or structure) is only distinguished through a figure which *itself* becomes background to another "figure" (for example, a porthole in the ship's side throws the ship into the background). In this "Gestalt" neither the figure nor the background are as important as the perspective which brings this tension to life: that is to say, the "situation."

The basic tenets of Gestalt, as is commonly known, are that the whole cannot be reduced to the sum of its parts, that the "part" (i.e. the "event") cannot be divorced from the whole (structure), and that therefore the "whole" is unanalyzable in its entirety. Merleau-Ponty gives the Gestalt experience an existential dimension by making speech and perception the "part" of the "whole" (the "whole," in this case, taking the place of the *Lebenswelt*). The "whole" is "unanalyzable" because the "parts" cannot be taken separately; that is to say, we cannot assemble all possible perceptions in order to arrive at an "objective perception" since all "figures" presuppose a background which is not yet fully known. In this respect we could say that there is a distinct similarity between the implied "ambiguity" of this gestalt and Nietzsche's perspectivism. Nietzsche's particular style of perspectivism did not presuppose a possible fusion of all perspectives into one universal perspective from which all its individual perspectives could then, in turn, be evaluated.[11]

But the difference between Nietzsche's "perspectivism" and Merleau-Ponty's gestalt model of perception is ultimately of the same nature as the difference between Merleau-Ponty's "divergence" and Deleuze's "phantasmatic" eternal return of difference. Nietzsche's critique of Truth as faith forces him to the conclusion that there can be no certainty about anything—of the "self" as much as of the "world"— for Nietzsche, only the "deed" is left. But this critique suggests *not that there is no certainty but merely that certainty is unattainable.* Similarly, Deleuze falls back on the Kantian "sublime" (that is, the representation of the "unrepresentable") in order to make this connection between reason and imagination, or between the "interior" and the "exterior," which we also see in his analysis of Bergson. As Nietzsche writes: "the antithesis of this phenomenal world is not 'the true world,' but the formless unformulable world of the chaos of sensations—another kind of phenomenal world, *a kind 'unknowable' for us.*"[12] Jean-François Lyotard comes ultimately to the same conclusion as Deleuze when he states that the central sentiment of post-modern aesthetics is characterized by the Kantian sublime. In fact, Lyotard goes so far as to suggest that the "Kantian theme of the sublime is a much earlier modulation of Nietzschean perspectivism."[13]

It must be recognized that there is a big difference between Deleuze's "phantasmatic uncertainty" (the lack of identity) and Merleau-Ponty's "phenomenological uncertainty" (or, more correctly, phenomenological contingency): although both are similar temporally, *they are completely dissimilar spatially.* Phantasmatic uncertainty is an uncertainty that is posed topologically from a future perfect position. This uncertainty is posed as a "lacking" that lags behind structure, placing limitations upon expression. This "lacking" solves the problem of passage, of temporality, by constantly eluding itself and thereby guaranteeing a perpetual flux. The eternal return of difference is like a bottomless pit that is constantly being filled. But according to this idea *nothing* must limit this lacking, this uncertainty: not truth, identity or the body. This is certainly what Merleau-Ponty would call "high-altitude thinking" (*pensée de survol*) since it is resolved to literally have no point of view. Phenomenological uncertainty, on the other hand, is grounded in the body of the present. This uncertainty is projected not as a "lacking," not as a hindrance to expression, but as the originary ekstasis of expression. Merleau-Ponty's greatness lies in his ability to demonstrate how that thing which has always frustrated thinkers from the beginning, namely, contingency (or "ambiguity"), is not accidental to thought but rather is constitutive of it. Expression depends on the fact that meaning is never complete (just as "perception" depends on the fact that we cannot see it all, for if we could see it all then we ourselves would be part of what we see, thus immediately depriving us of sight).

For Deleuze the autonomy of "difference" (the arbitrary nature of the sign which transcends thought) guarantees the ontology of Being when it is considered temporally as the eternal return of difference (the perpetual flux of meaning). In this sense Being as "becoming" is a purely formal (relational) construct with no content and as such should not be restricted by substance (space). In other words, temporal uncertainty assures the spatial uncertainty of identity (or rather, its "lack"). For Merleau-Ponty, on the contrary, the arbitrary nature of the sign guarantees the *contingency* of meaning by establishing the divergence between a spatio-temporal "figure" and a socio-historical background, as it does between what he called *parole originaire* and *parole parlée*. In this sense phenomenal Being is the material "hinge" between past and future and as such *must be* "restricted" by substance (space). Spatial groundedness is the guarantee of temporal uncertainty.

The implications of these two different strategies is readily apparent. Whereas Deleuze's "phantasmatic genealogy" has the strategic advantage of being able to break up the sedimentation of meaning (all attempts to "territorialize," as Deleuze would put it), it suffers from the fairly common delusion that this challenge is itself "positionless," that it cannot, nor should not, be "identified." The sublime version of truth admits to the temporal contingency of meaning but gives away its own hidden desire to escape that contingency by hypothesizing a space beyond representation—a speculation that must itself be sublime (and therefore, by definition, be positionless) in order to be credible. In the end this is essentially the same criticism that could be brought to bear against Nietzsche (and to a lesser extent, Foucault).[14] This "delusion," in Deleuze, is, as I have tried to show, at least partially the result of a combined inheritance of Nietzsche's "sublime" truth and structuralism's over-emphasis on the arbitrary nature of the sign.

What is lost in the Deleuzian and Foucaultian genealogy is the very thing which originally motivated it: politics. As Kerry Whiteside comments in his recent work *Merleau-Ponty and the Foundation of an Existential Politics:* "Foucault's refusal to think systematically about the values that his discourse serves entails a significant political cost . . . the problem is that, having lost his grip on the *situation,* the theorist undermines his own account of factors crucial to his political project" (emphasis added).[15] Merleau-Ponty's "divergence" never loses sight of our own political involvement in the world, not primarily because Merleau-Ponty is politically committed, as Whiteside seems desperately to want to suggest, but because this spatial and temporal contingency necessarily *requires* that one account for oneself socially and historically. The politics that emerges out of Merleau-Ponty's ontology cannot be reduced to a simple reflexivity, in which we deliberately set out to acknowledge our every prejudice. Nor can it be reduced, at a more abstract level, to universal axioms of human experience, which is often the charge laid against phenomenology. These two attitudes reflect the extremes of immanence and transcendency, both of which are caught up in the trap of spatio-temporal discontinuity. To confront contingency is to actively launch ourselves into the ongoing project of making the world—a project that admits as much to the fixed nature of our intention as it does to the unfinished quality of its expression.

Contrary to the revolutionary intent of Deleuze's radical, poststructuralist "hero," what we mean is not before us, hanging tantalizingly like an "empty space," nor are we doomed to the endless play of signifiers which perpetually deprives us of expression. Being sensitive, as he was, particularly in the latter part of his career, to the shortcomings of political over-zealousness Merleau-Ponty warns of this tendency to project ourselves outside our own situation. Against this teleological tendency, which ultimately empties itself of content, Merleau-Ponty suggests a form of political thought that is rich and expressive precisely *because* it is embodied.

> What we *mean* is not before us, outside all speech, as sheer signification. It is only the excess of what we live over what has already been said. With our apparatus of expression we set ourselves up in a situation the apparatus is sensitive to, we confront it with the situation, and our statements are only the final balance of these exchangés. *Political thought itself is of this order.* It is always the elucidation of an historical perception in which all our understandings, all our experiences, and all our values simultaneously come into play—and of which our theses are only the schematic formulation. All action and knowledge which do not go through this elaboration, and which seek to set up values which have not been embodied in our individual or collective history fall short of the problems they are trying to solve. Personal life, expression, understanding, and history advance obliquely and not straight towards ends or concepts. What one too deliberately seeks, he does not find; and he who on the contrary has in his meditative life known how to tap its spontaneous source never lacks for ideas and values (PLS 80, emphasis added).

Notes

1. Michel Foucault, "Theatrum Philosophicum" in *Language, Counter-Memory, Practice,* trans. Donald Bouchard and Sherry Simon, ed. Donald Bouchard (New York, Cornell U. Press, 1977), p. 165.

2. Ibid., p. 169–70.

3. In *A Thousand Plateaus* Deleuze writes: "the BwO is not opposed to the organs; rather, the BwO and its 'true organs,' which must be composed and positioned, are opposed to the organism, the organic composition of the organs." Deleuze, Gilles and Félix Guattari *A Thousand Plateaus,* trans. Brian Massumi (Minneapolis, U of Minnesota Press, 1987), p. 158.

4. In an editorial footnote to Kaufmann's translation to *On the Genealogy of Morals,* at a point where Nietzsche is attacking these so-called free spirits he asks, "Is Nietzsche here referring to himself?" Although Kaufmann goes on to say that this is probably a veiled reference to Nietzsche's friend Franz Overbeck and not a self-portrait there is no denying the correspondence, particularly in its existentialist resonances.

5. Friedrich Nietzsche, *On the Genealogy of Morals* (New York, Vintage Books, 1969), p. 151.

6. Friedrich Nietzsche, *The Will to Power* ed. Walter Kaufmann (New York, Vintage Books, 1968), p. 294.

7. Of course, there are those that pose the question whether Merleau-Ponty *was* in fact a structuralist. See particularly James M. Edie, "Was Merleau-Ponty a Structuralist?" in *Semiotica* IV, # 4 (1971), p. 297.

8. In this respect we could probably draw more parallels between Merleau-Ponty's interpretation of "difference" and Derrida's "différance," but this also deserves separate treatment not possible here.

9. Gilles Deleuze, *Nietzsche and Philosophy* (London, Athlone Press, 1983), p. 46.

10. See particularly *Phenomenology of Perception,* op. cit., p. 50 f.1.

11. Alphonso Lingis also comments on Nietzsche's perspectivism in the same way but, interestingly, contrasts this with another kind of perspectivism which he regards as "restricted" by its phenomenological approach. In *The New Nietzsche* he writes:

> "Perspectivism, then, in Nietzsche means something quite different from what it has come to mean in phenomenology: it does not mean that the appearances are profiles of an essential invariant; it means that there are only perspectives. Each appearance is not an appearance of a thing, but the apparition of a power. It is itself a power, it is itself generative." Lingis, Alphonso "The Will to Power" in *The New Nietzsche* ed. David Allison (New York: Delta, 1977), p. 43.

The problem with this idea is, of course, that it immediately ushers in the horrible spectre of "relativism": a problem that postmodernism seems to have inherited, a problem that Merleau-Ponty seems to have avoided.

12. Friedrich Nietzsche, *The Will to Power,* ed. Walter Kaufmann (New York: Vintage Books, 1968), p. 307.

13. Jean-François Lyotard, *The Postmodern Condition* Theory and Literature, Volume 10, trans. Geoff Bennington and Brian Massumi (Minneapolis: University of Minnesota Press, 1985), p. 77.

14. Foucault partially avoids the trap of the sublime by hypothesizing an "historical ontology" which, at least, admits to the historically contingency of Being. However, the same problem arises again since the historical ontology hides beneath it a "stable narrative" about our relationship to history—a narrative that is inherent in Foucault's own historical analysis. See particularly Derrida's critique of Foucault in both "Cogito and the History of Madness" in *Writing and Difference,* trans. Alan Bass (Chicago: University of Chicago Press, 1978), pp. 31–63, and "The Ends of Man" in *Margins of Philosophy,* trans. Alan Bass (Chicago: University of Chicago Press, 1982), pp. 109–136.

15. Kerry H. Whiteside, *Merleau-Ponty and the Foundation of an Existential Politics* (Princeton: Princeton University Press, 1988), p. 300–1.

13

Toward a Phenomenology of Politics:
Expression and Praxis

⋟⋞ ⋟⋞

Eleanor Godway

Because Merleau-Ponty's phenomenology takes us beyond (or be-hind?) the individual *cogito,* the autonomous self-willed subject, in what he says of politics as elsewhere in his philosophy we can recognize a "postmodern" trend in his thinking. But in emphasizing lived experience, recognizing there the emergence of meaning, he bears witness to the possibility of a "truth" in politics, the coming-to-be of norms in social experience which would surely set him at odds with other aspects of postmodernism. Phenomenology brings us back to experience, and I shall be concerned with political experience as lived, or what it is to experience politics, in particular what it can mean for such experience to reveal truth.

Kerry Whiteside begins his book by asking what he says is Merleau-Ponty's question, whether politics is thinkable.[1] Rather than go Whiteside's route into the application of Merleau-Ponty's insights to political theory—the thinkable—I have felt the challenge to be that of politics as praxis, and thus I draw on Merleau-Ponty to meditate on a slightly different question, namely whether politics is *possible.* What, first of all, is politics? If we use the word in a commonly accepted contemporary sense, to refer to the way socially constituted power relationships are worked out in larger or smaller communities through time, then politics is all too clearly actual. My concern, how-ever, picks up the older classical meaning of politics, as perhaps af-fording a possibility for meaningful action, an opening to a future where something like what used to be called the *polis* can come into being. I see it as picking up threads of Merleau-Ponty's own medita-tion on whether history is possible, whether there is any continuing meaning to be recognized in the wider social patterns of our intersubjective, intergenerational life. And politics could be our participation in, contribution to, even creation of such meaning. Thus, it will be clear, I shall be linking what I mean by politics with what Merleau-Ponty called expression, as he articulated it with reference to language and the arts.

Asking whether history is possible was among other things, to suggest that what we had thought of as history may have been misunderstood. One approach would be to say that it was an illusion to suppose that the sequence of events which historians have chronicled has any inherent intelligibility. This would be a hard-nosed empiricism allied to skepticism or nihilism. Some might say that this is the only credible postmodern view. To respond quickly in the affirmative, es, history must have been possible, since history already *is,* may be claiming too much, however, because it can suggest that what has taken place already has a meaning, that in a sense the past is finished, and we know what it was. To this *pensée de survol* ("high altitude thinking"), what has happened is over, complete; it has become what Merleau-Ponty called *histoire prosaïque* (PW 69/87), analogous to *parole parlée* or *secondaire;* by extension we could imagine that the history we participate in will have a meaning in this sense, at least afterwards, even if we cannot discern it now. But this version of history, which is apparent in parts of Hegel, is not ours as we live it: instead, Merleau-Ponty says, it sacrifices life to an idol of history (PW 83/117–8). The modernist perspectives evident in both of these views embody respectively the empiricist and intellectualist traditions. It is his transcending of this dilemma that makes Merleau-Ponty preeminently postmodern, and difficult to follow, because of the hold modernism still has on much of our thinking.

In terms of politics, or history in the making, the first account of history would result in the cynical conception of politics, namely the keeping and exercising of power; all political activity would be directed to getting the best deal possible, by whatever means seemed feasible—negotiation, intimidation, manipulation, violence, etc.[2] All political talk would be rhetorical, sloganeering, moves in a game; participants in the struggle, whether winners or losers, would be swept along, willy nilly, by forces or motives (outer or inner compulsions) which would not be open to reflection, or, if they were, would not be accessible to change (I myself used to think of all politics as like this; Merleau-Ponty helped me to see it differently.)[3] This view, as I have suggested, relies to a large extent on an empiricist, even Hobbesian account of human nature and social forces, in spite of the fact that there seem to be variants of it among so-called postmoderns such as Foucault.[4] In terms of such politics, political knowledge would be of the skills needed to arm oneself effectively to enter the arena. Or, from the theoretical point of view, one might be looking for the analytical framework which would give reliable insight into the mechanics of conflict with or without the means to deal with it. Here one would find hypotheses to explain what is going on in terms of, e.g., class, ownership of means of production, economic forces, even unconscious desires, gender or genetically inherited characteristics (race) etc. I do not mean that none of these have any bearing on our lives: indeed they are all extremely important, but as Merleau-Ponty consistently emphasizes, their significance will be in their meanings as lived by the people involved.[5] The point is that in discussions in terms of the view of politics I am considering now, these items are taken as causal factors which are sufficient to account for what goes on, and those who think such explanations are the whole answer do not in fact see history as having any point, any purpose. They see only means or techniques; seeking, keeping and exercising power (like seeking, keeping and spending money, taken as an end in itself) are thought of as the reason for politics. Yet in the case both of money and power, there is a problem with a fixation on means. If it does not make sense to inquire about ends, about whether or why such activity itself makes sense, we are stuck with non-reason, facticity, determinism—pick your label! That is to say, politics in the sense in which I want to articulate it is not possible because there is no room for praxis as the integration of thinking and action, no room for choice or change, no answers, because situations understood this way do not pose any real questions.

What about the other view, that, yes, it all does make sense, and History has a unified meaning. If we had to abide by the law of excluded middle, perhaps this would be the more appealing option—and of course, Merleau-Ponty's claim that we are "condemned to meaning" seems to push us in this direction. What we do has a meaning, has consequences, and we contribute to history, which Merleau-Ponty speaks of as "action" (PP 194–5). But does it follow that this meaning already exists and can be specified now? Some critics of Merleau-Ponty feel he ought to have given us a blue-print, and they either blame him for a wishy-washy withdrawal from politics, or carefully comb his political and other writings looking for such a blue-print, or for the means to create one for him. This way of thinking about politics needs to envisage an end to history, the perfect political state, where the conflicts of the present world will be overcome. Thus, if

Merleau-Ponty finds Marxism inadequate, he must, says Barry Cooper, be replacing it with another model or another goal.[6] Or, in order
to know that this situation is unjust, it is supposed that we must
already know what will constitute justice. Even, in order to know
that people are suffering, we must have a criterion of the beneficial,
says Sonia Kruks.[7] But if these ideas are already explicit, political
debate is in the realm of what Merleau-Ponty called intellectualism.
According to such a version of history, and *a fortiori* politics, there is a
correct answer already. The meaning of history is guaranteed, whether
by horizontal transcendence (understood as the unfolding of human
nature or by the result of the forces of dialectical materialism) or
vertical transcendence (in terms of some absolute value outside time,
how for example, God intends it to turn out (S 70–71/80).) Either way
thinking about history is dominated by the end: the living tissue of
human interaction is subordinated to a final truth according to which
it will all make sense. In contrast with the first, empiricist version,
where the means absorb the end, here the end swallows up the means.
Knowledge of the end (assuming we could have it, as some have
claimed to, while others still seek it) would remove uncertainties from
political discussion and justify political action. Whether we succeeded
or failed in our attempt to achieve the goal of history thus envisaged,
our actions would have meaning because the standard, or the *telos,*
would be recognized as having ideal validity. Looking back on history
so far, we would judge it as contributing (or failing to contribute) to
that goal, by which we would be able to evaluate its significance. And
this intelligibility, by the way, is or ought to be, available to us by dint
of a pre-existing universal rationality, which like the pre-existing idea
of justice, must somehow be already in place. Habermas's account
seems less realistic to us, perhaps, than Kant's did to his contemporaries.[8] Here, again, because what makes the answers right (or wrong)
is supposed as given in advance, there is no need to think about
politics. There is no problem to be solved *now,* except how to bring our
actions into line.

Whereas the first version of politics has no place for reason as
informing the events of history, and the second version depends on
the conception of a universal standard, a pre-existing logos, what we
are going to need is neither what the former denies nor what the
latter embraces, but another understanding of reason altogether.

Merleau-Ponty, as we know, criticizes both empiricism and intellectualism in *Phenomenology of Perception,* and as he moves beyond
both, shows how meaning emerges in the experience of perception.[9]
The gestalt, he explains, is the birth of a norm, and is not realized

according to a (pre-existing) norm (PhP 61/74). The figure appears in relation to the ground, and itself teaches how it is to be seen. Meaning is born, it is finite, vulnerable, incarnate in a context of contingency. We have to do here with the upsurge of reason in a world not of its own making (PhP 56/69). Merleau-Ponty's account of the birth of a norm in perception reveals a dynamic which is also at work in expression, namely the emergence of meaning in emotion, language, art. What he calls *parole originaire* (originating speech, speech as origin), the coming to be of new meaning, is exemplified in the first words of a child, the declaration of the lover, the achievement of the poet, thinker and artist, and also that of the leader of integrity and vision. This speech which institutes new meanings, (also called *parole parlante*) is distinguished from *parole parlée (secondaire),* spoken or secondary speech, in which we make use of already established, second-hand meaning. I have already alluded to this distinction in referring to *histoire prosaïque,* which he contrasts with *histoire sacrée* or *poétique.* To understand the past in this way is to relate to it as an action in which we are already implicated. What I am leading up to is something I am going to call *politique originaire,* of the same order as Merleau-Ponty's *parole originaire,* but as we shall see, with slightly different implications because it will not need an identifiable speaker, and it will fit better with some of his examples, and with his more "postmodern" thinking in *The Visible and the Invisible.*

Going back to the relationship between expression and history: to participate in history in this way is to be drawn into a gesture which allows a meaning to be born, creates possibilities, and, by making the present a turning point, opens up a future and changes the meaning of the past. When he says that Saussure's account of language implies a new conception of history, what he is pointing to is the possibility of meaning emerging out of the situation to which a number of varying factors contribute without specifying who is acting on what, or what on whom.[10] Analogously, in the case of a work of art, all the elements can suddenly link up to allow its meaning to come to be. What this implies is the possibility of an intersubjective praxis which cannot be accounted for—is neither explained nor justified by—the traditional conceptual frameworks of our culture. For here, just as in the emergence of the gestalt, there is neither a causal relationship between the antecedent conditions and the result, nor a reasoned connection, such that this action can be known to have that meaning. There is no necessity and no guarantee; it must be, as Geraldine Finn puts it, a politics of contingency. That is to say, we are ourselves at risk as we find ourselves taking up this gesture. What we may become and what we can do may be still uncertain, but in the face of this, there are still experiences of political meaning which are *originaire,* transformative or fecund. Picking up a thread from the beginning of the paper, we have to confront the question addressed by the poet Audre Lorde (in the poem "Power" which I shall say more about in a moment), namely how to tell the difference between poetry and rhetoric. Her concern, as we shall see, is not quite Merleau-Ponty's, but it will help shed light on what is lost by letting postmodernism persuade us that there is only rhetoric, only the play of signs, nothing significant to be said, no truth to be honoured or betrayed.

When Merleau-Ponty writes: "The truth of politics is only this art of inventing what will later appear to have been required by the times" (PhP 210), we need to ask both how is this "truth" accomplished, and what makes it truth. The originary gesture at the right moment, the action that is called for, is the one that will give our whole history, our past and our present a new meaning and a new direction, according to which new values will enter the situation. This is not the prosaic truth of *la pensée du survol,* but a vital change in the sense of our lives, a shift which opens a field, offers a future. Merleau-Ponty writes of a *vérité de demain,* "truth of tomorrow" (S 5/10) which speaks without saying, "which touches the springs of hope and anger in each of us—and will never be the prose of truth" (*ibid.*). It will turn out to be the truth which all are waiting for, which will make sense of what has happened to us, and because of us, such that we can act in terms of that future, such that we can go on. Merleau-Ponty says that what people need from the politician, as from the artist, is that "he draw them on towards values in which they will only later recognize their own values" (PW 86/121). These values are not pre-existent; they come to be because someone has enacted them. The politician who has made a difference, who has helped a truth like this come to be, is concerned with other people not as "empirical others" such as events have made them, nor from the point of view of what they may expect of him (as in the public relations we often see in election year), but with others as they might be, according to a vision of their becoming such that he can live with them (S 74/92). Merleau-Ponty seems to be thinking of leaders with a kind of authority, to which the rest of us respond. Gandhi, Martin Luther King, Bishop Tutu, Kate Millette, Germaine Greer, . . . names spring to mind, of people whose leadership promises something. What gives them this authority? Not history as Destiny, somehow fore-ordained, nor finding a formula which matches a pre-existing truth about our species—or our race—or our gender; rather, as Merleau-Ponty says, "the inner certainty of having said what in the situation waited to be said, and what consequently could not fail to be understood" (S 74/92–3). Once articulated, we recognize it, and it inserts into our thinking a dimension which henceforth we will not be able to ignore (S 17/25).

What matters, in fact, is not so much the articulation (*la parole*) as the meaning given to the situation as it is taken up by those who live it. Indeed, I think it is characteristic of Merleau-Ponty's overall development that his earlier work sounds more "modernist," whereas his later work explicitly transcends such a subject-object distinction as is implicit in the concepts of leader and led.[11] A striking example, mentioned twice in *Phenomenology of Perception,* has no reference to a leader at all; and as there are neither speaker nor hearers of any *parole,* I want rather to call it *politique originaire.* Merleau-Ponty is exlaining the relationship of the emergence of class consciousness to the lived situation of workers in Russia. A new future becomes possible when the factory workers in the towns make common cause with the farm workers, and henceforth the members of each group feel the others' oppression as their own (PhP 444f/507f; cf. 362f/416f). There emerges a new gestalt, a wider meaning, in terms of which their individual sufferings, and previous conflicts of interest, even mutual enmity and ill-usage, can all be understood in a different way. "Social space begins to be polarized, and a region of the exploited is seen to appear" (PhP 445/508). Their image of themselves is changed, they find themselves moving in a new direction, hitherto unimagined, and so, in Russia 1917, the revolution is born.

My own most vivid experiences of such transformation have been in the areas of gender and class, and it is appropriate in a paper in phenomenology to offer a description. This autobiographical sketch is quite different from Merleau-Ponty's example; it will, I hope for that reason, clarify the point I am making; and I want this discussion of praxis to include the immediacy of lived experience.

I was a student at Cambridge University (1958–61), concurrently part of the time with two older brothers. We had very different experiences of undergraduate social life, they and I. In the colleges, all male at that time, without it being overtly conscious, the men gravitated towards one another according to accent, style of dress etc., soon discovering they had been to the same kinds of schools. Though my brothers joined many organizations and participated in sports, their social world remained curiously narrow and static. It was not like this for me: women made up only 10% of the undergraduate population. Inside my college (New Hall), we were more conscious of

our academic achievement in winning a place at the University than
we were of family background. Outside the college, at parties and on
dates, it seemed that I had (at last) an advantage over my brothers. I
was not glamorous or popular, or even particularly sociable, but I had
an entrée into all social groups, from the most exclusively élite to the
most aggressively working class. In time, it dawned on me why this
was so: while men had a class-identity, women, who were relatively
scarce, were treated as class-less, and simply took on the status of the
men they were with. This revelation of my marginality opened up for
me a new dimension in the class/gender dynamic, a new sense of
sisterhood, and of the bad faith implicit in identifying with men whose
status I could thereby reflect.

As *politique originaire,* it was only a beginning, and as Merleau-
Ponty says of all expression "it is like a step taken in the fog—no one
can say where, if anywhere it will lead" (SNS 3/8). In politics, in the
present, we are caught up in social patterns, and we participate
without knowing the end of the story, since we at the same time
contribute to the story and so change its meaning. *Politique originaire*
is embodied in the acceptance of this responsibility, which commits
itself to a future with others. *Politique secondaire,* like *parole parlée,*
takes over what is already in place, and has no intimation of a future.
In reaffirming only what has already been said—what therefore, is
now said by no-one—it is, says Merleau-Ponty, a way of staying silent
(PW 20/30). This horizontal element, the "not yet" is a critical aspect
of our experience, of the present as lived, because we are always in
the midst of it, always, as the existentialists put it, inventing ourselves. Merleau-Ponty says somewhere that it is harder to live a life
than to write a book, which suggests to me that if we do not know
this, we have not yet noticed what living can ask of us. The lived
reality of politics is part of our experience, whether we deal with it
creatively or not. Adrienne Rich writes of the moment when she
"began . . . to feel that politics was not something 'out there' but something 'in here' and of the essence of my condition";[12] it is at such times
that *politique originaire* is possible.

Power and violence are part of our world—whether they have to
be is not here the question—we are born into this race, this class, this
nation, this family, this body of this sex; and these circumstances set
problems for us, whether or not we face them (or are forced to face
them). The tensions they generate are not going to go away, but to
respond to them creatively, to transform their meaning, is going to
cost us something, whether we see ourselves as privileged or as oppressed.[13] So I come to pick up a theme of Geraldine Finn's, namely

that the politics of contingency offers no safe place. Audre Lorde's poem, "Power," begins:

> The difference between poetry and rhetoric
> is being
> ready to kill
> yourself
> instead of your children.[14]

It is about a black woman who was a member of the jury (the rest of whom were white men) which acquitted a white policeman who had killed a 10 year old black boy. Ready to kill yourself instead of your children? Either way the outcome is tragic; no one can tell whether it will be "worth it," whether she will be (or be recognized as) a hero, but for all of us the possibility of a future may rest on our risking our whole present.

Notes

1. Kerry Whiteside, *Merleau-Ponty and the Foundation of an Existential Politics* (Princeton: Princeton University Press, 1988), p. 3.

2. Merleau-Ponty's reading of Machiavelli (S 211–223/267/283) is important in showing how Machiavelli is misunderstood by those who see him as cynical.

3. I entered on the path which has led to these reflections when I participated in a panel on Feminism and Ideology at the Canadian Association for Political Science, MacMaster University, June 87. In October 88, I presented a more developed version of those ideas at Eastern S.W.I.P. and the present essay is indebted to the challenging questions posed by women at that meeting.

4. This is true of some readings of Foucault. Even if Foucault does not think in terms of individual motivation, he evidently believes in "Leviathon."

5. See Merleau-Ponty's long footnote about Marxism and psychoanalysis at the end of the chapter on "The Body in Its Sexual Being" (PhP 171–3/199–202).

6. Barry Cooper: *Merleau-Ponty and Marxism: From Terror to Reform* (Toronto: University of Toronto Press, 1979), p. 3.

7. Sonia Kruks, *A Study in the Political Philosophy of Merleau-Ponty* (Garland, 1987), p. 37.

8. Geraldine Finn refers to Habermas's position as "nostalgic rationalism" in "Beyond Either/Or: Post-modernism and the politics of feminism", a

paper presented at the Conference on Feminism, Critical Theory and the Canadian Legal System, at the University of Windsor, June 1988, forthcoming in the *Canadian Journal of Women and the Law*. Cf. Merleau-Ponty: "Human society is *not* a community of reasonable minds, and only in fortunate countries where a biological and economic balance has locally and temporarily been struck has such a conception of it been possible" (PhP 56/69).

9. See my article "Perception and Dialectic" (published under the name Shapiro), *Human Studies I*, 1978, pp. 245–276.

10. (IPP 54/63): "The theory of signs as developed in linguistics perhaps implies a conception of historical meaning which gets beyond the opposition of *things* versus *consciousnesses*." And 55/64: "There is a rationality in contingency, a lived logic, a self-constitution which is exactly what we need to understand the contingency and meaning (*sens*) in history, and Saussure could well have sketched out a new philosophy of history."

11. Cf. Elaine Stavro-Pearce's comment that the distinction between leader and led is not ontological but historical. See her unpublished thesis *Towards a Philosophy of Humanism* (Toronto: University of Toronto, 1985), p. 116. I am grateful to Dr. Mildred Bakan for drawing my attention to this thesis.

12. Adrienne Rich, *On Lies, Secrets and Silence* (New York: Norton, 1979), p. 44.

13. Cf. the notion of "Surrender" developed by Kurt Wolff, in *Surrender and Catch* (Dordrecht: Reidel, 1976).

14. Audre Lorde, *The Black Unicorn* (New York: Norton, 1978), p. 108.

14

The Politics of Contingency:
The Contingency of Politics—On the Political
Implications of Merleau-Ponty's Ontology of the Flesh

ะ ะ

Geraldine Finn

**"What does this talk of flesh and chiasms
amount to politically?"[1]**

The argument of this paper is that Merleau-Ponty's ontology of
flesh and chiasms moves us well beyond the terms and relevancies of
traditional politics which I have described elsewhere as a "politics of
final solutions"[2]—which is the politics of Hegel and Marx and
Habermas as much as it is the politics of Hitler and the Ayatollah—
towards a radically new and yet to be articulated *politics of contingency*. By this I mean a politics theorised and practised from the
standpoint of *contingency* rather than necessity, of *ambiguity* rather
than apodicticity, of the intertwinings of the *flesh* rather than the
separations and negations of a would-be autonomous subject(ivity) or
individual consciousness. It is, in this sense, a politics of and for the
'people' rather than the Prince: a politics of and for those whose
experience of contingency, ambiguity and the flesh cannot be easily
disavowed (denied, distorted or dissimulated from themselves) or mys-
tified by the various rhetorics of transcendence, universality and necessity which maintain the power of Princes by masking the ambiguities of the particular flesh which is the specific and contingent
condition of their privilege. It is a politics which renders traditional
political discourse redundant, therefore, to the extent that it is spoken from the privileged position (the position of historical necessity
and final solutions, the position of the Prince) and to the extent that

it relies on the traditional ontological assumptions of high-altitude thinking, thinking forgetful of its contingent roots in particular persons, places and times.

Commentators on the political implications of Merleau-Ponty's philosophy of ambiguity have, I think, consistently underestimated the distance of his thought from the ontological assumptions which inform traditional politics (of necessity), and likewise the inadequacy of traditional political concepts and categories for articulating the very different politics it implies. Writers like Barry Cooper, Sonia Kruks, and Kerry Whiteside[3] for example (political scientists rather than philosophers by affiliation) have measured Merleau-Ponty's politics against the yardstick of traditional political theory—against Marx and Hegel and contemporary 'liberals' like Michael Walzer and Richard Rorty—and, not surprisingly, found him lacking. But this is surely to miss the point of Merleau-Ponty's retreat from and challenge to conventional politics, the very rationality of which is thrown into question by his ontology of chiasms and flesh: its roots in the ancient metaphysics of necessity—of consciousness and apodicticity, of affirmation and negation, of freedom and determinism, self and other, subject and object etc., as well as its implicit telos towards some form or other of "final solution"—of achievement and completion of a human project presumed to be immanent in history.

It is the argument of this paper that Merleau-Ponty's ontology of flesh and chiasms calls for a complete rethinking of politics: of how much of life (and history) is contained within its category, of its ground in human being and consciousness, of what in its light, therefore, constitutes the limits, the scope and the 'end' of political action. I will be suggesting specific ways in which the politics of contingency is both broader and narrower in its scope than the traditional politics of necessity which framed Merleau-Ponty's own (explicitly) political essays of the forties and fifties and which continues to determine and delimit contemporary political debate in general as well as the thinking of Merleau-Ponty's commentators in particular. My objective is twofold: to defend Merleau-Ponty from the common criticism that he exchanged politics for philosophy in his later years and thereby challenge the notion of politics implicit in that claim as well as the presumption of a disjuncture between political and philosophical engagement; and thence to consider the incidence as well as the rationalisations of political violence in the contemporary world (including the kind of account offered by Merleau-Ponty in *Humanism and Terror*) from the perspective of a politics of contingency rather than necessity and from the standpoint of its traditional victims (the 'people') rather than those who are or would be its agents and apologists (the Prince). The historical and continuing resistance of women to their particular 'occupation' by men and the historical and continuing resistance of blacks to their historical and continuing 'occupation' by whites supply the concrete contexts for these reflections on contemporary political violence and its relationship to the politics of contingency and necessity.

Beyond Traditional Politics

Merleau-Ponty did not wake up to the facts of power and the reality of politics as a necessary contingency of his own life until World War II and the occupation of France forced him up against it and made it impossible for him to any longer not-see and not-choose for or against a power in which he was implicated.[4] The relatively simple politics of the Resistance, however, where differences between one's political allies and opponents (between us and them, good and evil, freedom and domination, masters and slaves) were easy to recognize, at least in their larger configurations (of Nazi and Jew, occupier and liberator, dictator and democrat), gave way after the war to the increasingly complex, ambivalent and, for Merleau-Ponty, abstract and distant politics of the Cold War which ultimately led him to abandon political speech altogether in favour of philosophical reflection.[5]

In the light of that reflection and the political aporias that preceded (and possibly precipitated) it, I see Merleau-Ponty's withdrawal from political speech not so much as an abandonment of politics *tout court*—of the problematics of power, responsibility and resistance—as a deepening of his engagement with it. Faced as he was with the inadequacy of traditional political categories (inherited from Machiavelli, Hegel, Marx and Weber, for example) to make practical sense of the political situation he found himself in, Merleau-Ponty went back to the drawing-board so to speak, to renew his efforts to think beyond them: to think beyond the political divisions and philosophical aporias of Cartesian dualism and Hegelian dialectics which supplied traditional politics with its ontological and ethical reasons. I see this not as a retreat from politics but as a very particular retreat from a very particular politics, that of the Prince: a dominant politics which is also a politics of domination both theorised and practised by and on behalf of those who rule; those who have (or believe themselves entitled to have) political power (over others); who claim to have necessity, history, freedom, reason and right (all the grand universals) on their side. Merleau-Ponty abandoned this particular politics and its particular philosophical presuppositions for a very different philosophical project, an ontology of chiasms and flesh theorised from the standpoint of a "fold in being" the political implications of which have scarcely been considered.

Merleau-Ponty made few explicitly political claims in his later work and certainly offers no platform or program for a 'politics of the flesh'—requirements of politics in the abandoned traditional sense. But it is not difficult to identify the kind of politics his phenomenology of the flesh would exclude: all politics which rely on dualistic ontologies of subjects and objects, freedom and necessity, self and other, (perhaps even master and slave); all politics which assume a universal telos or essence to human being(s): some generalised human project or destiny the realisation of which is taken to be the particular task of politics as well as the transcendent meaning of History. The ontology of the flesh rules out, that is, all politics of what I have been calling necessity and/or final solutions: politics which postulate ideal ends which leave no remainder, which negate the present inasmuch as it is merely the means to a future which is forever deferred. It rules out all traditional politics inasmuch as they aim for closure (completion, fulfilment, ends) and seek thereby to suture all contingencies (differences, divergencies, disagreements, conflicts, confusions, possibilities, peoples and pains) into the seamless linear narrative of historical necessity, of some *'grand récit'*: a politics which leaves no openings for an other, for a future which can (must) be different, unknown, for life, for the world, for the flesh, for the "reversibility that defines the flesh" (VI 144) which is "always imminent and never realized in fact" (VI 147).

Thus, Merleau-Ponty's talk of flesh and chiasms puts out of play modernist and postmodernist politics alike to the extent that they both rely on the terms and relevancies and implicit metaphysics of traditional politics: of the Hegelian dialectic of Subjects and Objects (Man and History, Culture and Nature, Freedom and Necessity) and its ultimate realisation one way or another in some "Universal and Homogenous State." Modernist politics (liberal, marxist, nationalist, for example) continue to affirm and pursue traditional abstract political ends, like Freedom, Sovereignty, Subjectivity and Man, as if they were absolutes—categorical, necessary, immanent. Postmodernism's (would-be) abdication of *all* political 'sens' merely confirms the absoluteness of modernism's ends in its inability to think beyond them: to imagine a politics which is different from traditional politics, which is for and of the other(s) not the Same, for and of the people not the

Prince, for and of contingency (the flesh) not Necessity (consciousness). For both modernism and postmodernism alike, politics remains a question of all or nothing, of sink or swim, of necessity, of "final solutions" and all the practicalities this entails: what Sartre called "the liquidation of particularity" with reference to Stalinism, and Brian Fawcett, more recently and closer to home, "genocide"[6] with reference to the shared intentionalities (telos) of American television (slow) on the one hand and Cambodia's Khmer Rouge (fast) on the other. For both modernist and postmodernist politics tend in the same direction: away from the particularities and contingencies of the flesh and the future—which would have to be the point of departure for any politics consistent with Merleau-Ponty's ontology—and towards the universality, necessity and finality of Imperium: towards, that is, a politics whose totalising praxis renders individual memory and imagination superfluous, "creating in its stead a single focus on the monodic truth."[7] They tend, that is, towards what Lyotard has rightly called terrorism.[8]

Towards a Politics of Contingency

I have been arguing that traditional politics is at once a politics of necessity and final solutions *and* a politics articulated from and on behalf of the position of the Prince: a politics which assumes the standpoint of privilege and power (of autonomy, freedom, reason, universality, necessity, history, consciousness, Man, etc.), even when it puts itself at the service of the people. A politics of contingency, by contrast, would take its point of departure from the side of the Other of traditional politics, the side of Necessity's other, the Prince's other. Not to confirm its Otherness nor the Oneness of the Prince (of the Enlightenment ideal of the opposite and privileged pole) but to resist and subvert the already political polarisation itself and the obliteration of particularity and difference which speaking (and organising) the Universal from the side of the Prince, of the Subject, of the privileged pole (of Reason, Freedom, History, God etc.) always entails. Thinking (and acting) politically from the standpoint of those who have been the objects, the material, the instruments and the excluded of traditional politics will transform the very meaning and 'sens' of politics itself, as when the figure becomes ground and the ground the figure when we change the focus and intentionality of our perception of an ambiguous image. What emerges from the standpoint of contingency as 'political'—political experience, knowledge, vision, change, struggle, resistance and power, for example—will be phenomenologically distinct from what emerges as 'political' from the standpoint of necessity, offering a politics which is both broader and narrower in its scope than the politics of the tradition.

One of the ways in which politics as disclosed from the standpoint of the flesh (of chiasms and reversibility) is broader in its scope than traditional politics is that it cannot be reduced—without destroying the phenomena of experience itself—to the relatively simple question of taking sides in a conflict of opposites in a system of polarised differences: of self and other, us and them, subject and object, reason and violence, etc. This is because the experience of the flesh, of our being as a fold in being *including our experience of political power itself* is always ambiguous and reversible and cannot, therefore, support a politics which requires us to identify others as Others, as the Enemy *once and for all*. The politics of racism and sexism, for example, is quite literally a *politics of the flesh:* a hierarchy of power, privilege and control built on the absolutely arbitrary and contingent, but nevertheless real, differences of skin colour and genitalia. Racist and sexist power is thus inscribed on our very bodies and inseparable from who we are and the flesh of 'our' world(s). As far as sexist and racist power is concerned, it is we who are occupied by 'enemy' powers, not 'our' country.[9] Our struggle against that occupation is always, therefore, a struggle against ourselves *and those we love*—mothers, fathers, lovers, brothers, sisters, friends, children, neighbours: a sustained internecine struggle against the 'enemy' within and not an easy confrontation of opposites—us/them, right/wrong, self/other, good/evil, friend/foe and so forth.

Resistance to the politics of the flesh is therefore always as ambiguous and as reversible as the flesh it organises: as personal as it is political (personal because political, political because personal), as private as it is public, because it is grounded in as well as directed towards the very flesh of our own political being-in-the-world. It rarely takes so simple a form, therefore, as directing a gun at the 'other' or the 'enemy,' for the other and the enemy is within us as well as those we have grown to love, admire and rely on, and those whose lives we aspire to. Resistance in these circumstances takes forms unrecognized by and often invisible to traditional revolutionary strategists[10] who continue to theorize politics from the standpoint of the Prince—of necessity, of 'pensée de survol.' It is, for example, embedded in, intertwined with, the very minutiae of daily life: in how we wear our hair, our clothes, our face; in how and where and when we walk, talk, smile, listen, look and pass someone on the street. Nor are such resistances exclusive of 'collaboration' and 'collusion,' for the politics of contingency cannot sustain the rigid boundaries implicit in such exclusions. Performing 'woman' or 'native' well, for example, can be both subversive *and* submissive, rebellious *and* acquiescent in racist and sexist societies, at different times or even at one and the same time. Push-up bras, painted nails, lipstick and fuck-me shoes, for instance, can be used to rebel *against* the hierarchical divisions of man/woman, good/bad, white/black, labour/leisure, public/private, virgin/whore and the system of oppressions they organise, as well as to sustain it. Similarly, having or not-having a baby, an abortion, a husband, an education, a job, or going or not-going to church, to work, to vote, to the beach or the bar, can be revolutionary choices (choices from which the revolution will be created) depending on the specificities of circumstance and context. As can 'loving' the 'enemy.'

This means that politics experienced and practised from the standpoint of contingency is broader in its scope than the politics of necessity in that it is also a politics which has no place, no place proper to it. It cannot be restricted to the polis, for example, to sites of government and business, to the targetting of 'public' institutions as the only proper objects of political agency and change. On the contrary, from the standpoint of contingency (of chiasms, of the flesh, of subordination) politics encompasses the whole of one's life including its most personal and seemingly private moments, as suggested above. For, we do not slough off our skins or our genitals (or our class, our nationality, our language, our education, our wealth or even our good looks) on the doorstep of our 'homes' when we leave the 'public' sphere, nor drop their social and political meanings on the doormat with the mud from our shoes. The skin, the genitals, the class, the language, the nationality, the education, the wealth, the good looks and their social and political meanings remain with us wherever we are and whatever we are doing, feeling or thinking. They *are* who we are and our struggles against the political hierarchies built upon them, against racism and sexism, for example, is one which is waged within and against ourselves and our own 'subjectivity' and experience, as much as within and against the 'objectivity' of the institutions which govern us and the 'subjectivity' of those who rule. This makes the politics of contingency a profoundly radical politics in that it reaches to the very roots of our being. It is a relentless politics of everyday life and consciousness, a guerilla politics of everywhere in general and nowhere in particular.

This truth of politics and power—its lack of proper place—is often invisible to and unrecognized by those whose privilege protects them from it: the traditional spokesmen (*sic*) of traditional politics. As

Nadine Gordimer has observed of the different place of politics in the anti-apartheid struggles of whites and blacks in South Africa:

> We whites have still to thrust the spade under the roots of our lives: for most of us, including myself, struggle is still something that has a place. But for blacks it is every where or nowhere.[11]

In the same paragraph she cites the example of an overheard remark of a young black woman: 'I break the law because I am alive'; and in an earlier essay written from Johannesburg in 1976, two months after the Soweto killings, the words of a black intellectual "whose commitment to liberation no one would question, although he risks the violent disapproval of blacks by still having contact with whites":

> When I go home tonight, I don't know which to be more afraid of— the polic getting me when they shoot at anything that moves, or my own people getting me when I walk across the yard to the lavatory.[12]

This truth about the different place of politics in the lives of blacks and whites in racist society is true of the politics of all social hierarchies: of the experience and place of sexual politics in the lives of women and men, for example. Women in sexist society, like blacks in racist society, occupy Man's World on his terms and at his discretion—like guests whose invitation can be withdrawn at any time and for any reason. We run exactly the same risks when we go home as the black (male) intellectual cited above: not knowing which to be more afraid of—the men in the street who feel free to harass us when we are not escorted ('legitimized') by another man or 'our own people,' the men in 'our home' whose violence we are, as a matter of fact, most commonly subjected to. (Whose streets are they really, then? Whose people? Whose home?) Women do not have, as men have, a 'private' sphere into which we can retreat from the 'public' world of politics and power. The politics of our subordination and oppression is centred in our homes—in men's private sphere—where we are most likely to experience violence: to be beaten, raped and killed, in the bedroom and the kitchen (i.e., where we belong) by 'our own people' i.e., our male kin, on Sundays—their day of rest.[13]

It seems to me that this specific difference of political experience between men and women—that for women, it has no place, no polis— conditions the nature and direction and probably the incidence of violence in political struggles, coinciding as it must with a particular and specific consciousness of oppression and its place, of what of oneself and one's community is at stake in resistance to it, and the price one is prepared for what is understood to be 'liberation.' Women do not characteristically resort to the same kind of violence as men in either their liberation struggles and their struggles for justice, or in their various daily practices of conflict resolution—as mothers, for example, or as mainstays of the service industries. I think this is because women—as the Other of Man in sexist society—have no place from which to articulate a politics of necessity, of means and ends, of necessary destiny. They have no proper place, that is, no place proper to them, which is their own, which they *can* own (they take their father's or their husband's name, not their mother's), which defines who they are (some man's property) and with which they can I-dentify: no place to which they can retreat from the contingency, chaos and confusion of the flesh—from which they can organize 'attacks' on the same contingencies and over which they can imagine themselves to be in some sense Sovereign, Prince (not even our own bodies). Women, unlike men, have no place from which to assume the political standpoint of the Prince: no place which is exclusively their own, which *is* themselves and from which others can and must, therefore, be dis-placed, ex-cluded, dis-tanced and ob-jectified as Other. Having such a place—or at least, feeling entitled to claim such a place—seems to me to be a condition of political violence, which always flows one way: from and between would-be Princes, would-be Sovereignties, against whatever stands in the way of its (illusory) achievement. Political violence is always, in some sense, top-down, male and tribal: organised and articulated from the standpoint of the Prince (of necessity and historical destiny) against others who are clearly Other (the Enemies of the One) for the sake of an 'I'—an Identity—which is clear and distinct, and a place which that I-dentity claims as exclusively its own.[14]

Patriarchal social relations make this standpoint available to men—even necessary inasmuch as masculinity is defined in its terms: in terms of necessity, identity and difference—and not to women, who *as women* are confined to contingency and the ambiguity and reversibility of chiasms and flesh. This is not to suggest that women are not as capable as men of 'violence'—political or otherwise—but that there are significant differences and discontinuities between 'violences': between those perpetrated by and in the name of patriarchal tribes, for example, and those perpetrated by and in the name of specific individuals: between necklacing and dropping bombs, for instance, and having an abortion or beating a child.[15] These are differences which philosophers, philosophising from the standpoint of the Prince, have consistently obscured, and thereby the political relations which I have been suggesting constitute and coincide with them.

Theorising violence from the standpoint of contingency makes these relations and these discontinuities, these *specificities,* visible and brings them into focus for further reflection on the political possibilities 'inherent' in the 'human condition.'

Just as from the standpoint of contingency politics has no proper place, so also has it no proper time: no time proper to it apart from the local, particular and immanent, and therefore constantly shifting, temporalities of specific political actions and people. In other words, the politics of contingency is broader in its scope than traditional politics in that, just as it cannot be reduced to the taking of sides, so it cannot be reduced to the planning and pursuit of parties, platforms and programs which postulate definitive and transcendent (usually universal and historically necessary) ends to which present and past meanings ('sens')—and people—are subordinated as means, as contingent and particular instrumentalities. Instead of a politics of propaganda and programs, of means and ends and transcendent teleologies, the ontology of flesh and chiasms calls for a creative politics of 'bricolage' and original/originating speech (parole originaire) grounded in the local and historical specificities of particular people, places and times: for originating action which will disrupt the sedimented meanings/sens of the past, of history, power and necessity, and thus give birth to new norms and to futures which can be different. It calls, that is, for a *politique originaire* (to use the words of Eleanor Godway)[16] which when successful—and there is no guarantee of this—will invent what in the future will appear to have been required at the time.

Keeping alive local memory and imagination as a reservoir of meanings, truths and possibilities for a different future is thus absolutely central to a politics of contingency.[17] This means refusing all totalizations of destiny, universality, necessity and Reason, wherever they appear. In our own case, this means resisting not only television as Fawcett argues,[18] but also the lure of traditional political formations (both of which tend towards the liquidation of particular memory and local imagination) with ordinary (not now so ordinary) everyday speech. It means eschewing the old abstractions of universality, destiny and necessity by being present to each other (face to face) in all the ambiguities and reversibilities of the flesh in conversation and speech. It means, that is, resisting the old modernist and would-be-post modernist tendency to go global—with either one's projections or one's rationalisations of political realities. The best documented example I am familiar with of the strength, power, possibilities and in some sense success of this kind of local political resistance is that of Black Americans and South Africans, as evidenced in their music, for example, but especially as it is being currently disclosed in the poetry and fiction of Black American women.[19] I think the same kind of politics (of contingency) made possible the changes in Eastern Europe we witnessed in 1989, which took so many political commentators by surprise, and that the possibility of its continuing—as a politics of contingency—in the different locations (Romania, Poland, Germany, Czechoslovakia) will determine the direction and 'success' of these changes in the future.[20]

This aspect of the politics of contingency, that it has no place or time proper to it other than that of the specific and local practicalities within which it is realized, means that it can offer no necessities and no guarantees to its participants who must, therefore, assume responsibility for what they choose to do in its name. This means that there is an inescapable *ethical* dimension to the politics of contingency which can neither be abstracted from nor reduced to it, to politics itself, as is so often the case in a traditional politics of necessity. There, personal decisions, responsibilities and accountability are consistently denied, dissolved, disavowed and displaced—from individual actors onto political abstractions like History, Reason, Nature, Society, the State, the Struggle and the various necessities of Liberation. By contrast, a politics of contingency offers no safe place for the 'politically correct,' thus no way of protecting oneself from the exigencies of moral choice and 'political' responsibility within both the personal *and* the public sphere. Nadine Gordimer has observed that for whites in South Africa, this means:

> it is not simply a matter of follow-the-leader behind the blacks; it's taking on, as blacks do, choices to be made out of confusion, empirically, pragmatically, ideologically or idealistically about the practical moralities of the struggle.[21]

It means, that is, taking on choices and their consequences from the standpoint of the oppressed, the 'unredeemed,' those who know they do not know—from the standpoint of contingency; as opposed to the standpoint of power, of the 'chosen race,' of those who think they know—the standpoint of necessity, of the Prince. It means giving up the illusion of political purity or control and always running the risk of being in the wrong, and assuming responsibility for this.

This aspect of the politics of contingency is also relevant to the problem of violence in both its incidence and its various rationalisations. For, from the standpoint of necessity, wherein ends justify means and good (Reason, History, Freedom, Man) conquers all, and the present merely realizes the past and the future the present,

political violence can be done, has been done and is done 'innocently':
in both confidence and good faith as the necessary means to necessary ends, the necessary negation of the negation for the sake of an
ultimate affirmation presumed to be immanent in it.

It is in this precise sense that the politics of contingency is *narrower* in its scope than traditional politics in that it does not reduce
politics to ontology. It does not, that is, mask the concrete and contingent specificities of *political* violence which is always local and particular beneath the mystifying veil of an abstracted Universality and
Necessity supposedly immanent in History (Man, Freedom, Reason),
as does Merleau-Ponty himself, and the commentators who follow his
example, in his defense of violence in *Humanism and Terror* where
he assimilates political violence into the ontological necessities of an
"intersubjectivity" described, not in terms of chiasms and reversibility
as in his later work, but in terms of "encroachment" and "intrusion"
(e.g., HT 109). Both Merleau-Ponty and his commentators conflate
political rationality within which alone political violence makes 'sens'
with the falsely posited (and later repudiated) but familiar existential
rationality of the subject-object dichotomy and dialectic:[22]

> Political problems come from the fact that we are all subjects and
> yet we look upon other people and treat them as objects. (HT 110)

My point is not that Merleau-Ponty was wrong to defend the
necessity of political violence in the contingent (political) conditions
within which he was himself embedded and to which he felt himself
obliged to respond—I am not espousing an anti-violence position here—
but that he was wrong to do so on ontological grounds rather than
political ones: on the grounds, for example, that "Inasmuch as we are
incarnate beings, violence is our lot" (HT 109). I am objecting to the
tendency in traditional politics, exemplified by Merleau-Ponty in *Humanism and Terror,* to collapse all human conflict, suffering, force,
constraint, sacrifice, loss, pain, hurt, destruction and 'sin' into the
general undifferentiated category of a 'violence' presumed to be intrinsic to and ineradicable from the facts of corporeality itself, to a
"sort of evil in collective life" (HT xxxviii). I am objecting to this
tendency because it obfuscates the politics of particular acts of violence and the specific political and personal stakes of its agents,
objects, interests and intentionalities. It thus obscures the very phenomena of violence itself, pre-empting an interrogative phenomenology of violence in relation to politics by subordinating the question of
the contingent conditions of possibility of particular 'violences' to the
postulate of the necessities of an "elemental," "ineradicable" violence
inherent in the human condition. The practical-political-ethical prob-

lems posed by acts of real violence are thus forever forestalled by the abstracted philosophical problem posed to a 'conscience' of choosing between necessary violences: the necessary violence of the State, for example, or the equally necessary violences of those who would resist it? Our violence or theirs? The ethical standpoint of contingency, of personal responsibility, accountability and judgment is thereby forsaken for the frankly Macchiavellian standpoint of the Prince, of necessity, premised not on the lived ambiguities and reversibilities of the flesh but on the posited divisions and contradictions of subjects and objects, individual praxis and collective life.

It has been the argument of this paper that Merleau-Ponty's ontology of the flesh moves us well beyond the hypostasis of these old oppositions and aporia and the various political rationalities—of History, Freedom, Reason and Man—they have been called upon to support, towards a politics of contingency which takes both its point of departure and its always provisional 'ends' from the local and historical specificities of particular political experience. I have argued that the ontology of the flesh both requires and enables us to think politics anew and have suggested precise and significant ways in which this politics is both broader and narrower in its scope than the traditional political thinking which informed Merleau-Ponty's earlier work and continues to determine the interpretations of his principal political commentators. I have argued that the politics of contingency implicit in the ontology of chiasms and flesh is more radical than a traditional politics of necessity in that it extends to the very roots of our being— as men and women, blacks and whites, in racist and sexist society, for example—and leaves us with 'no safe place' for transcending our political status or the ethical implications of how we choose to live it out. Unlike traditional politics, the politics of contingency offers not only no safe place, but also no final solutions, no guarantees, no consolations and no crowning glories—no principles, programs or plans. Instead, it offers us a future and a world to be made, the resources for doing it, and the challenge of what Eleanor Godway calls a *politique originaire* in place of the *politique secondaire* of that which is already known. Couldn't this be the *post*-modern politics for which we have been looking?

Notes

1. This question is posed by Kerry Whiteside in the penultimate chapter of his recent book on *Merleau-Ponty and the Foundation of an Existential Politics* (Princeton University Press, Princeton 1988, p. 272), where he con-

cludes that Merleau-Ponty's late philosophy does not amount to much politically. He describes it as an "all-embracing ontology in which there is no obvious place for specific political demands" (p. 275), and continues:

> What is so dissatisfying in his late political writings is that, while not denying the necessity of political thinking, they conceive meaning and history in such a way that politics seems once again "impensable" . . .
>
> . . . We come to a theorist in the first place not to be told how we *must* think about political problems, but to receive some instruction about what political phenomena are important, about what unsuspected relationships may hold between them, about what action is necessary or permissable, about what values are worth pursuing and why. To be told that 'the task of the philosopher [is] . . . to elaborate such a concept of being that contradictions—neither accepted nor 'surpassed'—find their place in it' is to encounter a mode of thought [that] does little to help us to think politically. (pp. 276–277)

I think Whiteside is completely wrong here, both about what Merleau-Ponty's late philosophy amounts to politically and about the implied relationship between ontology and political thinking. He misses the point of Merleau-Ponty's *turn away from* traditional political categories and assumptions towards an 'originating' ontology which obliges us *to think politics anew*. Whiteside simply refuses this challenge and, along with others (Monika Langer, for example, in "Merleau-Ponty: The Ontological Limitations of Politics," in Alkis Kontos (ed.) *Domination* (Toronto: University of Toronto Press, 1975), insists on judging the political implications of Merleau-Ponty's late philosophy by the standards of his work in the forties. In this paper I reverse this procedure and read the earlier work in the light of the later and of what I take to be its implications for a 'politique originaire.'

2. See Geraldine Finn, "Beyond Either/Or: Postmodernism and the Politics of Feminism," unpublished paper presented at the workshop on Feminism, Critical Theory and the Canadian Legal System, held at the University of Windsor, Ontario, June 1988.

3. Barry Cooper, *Merleau-Ponty and Marxism: From Terror to Reform,* (Toronto: University of Toronto Press, 1979); Sonia Kruks, *The Political Philosophy of Merleau-Ponty* (Sussex: Harvester Press, 1981); Whiteside, *Merleau-Ponty,* op. cit.

4. "We knew that concentration camps existed, that the Jews were being persecuted, but these certainties belonged to the world of thought. We were not as yet living face to face with cruelty and death: we had not as yet been given the choice of submitting to them or confronting them" (SNS 139).

5. "Unity had been easy during the Resistance, because relationships were almost always man-to-man . . . And in this sense it must be said that the Resistance experience . . . fostered our illusions of 1939 and masked the truth of the incredible power of history which the Occupation taught us in another connection. We have returned to the time of the *institutions*. The distance between the laws and those to whom they apply is once more apparent; once again one legislated for X; and once again the good will of some resumes its class features which make it unrecognizable to others." (SNS 151).

6. Jean-Paul Sartre, *Critique of Dialectical Reason* (London: New Left Books, 1976); Brian Fawcett, *Cambodia. A Book for People Who Find Television Too Slow* (Vancouver: Talonbooks, 1986).

7. Fawcett, *Cambodia,* p. 63.

8. Jean-François Lyotard, *The Postmodern Condition: A Report on Knowledge* (Minnesota: University of Minnesota Press, 1984, pp. 63–64).

9. Or, to put it another way:

'Our country' . . . throughout the greater part of its history has treated me as a slave; it has denied me education or any share in its possessions . . . in fact, as a woman, I have no country. As a woman I want no country. As a woman my country is the whole world. Virginia Woolf, *Three Guineas* (Hogarth Press, 1938, p. 125)

10. I am paraphrasing Nadine Gordimer here but have been unable to locate the precise citation I have in mind.

11. Nadine Gordimer, *The Essential Gesture. Writing, Politics and Places,* edited by Stephen Clingman (New York: Alfred Knopf, 1988, p. 271).

12. Gordimer, *Gesture,* p. 131.

13. For further explorations of the different relationship of men and women to the incidence and rationalisations of 'violence,' see Geraldine Finn, "Reason and Violence: More than a False Dichotomy—A Mechanism of Patriarchal Power," *Canadian Journal of Political and Social Theory,* vol. vi, no. 3, 1982; and "Taking Gender into Account in the 'Theatre of Terror': Violence, Media and the Maintenance of Male Dominance," *Canadian Journal of Women and the Law,* Vol. 3, No. 2, 1989–1990.

14. There is clearly a connection between what I am suggesting here about the masculinity and tribalism of political violence and Nancy Jay's analysis of rituals of blood sacrifice, including the Christian Eucharist, as evidence of and at the same time means of constituting lines of patrilineal descent. See Nancy Jay, "Sacrifice as Remedy for Having Been Born of Woman," in Clarissa Atkinson, Constance Buchanan and Margaret Miles

(eds.), *Immaculate and Powerful* (Boston: Beacon Press, 1985). According to Jay, blood sacrifice only occurs in societies which trace their kinship relations through the fathers and not the mothers line. And only men sacrifice in these societies. William Beers maintains that men "are saying No to the mother" when they sacrifice (in William Beers, *Women and Sacrifice. Male Narcissism and the Psychology of Ritual.* A Psychoanalytic Essay on Gender, unpublished manuscript, undated). According to Eli Sagan they are both making and marking their transition from kinship to kingship: from anarchical matrilineal society to hierarchies of patrilineal status society. See Eli Sagan, *At the Dawn of Tyranny: The Origins of Individuality, Political Oppression and the State* (New York, Alfred Knopf, 1985). Ritual sacrifice is thus both the means and the expression of male bonding *over and against women.* It is a way of distinguishing men from women, masculinity from femininity, culture from nature and at the same time establishing a hierarchy of one over the other. It is always accompanied by the culturally prescribed fear and abjection of women (i.e., by misogyny) and of their capacity to give birth as the occasions of moral impurity and 'human' degradation. It is in the light of these analyses of ritual sacrifice that I am beginning to understand the more familiar incidence of ritual blood shedding by men in our own society: in wars and terrorism, mass murders, medical interventions, horror movies and so forth.

15. Acts of violence perpetrated by women are characteristically less 'senseless' less 'random,' less 'impersonal,' less bloody, less ritualised, less collective and less 'rationalised' than male-stream violence. They are most often directed by individual women at individual abusive men who are known to them, to save their own lives; or to particular children, sometimes to save theirs, through some tragic distortion of maternal care. See for example, Fay Weldon's *Praxis* (New York, Pocketbooks, 1978) and Toni Morrison's *Beloved* (Plume Books, New American Library, 1988) for two recent, powerful, fictional explorations of this theme.

16. Eleanor Godway, "Towards a Phenomenology of Politics: Expression and Praxis," in this volume.

17. Women's 'gossip' can thus be seen as a form of political resistance to men's 'reasoning,' keeping alive the local and particular memory and knowledge of women in the face of Man's totalizing histories which always leave them out.

18. Fawcett, *Cambodia,* op. cit.

19. See for example the various works of Audre Lorde, Alice Walker and Toni Morrison.

20. The plays of Vaclav Havel are perhaps the most obvious example of the kind of political resistance I am referring to here: keeping alive local imagination and memory in the face of the totalizing rhetorics of repressive institutions and knowledges.

21. Gordimer, *Gesture,* p. 268.

22. Monika Langer, for example, draws on a few key passages from *The Phenomenology of Perception* and *Humanism and Terror* to argue the following:

> It has emerged that there is a kind of violence inherent in the human condition as such. This elemental violence permeates all forms of human coexistence, from the simplest level of human perception to the most complex modes of human interaction . . . Given the ontological origin of violence, it becomes 'a law of human action' and 'a fact of political life' that human beings encroach, or intrude, upon one another . . . *No politics will ever be able to get rid of that violence which has to do with humanity's fundamental way of being in the world.*

(Langer, Merleau-Ponty . . . ," p. 105, original emphases).

15

Temporality: Merleau-Ponty and Derrida

≀▲ ≀▲

M. C. Dillon

"In the last analysis, what is at stake is . . . the privilege of the actual present, the now."

Jacques Derrida, Speech and Phenomena[1]

To raise the question of time at this time is to raise the question of the metaphysics of presence, the question whether the recognition of "the present or presence of sense to a full and primordial intuition" as "the source and guarantee of all value, [as] the 'principle of principles' " (SP 5) "conceals a metaphysical presupposition" (SP 4) which embodies a fundamental contradiction and, thus, is untenable. According to Derrida, who formulated the question as it is posed here, it is a momentous question because its answer signals the closure of Western metaphysics.[2]

Derrida's answer to this question is well known. Less well known is the fact that Merleau-Ponty contested in advance the viewpoint that was to eclipse his own in the minds of contemporary academics. My intent here is to review the crucial arguments on Derrida's side of this agon in order to expose a systematic flaw among his premises, and to attempt to resolve the paradoxes generated by this flaw with assistance from Merleau-Ponty.

Derrida's Argument[3]

The core tenet of Derrida's thesis is that "the movement of repetition . . . is irreducible in presence or in self-presence, that this trace of *différance* is always older than presence and procures for it its openness" (SP 68). The task at hand is to understand both the reasons for this claim and the consequences that follow from accepting it.

The argument presented in *Speech and Phenomena* cannot be dissociated from its context, that context being Derrida's critique of Husserl's conception of language and the notion of presence that drives it. Derrida's critique is deconstructive in the specific sense that it unravels the fabric of Husserl's discourse from within: Derrida acknowledges that he has "precisely formulated [his] question with Husserlian concepts" (SP 50) because the intent of the deconstruction is to show that his question is both (a) legitimated by the framework of Husserl's discourse and (b) unanswerable or aporetic within that very framework.[4]

Derrida's question concerns the how of the phenomenological principle of principles,[5] the principle that all truth or rationality or value in general is grounded in "primordial dator intuition" or "evidence-having," that is, the moment in which something presents itself to consciousness in "its bodily reality," that is, presence: presence both as (a) presentation of an object of intuition and as (b) the presence to itself on the part of consciousness which is required for (a) to take place. These two senses of presence coincide in the now moment of temporal presence. The present, the now, is the moment in which being and being-known coincide. That coincidence is one basis for the claim to apodicticity that Husserl makes for phenomenology: the lack of distance, the lack of any possible discrepancy, between the object-as-intuited and the intuition of the object precludes the possibility of error.[6] Derrida's deconstructive question is, simply put, how is that coincidence possible?

Derrida compounds the issue by raising further questions about the presentation, that is, about the dyadic structure, object-as-intuited/intuition-of-object. Specifically, he contests Husserl's claim that this is an unmediated presentation as distinct from a representation mediated by signs.

The initial focus of Derrida's critique is Husserl's distinction between expression (*Ausdruck*) and indication (*Anzeichen*). Derrida takes the main difference constituting this distinction to be the difference, "more functional than substantial," between signs that are necessarily bound up with meaning (*Bedeutung*)—these are the expressive signs—and signs which signify or indicate or refer—the indicative signs—but without necessarily being tied to meaning (SP 17–20). Thus a correlative distinction is drawn between meaning or *Bedeutung* or *vouloir-dire* in the sense that "a speaking subject" or "an expression . . . means or 'wants to say' something" (SP 18) and signification in the sense of indication or reference beyond itself or substitution: a sign may refer to another sign or substitute for another term without expressing any meaning of its own.

Derrida argues that, whereas Husserl acknowledges that the expressive function of signs is intimately involved or interwoven (*verflochten*) with the indicative function, he (Husserl) must for essential reasons contend that purely expressive signs are possible. The essential reasons here have to do with core tenets of phenomenological methodology, specifically, the aim of arriving, through the reductions, at the pure and unmediated expression of a meaning in the mode of evidence-having. Here is the connection with the doctrine of presence. As already noted, one claim for apodicticity lies in the absence of a difference between intuition and object or, in other words, the absence of a difference between the apprehension of a meaning and the meaning apprehended. According to Derrida's interpretation, presence, for Husserl, is "the presence of sense [or meaning] to a full and primordial intuition."

Derrida's counter-claim, truncated to its core, is that presence so conceived names an impossibility because there is always a *différance* between meaning and apprehension. The point of Derrida's counter-claim is inserted at the cleft of Husserl's distinction between expressive and indicative signs: if it is impossible to separate the two, if every expressive sign is essentially interwoven with an indicative function, then there must be a difference between meaning and apprehension, between object-as-intuited and intuition-of-object. The indicative function would necessitate a distancing of sign from meaning and would thereby entail some delay or deferral between what the sign wants to say and the fulfilling of that intention.

The crucial question is whether this *différance* between expression and indication is necessary. I shall turn to that question shortly, after a prior question has been posed. The prior question asks whether presence to meaning requires signs at all. Although Derrida acknowledges that "Husserl believes in the existence of a pre-expressive and prelinguistic stratum of sense, which the reduction must sometimes disclose by excluding the stratum of language" (SP 31), he (Derrida) proceeds on the assumption that presence to sense or intuition of meaning must, even for Husserl, involve the play of signs. As I hope later to show, this assumption is consequential. For the moment, let it suffice to point out that the equation of presence to meaning with expression or expressive sign is warranted by Husserl's extended use of the notion of soliloquy or interior monologue. Under Derrida's interpretation, "the reduction to the monologue is really a putting of empirical worldly existence between brackets" (SP 43). There is some uncertainty in my reading of his text as to what is intended by Derrida here. One interpretation would hold that the *epoché* is equivalent to a reduction to monologue in which the transcendentally meditating ego apprehends a meaning in a full intuition by means of an expressive sign; but, since this sign is conceived by Husserl as an imagined sign rather than a real sign, no mediation or distance between sign and meaning is held to be involved. Under this interpretation, imagination of the expressive word is equivalent to evidential self-presence of a meaning.

This interpretation strikes me as forced. As I read Husserl, the reduction to immanence achieved by the *epoché* does not require words, even imagined words. I concur with Derrida that Husserl's defense of the distinction between expressive and indicative signs requires him to stipulate something like an interior monologue to explain the possibility of entertaining a purely expressive sign quite apart from any intertwining with indicative signs. But I would not equate the presence to meaning in the reduced sphere in all cases to an entertaining of purely expressive signs.

This point is either trivial or of immense consequence. It is trivial in the context of Derrida's overall critique because, once one assents to Derrida's contention that all meaning is sign-dependent and that it is essential to the functioning of every sign that it include what is here called an indicative function, then it matters little whether one challenges the reduction on the basis of appealing to a purely expressive sign function or on the basis of appeal to an extra-linguistic apprehension of meaning: in either case, the indicative function (the function of differing and deferring) deemed essential to meaning is absent. On the other hand, the point *is* consequential if one does not assent to the thesis that meaning is language-dependent. But that issue is precisely what is at stake in the critique at hand, so let us now turn to it.

The question deferred above and the question now before us are the same. That is, the question as to the necessity of a *différance* in the relation of meaning and the intuition thereof and the question whether all meaning is necessarily sign- or language-dependent both come to rest on an understanding of the temporality of presence. Derrida presents his key ideas on this issue in chapters four and five of *Speech and Phenomena;* let us review his argument.

We begin with Derrida's conclusion. "The presence-of-the-present is derived from repetition and not the reverse" (SP 52). Presence is here taken as presentation (*Vorstellung*) as contrasted with representation (*Vergegenwärtigung*). Re-presentation is conceived as essentially involving repetition. The claim is then entered that the repetition constitutive of representation is essential to or presupposed by presentation. Why does presentation presuppose repetition?

The strategy employed by Derrida in the text at hand is to show how repetition functions in language, to show that the "philosophy of intuition and presence" attempts to eliminate that function, and to show that this philosophy of presence and self-presence depends on two constructs, self (or ego) and the now (or temporal presence), which themselves presuppose repetition. From this, two conclusions follow. The first is that the metaphysics of presence embodies a contradiction, since it defines itself by denying the primordiality of the repetition upon which it stands. The second conclusion is that, since repetition is itself made possible by *différance,* specifically by the differing and deferring which constitutes the play of signs, *différance* grounds the possibility of signification or meaning in general. From this, it should be clear that the crux of the argument rests on the notion of repetition and its function in the genesis of signification.

Here is a condensation of the text in which Derrida outlines his thesis of the primordiality of repetition.

> When I . . . use words . . .⁷ I must from the outset operate (within) a structure of repetition whose basic element can only be representative. . . . A sign which would take place but 'once' would not be a sign. A signifier (in general) must be formally recognizable in spite of, and through, the diversity of empirical characteristics which may modify it. It must remain the *same,* and be able to be repeated as such, despite and across the deformations which the empirical event necessarily makes it undergo. . . . It can function as a sign, and in general as language, only if a formal identity enables it to be issued again and to be recognized. This identity is necessarily ideal. It thus necessarily implies representation: as *Vorstellung,* the locus of ideality in general, as *Vergegenwärtigung,* the possibility of reproductive repetition in general, and as *Repräsentation,* insofar as each signifying event is a substitute (for the signified as well as for the ideal form of the signifier). Since this representative structure is signification itself, I cannot enter into . . . discourse without being from the start involved in unlimited representation. (SP 50)

In this passage, Derrida identifies "signification itself" (or meaning in general) with the representative structure of repetition. The basis for this claim is the assertion that an ideal formal identity which remains the same through changes in time and circumstance allows the sign to be re-cognized as the same.

Let me note here for future reference that this argument places meaning irrevocably within the sphere of ideality and, in doing so, trades on an ontological bifurcation:[8] the empirical is conceived as the domain of particularity and mutability, and is contrasted with the ideal as the domain of universality and immutability (SP 10). Without this presupposition, the identification of repetition and ideality would make no sense. I will return to this point later.

The philosophy of intuition and presence attempts to eliminate signs or, more accurately, regard them as "a modification of a simple presence" (SP 51) precisely in order to banish all difference between meaning and apprehension: the relation between intuition-of-object and object-as-intuited must be an immediate relation or an identity to ensure apodicticity. Derrida's claim is that this immediacy or identity is an impossibility,[9] and he supports this claim by attacking the two constructs he sees as foundational to the metaphysics presupposed by any philosophy of intuition and presence.

(A) The transcendental subject. The first of these is the concept of the transcendental subject or ego. The thrust of the attack is that any presentation requires objectification or presentification or distantiation of some sort between the act of intuition and that which is intuited. This is a point familiar to readers of Kant, Hegel, and their successors in the tradition of transcendental philosophy: it consists in asserting that consciousness of an object, be that object regarded as immanent or transcendent, is not to be confused with the object itself. Even in the case of immanent objects, which is the case under consideration in this critique of Husserl—indeed, especially in the case of immanent objects—there is something different from sheer presence or meaning, there is apprehension or consciousness of that present meaning. For Husserl, the substrate of consciousness is the transcendental ego. So there are two elements, ego and object. Husserl contends that they coincide in the intuition of immanent objects: presence to object is coincidental with presence to self. Derrida objects to this on two grounds.

In the first place, the subject is produced by the act, not *vice versa,* i.e., the subject held by Husserl to be a prior condition of intuition is, for Derrida, an ideality produced by repetition. The "primordial impression," he contends, "is already pure auto-affection" (SP 83) and auto-affection presupposes "that a pure difference comes to divide self-perception" (SP 82).

> This movement of [auto-affection or] *différance* is not something that happens to a transcendental subject; it produces a subject. (SP 82)

In the second place, the result of this coincidence is the apprehension (noesis) of an ideal or repeatable meaning (noema). Its meaning as ideality consists in its repeatability, and this repeatability is a reference to a potential infinity of other, non-present iterations. Thus, intrinsic to the apprehension of a meaning is a reference beyond itself to something not now present. From this, several things follow for Derrida. Reference beyond itself (indication) or signification is inextricably bound up with meaning or intention (wanting to say, *vouloir-dire*). And this signification requires a vehicle, a trace, to enable the same sense to be carried forward in time (deferred) to be posited at another time and in another context as the same (but differing from itself with regard to temporal and contextual displacement). Ultimately, this vehicle is the sign. For the reasons just stated, Derrida will contend, contrary to Husserl, that signs are prerequisite for meaning of all kinds, and that signification/indication is an intrinsic part of the sign function. Clarification of these issues will take us to the second of the two constructs attacked by Derrida and the titular subject of this essay, the temporality of presence.

(B) The temporality of presence. The position Derrida is intent upon deconstructing is the position taken by Husserl that self-presence excludes all mediation, including that of signs. The phase of the deconstruction I regard as crucial is that devoted to the temporality of presence and self-presence. Derrida embarks on this phase by asserting that the concept of presence

> . . . not only involves the enigma of a being appearing in absolute proximity to oneself; it also designates the temporal essence of this proximity—which does not serve to dispel the enigma. The self-presence of experience must be produced in the present taken as a now. And this is just what Husserl says: if 'mental acts' . . . do not have to be informed about themselves through the intermediary of indications, it is because they are 'lived by us in the same instant' (*im selben Augenblick*). The present of self-presence would be as indivisible as the *blink of an eye*. (SP 58–59)

The issue, then, concerns the indivisibility of the now, its identity with itself, its coincidence with itself in pure immediacy. Derrida's strategy in the text at hand is to challenge the claim of indivisibility through a deconstruction which displays the aporia at its root: the now can be thought as self-identical only if it is thought at the same time as differing from itself. The form of argumentation Derrida will employ is the same that we have witnessed throughout. Its formula depends on the key notion of repetition and might be expressed as follows: **identity presupposes ideality which presupposes repetition which presupposes mediation which presupposes non-identity.**

Derrida begins this phase of the deconstruction by pointing to a tension in Husserl's treatment of the now as moment of self-presence.

On the one hand, there is the abiding theme that the now must be
conceived as a punctum;[10] and, on the other, there is the contrary
assertion in *The Phenomenology of Internal Time-Consciousness* that
"it belongs to the essence of lived experiences that they must be
extended . . . , that a punctual phase can never be for itself."[11] Some
tenuous resolution may be found in Husserl's ambiguity in the doctrine of retention and protention: he asserts both that retention is to
be included in the perceptual moment and that it is the antithesis of
perception, i.e., non-perception; but this account culminates with the
thesis that there is a "continual transition" from perception to non-
perception (i.e., from perception to primary remembrance or retention), that the two "continually pass over into one another."[12] Derrida
concludes from this that "there is a duration to the blink," that the
now is not an instantaneous punctum, and "that nonpresence and
otherness are internal to presence" (SP 65–66).

The argument in support of this conclusion recapitulates the
formula stated above.

> The ideality of the form of presence itself implies that it be infi-
> nitely re-peatable, that its re-turn, as a return of the same, is
> necessary *ad infinitum* and is inscribed in presence itself. (SP 67)

There is a problem here that lies in the difference between retention
and representation. It is not at all clear that retention involves the
kind of repetition that is intrinsic to representation: retention names
the quality of lingering on or enduring through time that Husserl
exemplifies with the abiding quality of sound in the "tonal moment."
Husserl explicitly distinguishes retention from the re-calling or re-
appearance of something past which he calls "secondary memory"
and which does lend itself to the model of repetition of representation.[13] Derrida acknowledges this problem in speaking of "the abyss
which may indeed separate retention from re-presentation," but passes
over it by asserting "a priori" that "re-tention and re-presentation"
have "a common root" in "the possibility of re-petition in its most
general form, that is, the constitution of a trace in the most universal
sense" (SP 67).

This problem cannot be dismissed in this manner. The 're-' of retention does not provide sufficient warrant for subsuming it under
the general rubric of repetition conceived as the means whereby the
trace is constituted—when repetition has been modelled from the
start on the 're-' of re-presentation and the issue at stake is whether
the 're-' of retention can be assimilated to that model. The question
that must be addressed is whether there is an essential thickness to
the present that cannot be captured either in the now as punctum or

in the now as differing from and deferring itself (i.e., in the play of *différance* Derrida customarily cites as the means whereby the trace is constituted).[14]

Postponing this question for treatment below, I return to consideration of Derrida's thesis regarding repetition and the temporality of presence.

> . . . The presence of the present is thought [by Husserl] as arising from the bending-back of a return, from the moment of repetition, and not the reverse [i.e., repetition is not thought as arising from the presence of the present, even though the absolute primordiality of that presence is the "principle of principles" for Husserlian phenomenology]. Does not the fact that this bending back is irreducible in presence or in self-presence, that this trace or *différance* is always older than presence and procures for it its openness, prevent us from speaking about a simple self-identity '*im selben Augenblick?*' (SP 68)

Here is the completion of the deconstruction of the temporality of presence. The thesis of the primordiality and indivisibility of the presence of the present in the now deconstructs into the opposing thesis that presence is not primordial but founded upon a divisive *différance* that makes it possible. The question that remains in this phase of my argument concerns the manner in which the differing from and deferring of itself by the now procures for presence its openness.

Recasting Derrida's answer to this question in terms which may or may not be alien to him, we arrive at a conception of time in which each now moment—conceived as punctum—displaces itself with another now that is both the same in being a now but also differs from itself in its displacement of itself. This displacement is what Derrida calls the spacing of time.[15]

How does this displacement endow presence with openness? It provides "the possibility of a retentional trace"[16] defined as "the intimate relation of the living present with its outside, the openness upon exteriority in general" (SP 86). It is through the trace that the present relates itself to its displaced outside, but how?

The clue to the how is repetition. Each now repeats itself by differing from itself. The repetition provides the possibility for the constitution of an ideal unity. The ideality that effects the unity is the trace written as 'now.' But this is still cryptic. The sign 'now' is an ideal object constituted by repetition which unifies the nows that displace each other. But this cannot be a spoken sign, for it would pass with the moment and thereby not be able to range over passing moments and unify them. It must be a sign that is inscribed, and through that inscription capable of enduring.

Ideality is created by repetition. Thus, thought can create the ideality of sense only by virtue of that which can be repeated, the inscribed trace.[17] Again, thought, as the opening on to the presence of the present, effects that opening by means of the trace, that is, by means of signifying, that is, by means of indicating itself or substituting for itself. In other, perhaps alien, words, the now could never be re-cognized as such if each experience of the now exhausted itself in that experience and left no trace. The condition for the possibility for the experience of the now as now and, at the same time, the condition for the possibility of the unification of time as the synthesis of nows— is the inscription of the trace, the signifier 'now,' which enables the repetition of the now to be recognized as such.

And yet once again, this time in terms that are not as alien as they might first seem, the function of the synthesis of time which Kant assigned to the noumenal transcendental unity of apperception and which Husserl assigned to the play of transverse intentionality (i.e., retention and protention) originating within the transcendental ego—is now assigned by Derrida to the inscription of the trace. The inscribed trace effects the synthesis of time *as an ideal unity* through the repetition required for re-cognition in general.

If the openness on to the presence of the present presupposes re-cognition of something as abidingly the same, as every transcendental thinker from Kant to the present has maintained, then, assuming that his argument to this point is sound, Derrida can legitimately assert the following conclusion.

> The living present springs forth out of its nonidentity with itself and from the possibility of a retentional trace. It is always already a trace. . . . Being-primordial must be thought on the basis of the trace, and not the reverse. This protowriting is at work at the origin of sense. Sense, being temporal in nature . . . , is never simply present; it is always already engaged in the 'movement' of the trace, that is, in the order of 'signification.' (SP 85)

Critique

Derrida's conclusion sheds light on several dominant and characteristically enigmatic themes in his thought. (a) There is the reassignment of meaning from intuition (or the world as perceived) to language (sign or trace)[18] which has the consequence of rendering perception meaningless. (b) There is the denial of metaphysical foundations in either the subject[19] or the object of intuition.[20] (c) There is the displacement (or deferral) of truth to an indefinite future.[21] (d) There is the cryptic announcement that the signs upon which meaning, knowledge, and truth are now held to depend are themselves "originally wrought by fiction."[22] The list could be extended further, but there is one among the possible *sequiturs* that calls for reflection. In the process of concluding his discourse, Derrida writes the following.

> There never was any 'perception': and 'presentation' is a representation of the representation that yearns for itself therein as for its own birth or its death. (SP 103)

This is then followed by the allegory of the Dresden gallery in which there is a painting representing a gallery in which there is a painting representing a gallery in which . . . and so on. Derrida offers this as an allegory of origins: "everything," he says, "has, no doubt, begun" in that way. What are we to make of this?

The key thought, as I have tried to show, is that of repetition as origin. This is an elusive thought which I have tried to grasp with the formula given above: *identity presupposes ideality which presupposes repetition which presupposes mediation which presupposes non-identity*. The paradox is generated by the apparent contradiction between the first and last terms: identity presupposes non-identity. One might seek to eliminate the appearance of contradiction by searching for equivocity in the use of the term 'identity.' In the first instance, 'identity' refers to the selfsameness of a presentation. In the second, 'non-identity' refers to the difference from itself embodied in re-presentation: a re-presentation cannot coincide with itself because, as an ideality, its essence is bound to repetition. Might we, then, resolve the paradox by concluding that the identity or selfsameness of presentation presupposes the non-identity or non-self-coincidence of re-presentation? This is, indeed, Derrida's doctrine: presentation presupposes re-presentation. It is this doctrine that supports the claim that "there never was any 'perception' " and gives rise to the allegory of the infinitely regressive painting in the Dresden gallery.

Presentation presupposes re-presentation: what does this mean? Does it not generate the paradox once again, although in different terms? The answer to the second of these questions is contained in the answer to the first—at least, in the answer I have proposed in the interpretation set forth above. 'Presentation presupposes re-presentation' means, according to a founding precept of transcendental philosophy, that identification or cognition of an object presupposes recognition under a signifier or concept. And that precept has always been paradoxical for transcendental philosophers because it begs the question of the origin of the concept or signifier. In the book at hand, Derrida has exposed that paradox as generating a fundamental inconsistency in Husserl's thinking: in appealing to presentation or primordial dator intuition as the foundation of sense or meaning, Husserl begs the question of his own condition for the possibility of cognizing that presentation, namely synthesis under a noema or meaning.[23] But Derrida has gone further than that: given the conflict in transcendental philosophy between asserting the primordiality of concepts or ideality in general and accounting for the origin of those concepts, Derrida has (1) opted for the primordiality of ideality and (2) enshrined the problem of origins in paradox. The first of these options has already been explicated: the primacy of repetition is already, in Derrida's terms, the primacy of ideality. The second, however, requires further consideration of the role of temporality in the constitution of identity.

Derrida's argument here is simple. There can be no identification in an originating now moment because identity means sameness over time: nothing can be identified for the first time in an instant. But, why not? Let us consider an example.

In a social setting, I notice someone unknown to me. "Who is that person?" I ask a friend, who may reply with a name and a biographical sketch, thus providing me with a signifier which will assist in future recognition of this hitherto unknown person. However, even if my friend is not acquainted with the stranger and cannot provide an identity, I am still able to recognize the person moments later as the person whose name I still do not know.

Of course, the example is not decisive. My initial identification and subsequent recognition of the unknown person as a person unknown to me may be mediated by the signifier 'unknown person.' In any case, the whole encounter takes place in a language-saturated context, and may be inconceivable apart from it.[24]

But, let me persist a step further. The person I identify and then recognize as an unknown person is not a generic unknown person who is undifferentiable from all other persons unknown to me. In fact, if I were to try to provide a string of signifiers to a third party to whom the unknown person was also unknown in order to enable that third party to identify the unknown person (as witnesses to a crime try to provide descriptions of the perpetrator to police officers), the attempt might very well prove to be futile. But suppose I had taken a photograph and could produce that. . . .

Once again, the example is indecisive. The photograph is a representation, a signifier or trace of sorts, and repetition is involved.

But, persisting further, the original sight of the unknown person which the photograph re-produces better than words was not, itself, a photograph or a re-presentation; it was a perception. Why is this not an originating presentation?

Here is the crux of the issue. Why can there be no presentation that is not already a re-presentation? Recall Derrida's argument.

> When I . . . use words . . . , I must from the outset operate (within) a structure of repetition whose basic element can only be representative. . . . A sign which would take place but 'once' would not be a sign. (SP 50)

"When I use words. . . ." But, if my initial identification is visual, am I using words? Derrida is committed to an affirmative answer to this question, and his commitment to the affirmative answer is at the same time his commitment to the tradition of transcendental idealism. The commitment is grounded in the founding precept of transcendental philosophy articulated earlier: the precept that identification/cognition of an object presupposes re-cognition under a signifier or concept.

Why would anyone—much less thinkers on the order of Kant, Husserl, and even Derrida—adhere to such a precept when it inevitably renders the problem of the origin of signifiers or concepts insoluble? In the cases of Kant and Husserl, the answer to this question is well documented.[25] It is their quest for apodicticity that leads to the reduction to the sphere of immanence (where certainty is guaranteed by elimination of the error that can arise when intuition-of-object and transcendent thing do not coincide), and it is that reduction which grants primacy to concepts in the process of identification over time: since the transcendent thing has been bracketed, its real and enduring existence cannot serve as the ground for identification; this leaves the job of establishing the *simile in multis* (i.e., the job of establishing something which remains constant over the passage of time and diversity of evanescent appearances) to the enduring immanent object, the concept, representation, or signifier. But, what about Derrida?

The answer that I would hazard here is that Derrida has not freed himself completely from the ontology and methodology of his primary mentor, Husserl. As noted above, Derrida's deconstruction of Husserl's language theory operates from within the Husserlian conceptual matrix. It is my contention that, although Derrida challenges and alters that matrix, he does so within the overriding standpoint of transcendental methodology and idealistic ontology. In support of this claim, I offer the following set of interrelated arguments.

In the opening phases of my interpretation of *Speech and Phenomena,* I noted that, for Derrida, presence to sense or intuition necessarily involves the play of signs, and flagged this as a crucial assumption on his part. It has now been made explicit why he makes this assumption: presence to sense requires identification which, in turn, requires the repetition constitutive of the ideal unifier/identifier, i.e., the sign. Why does identification require the repetition granted by a re-presentation or sign? Because there would be no abiding meaning were it not for the ideal meaning provided by the sign which enables it to range over time. Why would there be no abiding meaning? Because the present, the now, is evanescent; because, in the absence of a time-unifying ideality, the present vanishes in the blink of an eye. If we abbreviate this line of argument, we arrive at the following: presence to meaning requires ideality because ideality is the sole source of meaning. Or: presence grants no abiding meaning because there is nothing abiding in presence. If we ask why ideality is the sole source of meaning or why there is nothing abiding in presence, it becomes evident that these presuppositions make sense only within the context of a prior reduction to the sphere of immanence.

Derrida's critique of the metaphysics of presence rests on his assertion that the repetition constitutive of re-presentation is essential to or presupposed by presentation. But this requirement of repetition applies only if presence to sense is understood within the immanent sphere, as presence to the object-as-intuited or object-as-meant (where the meaning or *Bedeutung* involved is that of *vouloir-dire,* wanting to say or intending). What if presence were taken as perceptual presence and perception were understood, as Merleau-Ponty understands it, that is, as an opening on to a world transcendent to the act of perceiving? Is the play of signs necessary under this assumption?

Let us grant, with Merleau-Ponty, that language is sedimented in culture, and that, for humans, at least, all perception takes place within a cultural horizon, can there still be room for perceptual experience which is not mediated by signs? Merleau-Ponty's answer to this question puts him at a distance from the contemporary thinkers in the Continental tradition who are still working within the framework of transcendental philosophy. The distance is created by Merleau-Ponty's rejection of the founding precept of transcendental thought to which I have alluded above, the precept that meaning presupposes identification which, in turn, presupposes subsumption under a concept or sign. And this grants him unique status among those of our contemporaries who, having made "the linguistic turn," contend that all perception is mediated by signs (and thus espouse what I have called the thesis of linguistic immanence).[26] What is this differentiating answer?

Merleau-Ponty's answer must be arrayed under two headings: (a) the problem of organization, and (b) his solution to it, the doctrine of autochthonous organization.[27] The problem of organization is the problem of accounting for the subsumption of a given perceptual experience under a given concept or sign. Continuing in the vein of the example given above, if I see a human being and recognize that person as a person and also as someone with whom I am acquainted [for want of a better name, let him be Alphonso], how do I account for the application of just this set of categories, concepts, or signs? How am I able to apply the signs 'human being,' 'person,' and 'Alphonso' correctly? Why did I not apply the signs 'automobile,' 'Edsel,' or some other? Either the signs were invoked by the percept (which demanded just these signs and excluded others)—in which case the percept has a perceptual meaning not derived from signs—Or the signs were applied arbitrarily—in which case I am entirely free to constitute my friend, Alphonso, as an automotive relic, or an orang-outang, i.e., as anything whatsoever.

The doctrine of autochthonous organization maintains that there is a fundamental organization to the world as perceived that is not constituted or projected through the act of perception. The organization of the world constitutes its meaning. Meaning thus conceived is grounded in the differentiation of objects, the principles or laws governing their interactions, the overall world horizon in which they are found, etc. This is not the place to set forth the ontology to which I am here appealing,[28] but there are several points which apply to the issues before us and should be mentioned.

(1) Meaning is held to originate in the world instead of being conceived as a projection onto the world of intentions whose origins are obscured by paradox. Human cognition is, thus, regarded as an evolutionary process aimed at accommodating the organisms to its environment instead of being taken as a process of constituting the world through the supervenience of an extra-mundane a priori.

(2) Perception is conceived as an opening on to the world of which it is a part. Thus conceived, openness presupposes cognition at the level of perception rather than requiring a doctrine of original recognition which subsumes reality under ideality by making repetition a prime condition for cognition.

(3) The object of perception is conceived neither as immanent object whose meaning is entirely constituted by intention or signification, nor as transcendent thing whose meaning could be known only to divinity, but rather under the heading of phenomenon with that term taken to betoken coincidence of immanence and transcendence in perception. The phenomenon or perceptual object is immanent to

the extent that it manifests itself and transcendent to the extent that its self-disclosure is partial and intrinsically involves withholding and self-concealment. In Merleau-Ponty's ontology there is a deliberate intent to undercut the classical binary oppositions of immanence and transcendence, idealism and realism, for-itself and in-itself, etc. This list could also be extended, but I will confine my discourse to the two points I regard as decisive.

The first of these has already been mentioned and needs only brief comment. It is the transcendent aspect of the phenomenon that resolves the problem of organization by calling for certain concepts or signifiers and excluding others. Alphonso demands to be perceived as a human being and not as a means of transportation. There are practical and moral as well as epistemological and ontological implications in this demand that serve further to differentiate Merleau-Ponty from contemporary thinkers such as Derrida. The point to be emphasized here is that the demand to be recognized in some ways rather than others originates in a mode of self-presentation that is direct, perceptual, and, albeit fallible, nonetheless compelling. In our encounter, Alphonso presents himself to me and I see him; my antecedently formed representations are too fragile to sustain themselves in the face of his bodily presence.

The second point takes us back, for the last time, to time. Several pages back, I argued that, for Derrida, the inscribed trace effects the synthesis of time *as an ideal unity* through the repetition required for re-cognition in general. Time must be an ideality because, in Derrida's doctrine, the now cannot be experienced as a presence. Time is the name given to the repetition of the now in differing from and deferring itself. But that which is constituted by repetition is an ideality. Again, in terms that are, perhaps alien to Derrida, the being of time is relational and relations are held to be ideal.

The thesis of the ideality of time raises the question of the experience of time. For Derrida, there can be no experience of time in the ordinary sense of the word 'experience' because, within the context of the metaphysics of presence, that ordinary sense of 'experience' is understood as presence. But there is a further reason. As it is in the case of all meaning, so it is with time, there never is any direct perception or evidential presentation, there is only re-presentation or mediation through signs, and that mediation involves an indefinite deferral of evidential fulfillment. Thus, the experience of the passage of an hour or a day, at one end of a continuum, and the understanding of the rings in the cross section of a tree trunk or the dating process based on the half-life of carbon-14, at the other—and everything in between—depends on the play of signifiers.

The now, as signifier, is constituted by the nothing that differen-
tiates one now from another, the *différance* that *is* not. This doctrine
raises questions at both ends of the spectrum. Is it nothing that
determines the age of a tree or the Dead Sea scrolls? Is it nothing
that determines the length of a day for a child and an adult, the
length of an hour spent tacking upwind in a brisk wind as against an
hour spent listening to a discourse such as the one presented here?

Heidegger allows for the measure of time by nothing experienced
in the mode of boredom. What is the experiential correlate of Derrida's
nothing? His answer is nothing present, nothing that can be experienced as presence, even oppressive presence. Venturing to the border
between exegesis and speculation, however, I might offer the following for consideration. It is the displacement of the now by itself that I
find at the basis of Derrida's understanding of time. My interpretation has already been set forth, together with my claim that it is this
understanding of time that informs the notions of *différance* and
trace and drives the Derridean enterprise directed against the metaphysics of presence. I want to suggest now that this notion of time as
self-displacement has strong kinship relations with antecedents to be
found in Husserl, specifically, in Husserl's doctrine of retentional and
protentional modification.[29]

My suggestion is that Husserl's description of the "shoving back"
of primal impressions in retention—when coupled with the futural
displacement involved in protention—provides some insight into
Derrida's model of the self-displacement of the now in the modes of
differing and deferring.

There is, however, a profound difference between the two accounts. Although time, for both Husserl and Derrida, is an immanent
structure or an ideality or a synthetic unity, Husserl models his conception on perceptual experience (for the most part, the experience of
a melody) as well as on theoretical considerations, whereas Derrida's
theory precludes the possibility of direct experience of time. As argued above, it was his attempt to correlate the experiential presence
of the now as "primal impression" with the ideal retention of the now
in primary memory that led Husserl into the ambivalence (or out-
right contradiction) on the issue as to whether retentions are perceptions or non-perceptions. And it was this ambivalence that allowed
Derrida to restore theoretical integrity by removing the now from the
domain of perception altogether.

Once presence has been banished to the realm of theoretical
impossibility, theoretical room is opened to allow limitless work upon
the re-presentation prior to its appearance. Dreamwork, political work,
the work of archaic and metaphysical structures—all this and more

can infiltrate the system of signifiers bequeathed to us by history and work upon the re-presentational matrix through which our experience is always already filtered. And it can do this without the counterbalancing influence of the perceptual presence which would compel us to see a thing or person or world in some measure according to its measure.

The actual present does, indeed, acquire a privilege if one accords to the phenomenon of time its transcendent dimension. It was no accident that Husserl privileged the now of primal impression: its perceptual grounding demanded that the presence of the present be accorded a modicum of reality which sets it apart from past and future. And it was finally that modicum of reality that created the tension within Husserl's transcendental idealism upon which Derrida capitalizes. Suppose, however, that one alters Husserl's doctrine, not by banishing the transcendent dimension of time, as Derrida did, but by reconciling it with its immanent dimension, as Merleau-Ponty did.

I have already alluded to transcendent aspects of time which become unintelligible under the Derridean model, and there is much more that needs to be brought out under that heading.[30] Instead, I will briefly point to two related issues that strike me as decisive.

The fundamental issue is whether presence requires the assumption of a translucent now moment conceived as a punctum. Husserl, as we have seen, waffled on the issue. There had to be a source point to define the moment of primal impression, the moment of evidence-having. And this had to be both same and different from the now moments being "pushed back" in primary memory by the onslaught of each succeeding primal impression. The now, as punctum, is defined by the separation of primal impression and retention. Husserl had both to maintain and deny that separation: he had to deny it in order to assert the thesis of the continuity of time, and he had to maintain it in order to keep the sensuous present distinct from the retention.[31] Husserl is thus left with two alternatives, neither of which is acceptable. The first would be to abandon the thesis of primal impression—which is the option chosen by Derrida—and forsake the "principle of principles" of phenomenology. The second would be to acknowledge something like a doctrine of the specious present—which Husserl does mention in *The Phenomenology of Internal Time-Consciousness*[32]—but this option held no promise for him: as set forth by James,[33] it embodies a realism that Husserl would consider naive.

Within the context of an ontology that regards the phenomenon of time as both immanent and transcendent, the doctrine of the specious present poses no problem. It means, simply, that there is no natural measure of time.[34] That is, one is not forced to acknowledge a sharp boundary between the actual primal impression (perception) and its retained antecedents (non-perception). But it is just this distinction that commits Husserl to the language of puncta. And it is just this language of puncta that Derrida must presuppose in order to deny the possibility of perceptual presence: for the model of the displacement of nows, the model of the primacy of repetition, there must be discrete now moments, moments separated by their differing and deferring. The point at stake here is this: Derrida's critique of perceptual presence presupposes a temporal atomism that, although it has had adherents in the history of metaphysics, in no way dominates or defines that tradition. That temporal atomism does, however, define the short history of deconstructionism insofar as the key notions of trace and *différance* depend upon it.

My final point concerns the issue of privilege. As already acknowledged, the conception of temporality I am defending here does accord a privilege to present over past and future. Viewed *sub specie aeternitatis,* this privilege is a matter of accidental perspective, a kind of unwarranted 'temporocentism.' But, if one rejects the standpoint of eternity, and adopts the viewpoint of finite worldly unfolding, there is a necessity to the vantage of the present that is not accidental. The privilege of presence is evident in the very attempt at temporal decentering: one can move away from a given piece of space and move about in cultural geography, but one cannot live another position in time.[35]

To conclude. I have attempted here a deconstruction of Derrida's critique of the metaphysics of presence. I have also attempted to provide a rough sketch of a conception of presence that would not unravel under deconstructive analysis. Neither attempt is complete. It remains to show the extent to which the Derridean edifice is shaken by the exposition of his own presuppositions. And the sketch needs to be developed into a coherent thesis. That will require time. Phenomenal time.

Notes

1. Jacques Derrida, *Speech and Phenomena,* trans. David B. Allison (Evanston, Ill.: Northwestern University Press, 1973), pp. 62–63. Henceforth cited as SP. *La Voix et le Phénomène* (Paris: Presses Universitaires de France, 1967).

2. ". . . *Within* the metaphysics of presence, within philosophy as knowledge of the presence of the object, as the being-before-oneself of knowledge in consciousness, we believe, quite simply and literally, in absolute knowl-

edge as the closure if not the end of history. And we believe *that such a closure has taken place*. The history of being as presence, as self-presence in absolute knowledge, as consciousness of self in the infinity of *parousia*—this history is closed." (SP 102)

3. The argument to be presented here is the one Derrida presents in chapters 4 and 5 of *Speech and Phenomena*. Later, in the essay "Ousia and Gramme: Note on a Note from Being and Time" [in *Margins of Philosophy*, trans. Alan Bass (Chicago: University of Chicago Press, 1982)], he presents another argument in support of the conclusion that the metaphysics of presence rests on a conflicted understanding of temporality. That argument differs significantly from the one to be considered here, and I have set forth an interpretation and critique of it in "The Metaphysics of Presence: Critique of a Critique" (publication data unavailable at this time).

4. The focus of the deconstruction is presence. Following a straightforward Husserlian identification. Derrida equates presence with "primordial dator intuition" or "primordial representation." He then describes his deconstructive strategy of unraveling from within as follows.

"What we are describing as primordial representation can be provisionally designated with this term only within the closure whose limits we are here seeking to transgress by setting down and demonstrating various contradictory or untenable propositions within it, attempting thereby to institute a kind of insecurity and to open it up to the outside. This can only be done from a certain inside" (SP 57, n. 6).

5. See SP 62, n. 3 where Derrida quotes Husserl's statement of the "principle of principles" from section 24 of *Ideas I*.

6. This is the position Husserl takes in the earlier works. Later, notably in the *Cartesian Meditations*, Husserl will realize that the instantaneous nature of immediate intuitions cannot provide a basis for claims that are universal and atemporal in scope. A further support for the apodicticity of these latter claims is needed, and to provide this Husserl reverts to the classical (Kantian) grounding of apodicticity in inconceivability of the contrary.

"Any evidence is a grasping of something itself that is, or is thus, a grasping in the mode 'it itself,' with full certainty of its being, a certainty that accordingly excludes every doubt. But it does not follow that full certainty excludes the conceivability that what is evident could subsequently prove to be illusion—indeed, sensuous experience furnishes us with cases where that happens. . . . An *apodictic* evidence, however, is not merely certainty of the affairs or affair-complexes (states-of-affairs) evident in it; rather it discloses itself, to a critical reflection, as having the signal peculiarity of being *at the same time the absolute unimaginableness* (inconceivability) of their *non-being,* and thus excluding in advance every doubt as 'objectless,' empty." Edmund Husserl, *Cartesian Meditations: An Introduction to Phenomenology,* trans. Dorion Cairns (The Hague: Martinus-Nijhoff, 1960), pp. 15–16.

Derrida does not take up this notion of apodicticity in Husserl, but rather seems to regard all certitude in Husserl as grounded in the immediacy of self-presence in intuition.

The source of certitude in general (for Husserl) is the primordial character of the living now (SP 67).

7. The text reads, "when in fact I *effectively* use words." 'Effective' is here meant to be contrasted with 'imaginative.' But a page later Derrida writes that "by reason of the primordially repetitive structure of signs in general, there is every likelihood that 'effective' language is just as imaginary as imaginary speech and that imaginary speech is just as effective as effective speech" (SP 51). Hence, I do not think it unwarranted to omit the qualification regarding effective use in the passage I am here condensing.

8. Or, as some might characterize it, a "binary opposition."

9. See SP 92 where Derrida writes that the possibility "that the unity of intuition and intention [i.e., meaning as *vouloir-dire*] can ever be homogeneous at all" must be "excluded from the start."

10. "The actual now is necessarily something punctual and remains so, a form that persists through continuous change of matter." Edmund Husserl, *Ideas: General Introduction to Pure Phenomenology,* trans. W. R. Boyce Gibson (London: George Allen & Unwin, 1931), p. 237. Quoted by Derrida, SP 62.

11. Edmund Husserl, *The Phenomenology of Internal Time-Consciousness,* ed. Martin Heidegger, trans. James S. Churchill (Bloomington, Ind.: Indiana University Press, 1964), p. 70. Cited hereafter as ITC. Quoted by Derrida, SP 61.

12. The relevant texts from ITC are quoted by Derrida in SP 64–65.

13. "Retentional consciousness includes real consciousness of the past of sound, primary remembrance of sound, and is not to be resolved into sensed sound and apprehension as memory" (ITC 54).

14. At one point in his text, Husserl argues that the meaning retained is retained "precisely in the now"—which I take to be a now that is continuous with the original appearance of the meaning.

"When a sound dies away, it is first sensed with particular fullness (intensity), and thereupon comes to an end in a sudden reduction of intensity. The sound is still there, is still sensed, but in mere rever-

beration. This real sensation of sound should be distinguished from
the tonal moment in retention. The retentional sound is not actually present but 'primarily remembered' *precisely in the now.*" (ITC
53, emphasis added.)

Furthermore, if repetition implies a genuine differing between the now
and its recurrence, this seems to be ruled out from the very start by Husserl.

"With regard to the running-off phenomenon, we know that it is a
continuity of constant transformations which form an inseparable
unit, not severable into parts which could *be* by themselves nor
divisible into phases, points of the continuity, which could *be* by
themselves. The part which by a process of abstraction we can
throw into relief can *be* only in the entire running-off. This is also
true of the phases and points of the continuity of running-off" (ITC
48, emphasis added.)

In fairness to Derrida, it should be noted here that I concur with his
claim that Husserl is ambivalent and unclear on this point, and that I agree
further that there is an essential reason for this ambivalence. Derrida and I
do not agree, however, in our assessments of what that essential reason is.
As promised above, this is a point to which I shall have to return.

15. "This being outside itself proper to time is its spacing: it is a proto-
stage [*archiscène*]. This stage, as the relation of one present to another
present as such, that is, as a nonderived re-presentation (*Vergegenwärtigung*
or *Repräsentation*), produces the structure of signs in general as 'reference,'
as being-for-something (*für etwas sein*). . . ." (SP 84).

16. SP 85. Note that retention is here conceived in terms of the repetition of differing now moments, puncti-form moments that are spaced apart;
retention is not conceived in terms of temporal thickness or lingering on or
perduring. See n. 14 above.

17. "By means of this written inscription, one can always repeat the
original sense, that is, the act of *pure thought* which created the ideality of
sense" (SP 81).

18. ". . . We might be tempted to maintain not only that meaning does
not imply the intuition of the object but that it essentially excludes it." The
phrase 'might be tempted' distances Derrida from the point, but, later in the
same paragraph, he closes that distance in asserting that, "for reasons that
are essential and structural," the possibility "that meaning can be fused into
intuition without disappearing" must be "excluded from the start" (SP 92).

19. "When I tell myself 'I am,' this expression . . . has the status of
speech only if it is intelligible in the absence of its object, in the absence of
intuitive presence—here in the absence of myself" (SP 95).

20. "The absence of intuition—and therefore of the subject of the intuition—is not only tolerated by speech; it is required by the general structure of signification, when considered in itself. It is radically requisite: the total absence of the subject and object of a statement . . . does not prevent a text from 'meaning' something. On the contrary, this possibility gives birth to meaning as such, gives it out to be heard and read."

21. ". . . The difference that separates intention from intuition would . . . have to be *provisional*. And yet this provision would constitute the essence of meaning. The *eidos* is determined in depth by the *telos*. The 'symbol' always points to [*fait signe vers*] 'truth,' it is itself constituted as a lack of 'truth' (SP 97).

22. ". . . If it is admitted that, as we have tried to show, every sign whatever is of an originally repetitive structure, the general distinction between the fictitious and effective usages of the sign is threatened. *The sign is originally wrought by fiction*" (SP 56). This pronouncement is not as frighteningly portentous as it seems when taken in isolation; in context, 'fiction' is roughly equivalent to 'imaginative representation.' What might be inferred from the proposition that signs are originally wrought by imaginative representation? It would seem that this is a denial of natural signs—which, for some of us, is portentous enough—and, perhaps, a commitment to some version of the thesis of conventionalism.

23. This is but another variation on the well-known problem Husserl encounters under the heading of passive synthesis.

24. Although it is significant to me that organisms held to be without language are evidently capable of recognizing or re-identifying other objects and organisms.

25. See *Merleau-Ponty's Ontology* (Bloomington, Ind.: Indiana University Press, 1988), pp. 26–34 for my account.

26. See my essay, "Beyond Signifiers," forthcoming in *Writing the Politics of Difference*, eds. Silverman and Welton (Albany: State University of New York Press).

27. Since I have written extensively on these subjects, my treatment here will be brief. See "Merleau-Ponty and the Transcendence of Immanence: Overcoming the Ontology of Consciousness," *Man and World*, Vol. 19 (1986), pp. 395–412.

28. That task is undertaken in *Merleau-Ponty's Ontology*.

29. "The 'source-point' with which the 'generation' of the enduring object begins is a primal impression. [Husserl then takes up his extended example of the experience of a melody, and identifies the primal impression as the now or the tonal now.] The now changes continuously from retention to retention. There results . . . a stable continuum which is such that every

subsequent point is a retention for every earlier one.... Each subsequent retention ... is not merely a continuous modification arising from the primal impression but a continuous modification of the same beginning point.... There continually takes place ... a shoving back into the past." ITC, section 11, pp. 50–52. The excerpts quoted above are widely scattered throughout the section, but, I trust, there has been no violation of the doctrine in the process of selecting the excerpts.

30. The transcendent aspect of time provides a measure whereby we can evaluate the validity of normal v. morbid (Alzheimer's disease) temporality, infantile v. mature, primitive v. science-informed. We are always already temporal in our experience, but we can learn to live time differently and better (e.g., by abjuring the mode of eternality).

31. The "real sensation of sound should be distinguished from the tonal moment in retention" (ITC 53).

32. ITC 41. Husserl cites the work of W. Stern (1897, 1898), but makes no reference to James.

33. "... The practically cognized present is no knife-edge, but a saddle-back, with a certain breadth of its own on which we sit perched, and from which we look in two directions into time. The unit of composition of our perception of time is a *duration,* with a bow and a stern, as it were—a rearward- and a forward-looking end." William James, *The Principles of Psychology* (New York: Dover Publications, 1950), Chapter XV, p. 609. This work was first published in 1890.

34. The limits of the specious present are fluid and necessarily vague: 'natural seasons,' events, etc. are all constructs; there is no given unity—or, rather, there are many natural units of measure (day, month, year, radioactive half-life, etc.)—but one can usually determine what has passed or is yet to come.

35. Unless, of course, one adopts an Einsteinian perspective and develops the means of traveling at the speed of light.

16

Two Reversibilities: Merleau-Ponty and Derrida

ટા ટા

Mark Yount

Merleau-Ponty is not among the philosophers whose texts Derrida has written about. I find this a conspicuous absence because, as I will argue in this paper, there are striking similarities between the projects of the two authors, and between the new terminologies and logics they evolve toward their ends. I will focus here on a particular point on which that convergence might turn: reversibility. My argument will not be that these authors say the same thing, or that the earlier influenced the later. While both attempt a break from the fundamental errors of inherited philosophy, the *point* of that break is not the same. What I will do is retrace the trajectories of these writings to examine the point at which they cross; only then can we consider whether they are pointed in different directions. I will argue that the structures described by Merleau-Ponty and by Derrida are not decidably different beyond a certain point, but that the *medium* in which the two authors locate that structure is decidedly, perhaps critically, different. We will see, finally, that this juxtaposition of two sets of texts has implications for the reading of each, and for the more general question of the relation between deconstruction and phenomenology.

From *The Structure of Behavior* on Merleau-Ponty attempted in various ways to escape the procrustean oppositions of academic philosophy. Perhaps his most direct attack was on the subject-object dichotomy. Working "from below" with evidences drawn from studies of behavior and perception, he was able to show that "form," which gestalt theory had shown to be the fundamental order of perception, resists classification as physical structure or meaning, as objective or subjective. *Phenomenology of Perception* extended the scope of this

philosophy of ambiguity, to a reflection made more radical by plumb-
ing the depths of the perceived world (which would be equated with
the "brute being" of the last writings) (VI 170). Both empiricism and
intellectualism were again put through sustained critique, with the
emphasis shifted to the critique of intellectualism as Merleau-Ponty
diverged from Husserl's findings in order to carry out Husserl's project.
Husserl's theory of language, for instance, is just as much refuted as
the empiricist theory by the admission that *the word has a meaning*
(PhP 177). A thought independent of the constraints of speech would
disappear instantaneously, would not even exist for itself:

> Thought is no 'internal' thing, and does not exist independently of
> the world and of words. What misleads us in this connection, and
> causes us to believe in a thought which exists for itself prior to
> expression, is thought already constituted and expressed, which we
> can silently recall to ourselves, and through which we acquire the
> illusion of an inner life. But in reality this supposed silence is alive
> with words, this inner life is an inner language (PhP 183).

The "inner life" is an illusion, just as there is no inner man.

But these efforts to resist the dichotomy of subject and object did
not go far enough to suit their author. In a Working Note of July 1959
Merleau-Ponty wrote that the problems posed in *Phenomenology of
Perception* are insoluble because he started there from the "conscious-
ness-object" distinction (VI 200): Perhaps such a starting point made
unavoidable what he admitted in a note from February of 1959: that
he had "in part" retained the philosophy of consciousness (VI 183).
The same Note does point a way out: what is needed is to bring the
results of the earlier work to "ontological explicitation." A Note of
January 1959 proposes that such an ontology "would be the elaboration of the notions that have to replace that of transcendental subjectivity, those of subject, object, meaning . . ." (VI 167). A Note from the
following May marks one stage of this developing ontology. Because
the flesh of things speaks to our flesh, and to that of the other, "my
look" defies analysis into the categories of consciousness or thing.
Merleau-Ponty sees the implication of this: it requires "a complete
reconstruction of philosophy" (VI 193).

The reconstruction of philosophy was very much incomplete at
the time of Merleau-Ponty's death. Since then, Derrida has offered us
indications of the *de*construction of philosophy. Deconstruction goes to
the heart of philosophy, and to phenomenology in particular, largely
through critique of the notions of meaning and presence. Derrida's
readings of Husserl in his introduction to *The Origin of Geometry* and
(especially) in *Speech and Phenomena* inaugurate the moves that

have defined deconstruction as a movement. I will offer only a summary.

Derrida's critique of Husserl's theory of meaning recalls Merleau-Ponty's, especially in summary form. Husserl takes meaning to be an ideality which can be united to the sensible aspect of a signifier that in itself it does not need. But the signified has its meaning only within the signifying system, by means of the diacritical oppositions subsequently described by Saussure. A signified meaning is not possible as an individual, positive, ghostly being that would then find its way *to* language. But this is what *The Logical Investigations* require, Derrida argues: that meaning be uprooted from the medium of difference in order to institute the ideal *of* the ideal, the identical, the spirit unconstrained by its body. It is not the case that the ideality of meaning makes possible the repetitions of language; it is the opposite: it is repetition that creates the effect of the ideal. By the rigorous logic of what Derrida calls "the supplement," the copying is what makes the original possible.

It is not by accident that Husserl, and philosophy generally, would free both meaning and consciousness from the effects of their flesh. For Husserl, the matrix of that transcendental freedom is the "now" as source point and as living present. The present is also the locus of the *self*-presence of experience, even of transcendental experience, of intuition, of all that is invoked in phenomenological evidence. Thus:

> If the present of self-presence is not *simple,* if it is constituted in a primordial and irreducible synthesis, then the whole of Husserl's argumentation is threatened in its very principle.[1]

This is just what proves to be the case, and *by* Husserl's own principles. The present is not undivided; it bears in its structure the retentional trace of the past and a protentional cut toward the future. Presence is continually compounded by the trace of a nonpresence, a nonperception—a trace more primordial than what is phenomenologically primordial. The living present is effectively deferred *ad infinitum;* the subject who would *be* present is deferred and divided by this difference that is prior to any identity.

This entwining of differing and deferring yields *différance,* the logic that issues in deconstruction. But this rationality "no longer issues from a logos";[2] it is a strategy, and a double one. On the one hand, deconstruction contests the hierarchical orderings of philosophy, resists, lends its force to an overturning. Because of this it is necessarily engaged in the philosophical field; it must use meaning even as it writes against the authority of meaning. But on the other

hand there is an attempt to write differently, to play somewhat outside the rules, beyond the bounds of propriety. The attempt to put the
question of meaning carries writing toward a point at which *it* must
literally *mean* nothing.[3] Deconstruction pushes the rational to the
reach of its furthest questions, finds its echo in the call of the wild.
For Derrida the figure of the double gesture is the chiasm, an asym-
metrical forking in which one point extends its range further than
the other.[4]

But which?

One of our authors has written that "what we need to do is
determine *otherwise,* according to a differential system, the *effects* of
ideality, of signification, of meaning and of reference."[5] What ontology
will elaborate the notions to replace those of subject, object, meaning?
A Working Note of December 1959 suggests a way to "replace the
notions of concept, mind, idea, representation" (VI 224). The point of
departure it suggests is the critique of *positive* signification—a critique to be modeled on Saussure's diacritical conception of language.
The linkage hinted here is fascinating: The differential structure of
signification precludes meanings positively determined in their individuality; just so, this differential logic would displace the positive
characterizations of subject, object, and the other terms Merleau-
Ponty has tried to break open or slip between. What I will argue now
is that this new point of departure in the diacritical is precisely what
opens the motif of reversibility beyond phenomenology and into the
ontology of *The Visible and the Invisible.*

The most evident predecessor to reversibility is the phenomenon
of touching-touched (or more generally of the sensing-sensed), already analyzed in *Phenomenology of Perception.* What I must stress
is that the earlier analysis is precedent: it does not yet bear the
designation or the full reflective force of reversibility. The phenomenon noted in the earlier work is this: I can, with my left hand, touch
my right as it feels an object. In such 'double sensations' the body is
at once the touching and the touched; my two hands can reverse the
two roles, and I can identify the touching hand as the one that a
moment ago was the touched. Now, this doubling already points beyond the dichotomy of subject and object. The same flesh envelops
both, and Merleau-Ponty notes that here I apprehend my body as
"subject-object" (PhP 95). But the touching and the touched do not
coincide: the right hand as I touch it is not the right hand that
touches. It is not the *touching* hand that I am able to touch. In the
language of *Phenomenology of Perception,* it is the objective body that
I touch; the lived body that touches. The reflexivity of the touching-

touched thus exceeds the logic of dichotomy: the two are not entirely distinguished, since the roles can be reversed; but the two are not identical, since touching and touched can never fully coincide.

Why is this not yet the reversibility of *The Visible and the Invisible?* Because what holds for the body is not yet extended throughout the more pervasive hold of being. The flesh of the body must be situated in the elemental "flesh" whose being envelops both body and world. The *phenomenon* of the body's reflexivity must become the *ontology* that turns on the reversibility of visible and invisible. The *stuff* of that ontology is already embraced by the phenomenology of perception; the perceived world is equated with brute being by a late working note. But what is needed for the later ontology is a key to the *structure* of this stuff already under investigation, a structure that will break more entirely with the alternatives of subject and object. Diacriticity offers just that structure. The diacritical is not itself a "stuff," but neither is it an ideality that could be free of the various media structured by its rule. While it offers a model for the diverse attempts of structuralism to secure objectivity, it offers Merleau-Ponty a more powerful means to displace that objectivism.

Let us first consider the diacriticity of language, since Saussure's analysis of the signifying system figured in Merleau-Ponty's rethinking his own work. A Working Note of January 1959 concludes that the "tacit cogito" of *Phenomenology of Perception* is impossible (VII 71). It is by a combination of words that I *form* the standpoint of constituting consciousness. But these words do not refer to positive significations and to *Erlebnisse* as self-given: there are only differences between significations. Between these last two observations Merleau-Ponty notes this implication: "Mythology of a self-consciousness to which the word 'consciousness' would refer." Thus, as we saw in Derrida's reading of Husserl, this differential structure displaces the subjectivity of the subject as well as the ideality of meaning.

In a Note dated the following September, Merleau-Ponty detects in Saussure's analysis a rediscovery and confirmation of the idea of *perception* as divergence (VI 201). Another Note from that month concludes that the *Gestalt,* including the relation of the perceiving body to the sensible, is "a diacritical, oppositional, relative system" (VI 206). It is not always clear in these Notes whether Merleau-Ponty takes the differential character of perception to be the *same* as the differential of signification, but he pursues this coincidence—whether as equivalence or equivocation. A Note from May 1959 remarks the need to pass from the thing as identity to the thing as difference (VI 195). We recalled earlier the December Note that proposed diacriticity as a point of departure in order to critique the conceptions of the thing and the subject. Each of these is a fragmentary indication; taken together they are markings of an emerging ontology. The positive terms that constitute the dichotomies of philosophy are not at bottom positive after all: Through a radical reversal of figure and ground, the beings that had been figured as individual things assume their values as differentials of the ground of being.

This shift from positively conceived entities to constitutive difference is thus itself a sort of reversal. It stands out *as* reversibility when it is joined to the motif of touching-touched reflexivity. These two motifs are inseparable in the reversibility of the visible and invisible. On the one hand, the diacritical ultimately derives from the twoness involved in hands touching and touched. A Working Note of November 1959 observes that the *pair,* as right and left, as two eyes or two ears, is the advent of difference—the fragmentation of being that makes possible *all* discrimination and all separation, including the use of the diacritical (VI 216–217). On the other hand, the touching-touched remains a local phenomenon of touch until this reflexivity becomes reversibility, and it is diacriticity that makes this ontological extension possible.

The idea is not fleshed out all at once. The 1959 article "The Philosopher and His Shadow" refers to the reflexivity of touching and touched as "a sort of reflection" (S 166). A Working Note of that September shows this to be a special sort indeed, since *all* reflection is modeled on it (VI 204). A Note of April 1960 uses the expression "reciprocity" (VI 245); one dated that May speaks of a sort of "reflectedness," of a quasi "reflective" redoubling, of the reflexivity of the body (VI 249). This evolving terminology articulates the touching-touched motif more and more as a pervasive structure of flesh. A Working Note of May 1960, for instance, takes the *non*coincidence of touching and touched as an opening on the new ontology (VI 254). The touching and the touched are not joined in perception or at some level of consciousness; they can only have their junction in the *untouchable.* This untouchable is not a positive that is elsewhere, but the ungivenness of givenness, coextensive with the sensible: the invisible of the visible.

Between the visible and the invisible, there is reversibility, through which they implicate each other. One locus of this reversibility is the relationship between signifying and signified in language: Between sound and meaning, speech and what it means to say, there can be no question of priority.[6] But any visible, not only the signifier, is a certain differentiation, less a thing than a difference between things, an opening between interior and exterior horizons of invisibility (VI 132). These horizons are the invisible *of* the visible, only *in* the visible. In coiling back on itself the visible forms an invisibility that sees, an untouchable that touches. This "strange adhesion of the seer and the visible" forms a Visibility "as upon two mirrors facing each other," a couple more real than either of them (VI 139). If we are tempted to translate this unfamiliar language into more traditional categories we must not: Merleau-Ponty writes that this is what "we have previously called flesh, and one knows there is no name in traditional philosophy to designate it" (VI 139).

But that was just the point: to work free of those traditional designations—subject and object, for instance. There is not just our flesh but a flesh of the world, and these are not distinct, even if they cannot be identified: "[O]ur flesh lines and even envelops all the visible and tangible things with which it nevertheless is surrounded" (VI 123). Self and non-self are obverse and reverse (VI 160). "Perhaps," writes Merleau-Ponty, just a few pages before his writing comes to its sudden end,

> . . . perhaps our own experience *is* this turning round that installs us far indeed from 'ourselves,' in the other, in the things. Like the natural man, we situate ourselves in ourselves *and* in the things, in ourselves *and* in the other, at the point where, by a sort of *chiasm,* we become the others and we become world. (VI 160)

Again, this is possible because neither I nor the other is a positive subjectivity. The first Working Note with the heading "reversibility," dated November 16 1960, offers the image of the finger of a glove turned inside out. The end of the finger of the glove is a nothingness one can turn over, and the negative would only *be* in the fold, "the application of the inside and the outside to one another, the turning point—" (VI 263–264).

This turning point is the chiasm—I-world, I-other, my-body-things. Because my body doubles up into inside and outside and outside and inside are doubled up in things by the same chiasm, my body inserts itself *between* the two leaves of the world, which itself is inserted between the leaves of my body (VI 264). "Start from this," writes Merleau-Ponty: "there is not identity, nor non-identity, or non-coincidence, There is inside and outside turning about one another."

Another statement about turning outside and inside is there, in Derrida's text, where he writes that the chiasmus can be considered "a quick thematic diagram of dissemination."[7] Dissemination, "seminal difference," replaces the hermeneutic concept of polysemy. Its inexhaustibility is no longer that of meaning, so it cannot be gathered into "the calm unity of the verbal sign."[8] In "The Double Session," Derrida argues through a reading of Mallarmé's *Mimique* that the "phenomenological, hermeneutic, dialectical project of thematicism" will not hold.[9] This consequence can be drawn from the diacriticity that traverses the text through and through. Recall from Derrida's deconstruction of Husserl's theory of meaning that no signified can be a pure ideality, its identity independent of the differential field of signifiers. But that is precisely what 'the signified' has always signified; that has always been the soul of meaning. So this is the end of the sign as we know it: there is no decidable difference between signifier and signified. The order of the sign gives way to a difference without irreversible terms.[10]

One example of what for some is a theme in Mallarmé's text is the blank. In Derrida's text thematicism unravels on that point. What is the meaning of the blank? The blank is not the word but the between of words; not a presence but, more than absence, the spacing that makes the *effect* of meaning possible. The blank is the transcendental space of inscription, into which all marks are folded. The blank *is* this fold: it applies to the semic set of white things, but as the asemic spacing of every seme, it applies to itself as well, folds over on itself. Fold and blank are not distinguishable, then: the fold folds itself.[11]

This *is* a touching-touched, but one that cannot be made present, cannot have a phenomenology: a touching-touched of the trace, of spacing, of text. Derrida reads this fold in Mallarmé's text, in a seme of flesh:

> in a hymen (out of which flows Dream), tainted with vice yet sacred, between desire and fulfillment, perpetration and remembrance: here anticipating, there recalling, in the future, in the past, under the false appearance of a present.[12]

The hymen joins and confuses two incompatible senses: it names both marriage and the membrane broken by the consummation; both an identity and the division of that identity, a fold folded. It is thus undecidable, not either one of its defined meanings, but the enveloping medium of their difference, the *between*. Between the two there is both confusion *and* distinction; both contradiction and noncontradiction, and the contradiction and noncontradiction *between* contradiction and noncontradiction:

> What is lifted, then, is not difference but the different, the differends, the decidable exteriority of differing terms. Thanks to the confusion and continuity of the hymen, and not in spite of it, a (pure and

impure) difference inscribes itself without any decidable poles, without any independent, irreversible terms.[13]

These effects do not depend on the signifier 'hymen' but on the entré-logic of the between. Derrida's readings of other texts find this through the workings of *pharmakon* 'supplement,' and 'gram,' all of which are undecidables. What Derrida says of the *pharmakon* would extend to any undecidable: that it constitutes "the medium in which opposites are opposed, the movement and the play that links them among themselves, reverses them or makes one side cross over into the other . . ."[14] What Derrida writes is not an argument meant to stand free of context; Derrida's writing draws out what is undecidable in the text in order to unleash effects not recognized there before. Derrida's texts turn on these "points of indefinite pivoting"[15] in the texts his writing reads. But the point of deconstruction is not to privilege these particular points, which are no longer strictly signifiers. The point, rather, is that if there is no decidable difference of signifier and signified, then "a text is never truly made up of 'signs' or 'signifiers.' "[16] Everything we have called a sign is a cipher, and every cipher is, as Derrida quotes Mallarmé, "a cipher of pirouettes."[17] Each refers in its turn to another pirouette; each in its turn is the mark of another, "totally other and yet the same."[18] This is the dance of the diacritical, and this is reversibility. The two motifs are joined and separated in the undecidable, turned on "the invisible axis of writing."[19]

The writings of Merleau-Ponty and Derrida cross at the point of reversibility. Both pass through such a point as a way out of traditional philosophy, with its logic of dichotomy and the hierarchies that logic has always entailed. They have even drawn from common sources in that tradition, Husserl and Saussure, both doing so in highly critical and original ways. Arriving at points of reversibility, the structures they find mirror one another: a point at which there is neither identity nor non-identity, a difference without irreversible terms. I suggested at the outset, though, that the *point* of these writings is not the same. If they approach convergence, even if they stand somehow in this relation of reversibility, reversibility is always imminent and never realized in fact. I want to suggest now what the main lines of difference between these two reversibilities might be.

For one, Merleau-Ponty and Derrida have different angles of attack. If Derrida can be roughly classed as post-structuralist, Merleau-Ponty's post- is to the gestalt. Grammatology traces its structure in the field of writing, the medium of text. For Merleau-Ponty, phenomenology, and the ontology to which it leads, must find their truths in the medium of perception. Here is how I see the point: the reflective

structures these two describe are not decidably different *in* their
structure—in the kinds of relation they define, the extent of their
operation and their upheaval of the more definite relations of prior
philosophy. The difference lies in the *medium* in which that structure
is found. Derrida writes the reflexivity of reading as writing and of a
writing that refers to itself, while Merleau-Ponty sees a reflexivity of
the body, a touching of touch that lends its "inspired exegesis" to the
always unfinished birth of a world (VI 133). For Derrida, the medium
must be understood as *text* (though not in the "narrow" sense); for
Merleau-Ponty it must be understood as being (though not in any
traditional sense). This, I think, is a critical difference, and one which
offers a clue to the implications of deconstruction for phenomenology.

Before addressing the implications of this difference, we must
first note that we cannot parcel out a *domain* of truth to each: we
cannot say that Merleau-Ponty describes the structure of one kind of
thing or one part of the world while Derrida describes another. The
reason is this: there are not *two* media at stake. For Merleau-Ponty,
brute being with its wild logos is the encompassing; nothing exceeds
its reach. For Derrida, nothing eludes the economy of arche-writing
(variously called trace, *différance,* arche-trace); there is no region or
sector free of its play of forces. Nor does it seem we can reconcile
these two approaches: Merleau-Ponty never gives up the *stuff* of experience; Derrida reminds us that the last thing to go is the the
transcendental signified we dream to be origin and end. There is no
phenomenology of the hymen.[20]

The critical point, then: Does Merleau-Ponty's insistence on the
stuff of experience show his text to be yet another variant of
philosophy's dream of presence, of a transcendental signified? Must
the structure he describes be deconstructed of its stuff, stripped of its
flesh? No. At least not *simply,* and that is perhaps the most that could
be established here.[21] As we saw in discussing the "double gesture" of
deconstruction, no text works *entirely* free of the force and discourse
of metaphysics. The flesh of *The Visible and the Invisible* is the stuff
of the "transcendental," but it is no more a transcendental signi*fied*
than a transcendental signi*fier*—just as differance is "not more sensible than intelligible."[22] Neither conforms to the dualism of the sign.
Merleau-Ponty reinscribes the language he takes from the tradition;
he writes of being, but in a way that disrupts every metaphysics of
presence.

For deconstruction to consign Merleau-Ponty's last writings to
the tradition to *be* deconstructed, it must assert something like this:
that it is not enough for a text to explicitly break with traditional

philosophy, to reject oppositions or hierarchies, or even to formulate a "logic" isomorphic with *différance*. But in that case what kind of writing *would* satisfy the demands of deconstruction? One possibility is that we must simply break with *all* talk of "what is": of presence, being, experience, perception or *any* such term. If every one of these terms derives its meaning from the philosophical tradition, it might be argued that their very use thereby sustains what must be deconstructed. This in turn could have either of two points of emphasis: 1) that no writing using these terms could be *true* (since they embody the errors of philosophy); 2) that writing using these terms would have the wrong practical, *strategic* effects (thus abetting the enemy). Neither version will work.

While deconstruction might claim that every use of "being," "presence," "experience," or "perception," has been misguided, it cannot simply dismiss the referential function of these terms. They may refer misleadingly, poorly, but they *do* refer. To dismiss every ontological claim ever made would still not amount to a dismissal of "what is"—and such a dismissal would itself involve an ontological claim. Nor can all possible *talk* of what is (even of the "isness" of what is) be dismissed. To claim that the terms in question cannot be used in *any* context without perpetuating error, to deny they could ever be grafted to a truth, is to presuppose a vantage from which we can calculate every possible use. But it is deconstruction that best reminds us that that such mastery is impossible, that nothing can check the play of dissemination. Thus, neither vocabulary nor what Merleau-Ponty is writing *about* can be sufficient reason to assimilate his late work to the errors of a flawed tradition.

Questions of strategy are harder to decide. This very difficulty, though, argues for a keener look at less practiced possibilities. We have seen that the strategies of deconstruction are multiple, and it is worth noting that Derrida takes the philosophical questions Merleau-Ponty has pursued to be indispensable. Derrida has written that we must exhaust the resources of the concept of experience in order to attain by deconstruction its ultimate foundation; that only through discovery of a field of transcendental experience can we escape both empiricism and objectivism; that "a thought of the trace can no more break with a transcendental phenomenology than be reduced to it."[23] Deconstruction has well established that it is not reducible to phenomenology; no one is likely to miss that point. What has been less evident is the other hand of this relationship, that deconstruction depends on phenomenology's break with the natural attitude (and its hidden philosophical assumptions). This complicity of the two is more

easily missed or misrepresented—largely, I think, because many prac-
titioners of deconstruction attend to a very limited set of texts in
phenomenology, and read them only to verify the logocentrism they
know can be found there.

Merleau-Ponty's late texts can be especially helpful in reasserting the more positive connection between phenomenology and
deconstruction. Those texts hold open the direction of deconstruction
(just as Derrida has defended phenomenology). In introducing the
last chapter of which we have even a fragment, Merleau-Ponty makes
this remark entirely emphatic:

> *This does not even exclude the possibility that we find in our experience a movement toward what could not in any event be present to
> us in the original and whose irremediable absence would thus count
> among our originating experiences.* (VI 159)

This is just the possibility Derrida has pursued in his tracings of
différance, without the language of experience so prevalent in Merleau-
Ponty. Derrida puts out of play precisely what Merleau-Ponty wants
to focus on and elucidate as flesh—to reduce this being to its
grammatological structure. I would not find that structure in Merleau-
Ponty's text if I had not read Derrida's, and this is why the similarity
of structure between these two authors is not simply a one-way de-
pendence. Derrida creates his precursors, as Borges said of Kafka.
But if Derrida shows us this strange logic in more striking form,
Merleau-Ponty gives us a better sense of its *body,* as well as how it
relates to the enduring concerns of philosophy.

I have argued that deconstruction cannot simply dismiss every
conceivable ontology and that it cannot (even more) deny the experienced being that ontology seeks to explain. Given this priority (which
is surely contested by some), one virtue of Merleau-Ponty's late work
is that it calls attention to the "stuff" in which *différance* accomplishes its differing. Perhaps it is *différance* that *constitutes* this medium: perhaps flesh is even an "effect" of an economy of forces. But
what Merleau-Ponty points to as flesh *is* nonetheless, and this medium is usually obscured by the emphasis of deconstructive texts—
even Derrida's. What I hope I have shown here is that the logic of
deconstruction does not preclude either ontology or phenomenology;
that, at the same time, description of experienced being (or the being
of experience) must take into account structures which the category
of experience might not comprehend. We must find the chiasm that
will give us both sides: *différance in the flesh.*

This chiasm is open to interrogation, open to dissemination. What
does it suggest for our readings of Merleau-Ponty and Derrida? To

read Merleau-Ponty under the influence of Derrida calls our attention to the *extent* of Merleau-Ponty's departure from traditional philosophy in his last works. These similarities between Merleau-Ponty and Derrida should point us to the nuances of Merleau-Ponty's escape route and make us less confident that we can explain the later thought in more familiar terms. By letting *The Visible and the Invisible* stand in its strangeness, our readings might be more pointed to the extremities of its questions. By this same association, though, perhaps it is Derrida's texts that will read somewhat differently. The more commensurable Derrida to Merleau-Ponty, the more we might be reminded of Derrida's own insistence on philosophy; the less opposed to philosophy a work of deconstruction might seem. Perhaps a work issuing from the intersection of phenomenology and deconstruction will find yet other trajectories for thinking, will read and read differently of this flesh of *différance*.

"The point to be noted is this: that the dialectic without synthesis of which we speak is not therefore skepticism, vulgar relativism, or the reign of the ineffable."[24] There is no absolutely pure philosophical word; yet philosophy is not immediately non-philosophy. Irrationalism does indeed have philosophical meaning, but hidden from itself.[25] To renounce the order of philosophical discourse because of its inherent violence is to fall into the worst violence of all, the unimaginable night of a primitive and prelogical silence.[26] Philosophy can only let itself be questioned.[27]

Notes

*This article is an expanded version of a paper presented to the Merleau-Ponty Circle at our conference in September of 1988. My thanks to Tom Busch for support, as well as to Hugh Silverman, Jack Caputo and Martin Dillon for posing helpful questions.

1. Jacques Derrida, *Speech and Phenomena,* David Allison, trans. (Evanston: Northwestern University Press, 1973), p. 61.

2. Jacques Derrida, *Of Grammatology,* Gayatri Spivak, trans. (Baltimore: The Johns Hopkins University Press, 1974), p. 10.

3. Jacques Derrida, *Positions,* Alan Bass, trans. (Chicago: University of Chicago Press, 1981), p. 14. There is also a helpful disucssion of deconstruction as critique of meaning at p. 49.

4. Ibid., p. 70.

5. Ibid., p. 66.

6. See VI 118, 145 and 154–155.

7. Jacques Derrida, *Dissemination,* Barbara Johnson, trans. (Chicago: University of Chicago Press, 1981), p. 44.

8. Ibid., p. 255.

9. This characterization appears at ibid., p. 249.

10. Ibid., p. 210.

11. Ibid., pp. 250–259.

12. Derrida quotes this at ibid., p. 209.

13. Ibid., p. 210. See especially pp. 209–222 for Derrida's discussion of "hymen" and "between."

14. Ibid., p. 127. Derrida is writing of *pharmakon* here.

15. Ibid., p. 221.

16. Ibid., p. 261.

17. Ibid., p. 240.

18. Ibid., pp. 240–241.

19. Ibid., p. 241.

20. *Dissemination,* p. 265.

21. Nancy Holland has reported some comments Derrida made on Merleau-Ponty's work. In her article "Merleau-Ponty on Presence: A Derridean Reading" (*Research in Phenomenology* Vol. XVI, 1986), she writes: ". . . [Derrida] left us with an interesting thought—if one might argue that the *Phenomenology of Perception* falls within the metaphysics of presence, with *The Visible and the Invisible* it is even harder to say." (p. 111)

22. *Of Grammatology,* p. 62.

23. Ibid., p. 62. This passage, pp. 62–65, is especially important for understanding the relation between deconstruction and phenomenology.

24. VI 94–95.

25. VI 266.

26. Jacques Derrida, *Writing and Difference,* Alan Bass, trans. (Chicago: University of Chicago Press, 1978), p. 130.

27. Ibid., p. 131.

17

Phantom Equator

ea ea

Alphonso Lingis

The movement of disengagement from and return to the sensible field and levels of the world, which Merleau-Ponty maps out in the advance of objectifying thought, he already finds in perception. "The relation between the things and my body is decidedly singular; it is what makes me sometimes remain in appearances, and it is also what sometimes brings me to the things themselves; it is what produces the buzzing of appearances, it is also what silences them and casts me fully into the world. Everything comes to pass as though my power to reach the world and my power to entrench myself in phantasms only came one with the other; even more: as though the access to the world were but the other face of a withdrawal and this retreat to the margin of the world a servitude and another expression of my natural power to enter into it" (VI 8). The body that advances to and retreats from the levels at which things are found is the competent body, which can have objectives because the future and the possibilities of things are open-ended and because the imperative that makes each thing an objective leads into the field of things, and because the levels do not hold the body unless it takes hold of them. Merleau-Ponty's phenomenology makes perception a *praktognosis,* makes our existence a stance whose posture is directed upon objectives, makes our body occupied and laborious.

What of the disengagement from things, from the levels and planes which engender things, toward those refuges from the space of the practicable world where the phantomal doubles of monocular vision, perceptual illusions, mere appearances, refract off the surfaces of things; what of the dream-scene, the closed theaters of delirious apparitions, that realm of death in which the melancholic takes up his abode? What of the detachment from practicable things and from the trafficking in their trade and toil-worn paths with which the visionary consciousness is transported into realms of color and light, the dancing vitality is rapt into rhythmic spaces where there is no telos and no task, where movement is not movement going any where? What of the possibility of releasing one's hold on the levels, drifting into a sensible apeiron without levels, or into that nocturnal, oneiric, erotic, mythogenic second space which shows through the interstices of the daylight world of praktognostic competence? Might not the body that lets go of the things and retreats from the planes and axes of the world be ordered by other imperatives?

The One-World Hypothesis

The practicable world of perception is for Merleau-Ponty the one world and it contains the corridors, dreams, hallucinations, erotic and psychedelic phantasms open in it, like the dimensions of the canvas contain the dimensions of the scene painted on it, even though there is not one universal set of geometrical dimensions upon which the spaces opened in dreams and in erotic obsessions can be measured. These are absorbed into the geography of the practicable world, "as the double images merge into one thing, when my finger stops pressing upon my eyeball" (PhP 329).

> I perceive everything that is part of my environment, and my environment includes 'everything of which the existence or non-existence, the nature or modification counts in practice for me': the storm which has not yet broken, whose signs I could not even list and which I cannot even forecast, but for which I am 'worked up' and prepared—the periphery of the visual field which the hysterical subject does not expressly grasp, but which nevertheless co-determines his movement and orientation—the respect of other men, or that loyal friendship which I take for granted, but which are none the less there for me, since they leave me morally speaking in mid-air when I am deprived of them (PhP 321).

> The world remains the same world throughout my life, because it is that permanent being within which I make all corrections to my knowledge, a world which in its unity remains unaffected by these corrections, and the self-evidence of which attracts my activity toward the truth through appearance and error . . . I may be mistaken, and need to rearrange my certainties, and reject the being to which my illusions give rise, but I do not for a moment doubt that in themselves things have been compatible and compossible, because from the very start I am in communication with one being, and one only, a vast individual from which my own experiences are

taken, and which persists on the horizon of my life as the distant roar of a great city provides the background to everything we do in it (PhP 327–28).

And since the unity of the world is not that of an intelligible system, not grasped in synthetic concepts and principles, but that of a style (as we recognize the style of a city while all the things in it are rearranged and replaced), it is the style in our perception, the postural schema with which we integrate our own sensory-motor exposure to it, that prehends it. The world that is one individual that encompasses everything is the practicable world, and if it is not there as a given but as an imperative, it is an imperative that our sensibility be a praktognosis, and that we maintain ourselves integrally as practical organisms.

But not only do monocular images, phantom visual forms, mirages, drifting tones, obsessive erotic phantasms break free from the carpentry of the practicable world, but they extend fields about themselves—purely visual, purely sonorous, oneiric, erotic, nocturnal spaces—whose axes disconnect from the dimensions of the practicable field. When we get caught up in one of these ungraspable apparitions are we not drawn into unpracticable spaces whose directions are directives?

For Merleau-Ponty this multiplicity of fields each with its own ordinance does not contravene the primacy of praktognostic perception or confound the normative force of the practicable world. "I never wholly live in varieties of human space, but am always ultimately rooted in a natural and non-human space." (PhP 293). The images, doubles, masks, caricatures, phantasms that populate multiple unpracticable fields owe their presence to the grain of the sensible made contact with in perceptual prehension. "Even if there is perception of what is desired through desire, loved through love, hated through hate, it always forms round a sensible nucleus, however small, and it is in the sensible that its verification and its fullness are found" (PhP 293). The perceptible things show through their dream-doubles, hallucinatory caricatures, erotic mists, like the canvas shows through the painted landscape, the crumbling cement under the building, or the tiring actor under the dramatic character. And "human spaces present themselves as built on the basis of natural space" (PhP 294); this is true of spaces explored in dreams or hallucinations or erotic obsessions, as it is true of the all-encompassing metric space in which the scientist elaborates his representation of reality. Not only does the dreaming consciousness have no access to entities save the awakened perception (or the peripheral sensibility that never fully sleeps and continues to be sensitive to the levels and sensorial regions of the world), and has nothing but drifting fragments of perceived things to materialize in the vital and erotic dimensions in whose tides they rise and fall, but the dream-field itself owes its existence to the waking state that recalls it. "During the dream itself, we do not leave the world behind: the dream-space is segregated from the space of clear thinking, but it uses all the latter's articulations; the world obsesses us even during sleep, and it is about the world that we dream." "Though it is indeed from the dreamer that I was last night that I require an account of the dream, the dreamer himself offers no account, and the person who does so is awake. Bereft of the waking state, dreams would be no more than instantaneous modulations, and so would not even exist for us" (PhP 293).[1] Dreams, hallucinations, erotic obsessions, and psychedelic intuitions "endeavour to build a private domain out of fragments of the macrocosm, . . . the most advanced states of melancholia, in which the patient settles in the realm of death, and, so, to speak, takes up his abode there, still make use of the structures of being in the world, and borrow from it an element of being indispensable to its own denial" (PhP 293). The carnal physiognomy to which the eroticized perception is directed is indeed different from the physical shape of another as envisioned in a practical perception and coded by pragmatic and polite forms of social interaction, and the voluptuous tones that give it its sultry density are different from the colors that make its texture and pliancy visible to a perception that synergically focuses in on it. But it is the perceptible anatomy of the other that anchors the voluptuous phantasm for concupiscent longing.

The world of real things then admits monocular images, reflections, mirages, noises and fleeting tactile impressions, which the deviant consciousness elaborates into another space. The world "takes in without discrimination real objects on the one hand and individual and momentary phantasms on the other—because it is an individual which embraces everything and not a collection of objects linked by causal relations. To have hallucinations and more generally to imagine, is to exploit this tolerance on the part of the antepredicative world, and our bewildering proximity to the whole of being in syncretic experience" (PhP 343).

Masks of Masks

But is it true that the unpracticable spaces are constructed with fragments of real things lifted off them and elaborated into a private space by the deviant consciousness? Is it not true that the things themselves engender their doubles, the reflections and mirages that play off them, their shadows, the layers of images and simulacra? Merleau-Ponty says the the sensible is not in simple location, but exists in transcendence, by presenting itself here and now it at once presents itself out of a prior moment and extends itself into a future moment; the water of the pool is there by sending the streaks of light it has captured across the screen of cypresses at the back of the garden. The sensible takes form before us by giving form to the postural schema of our forces. But then it is a transcendence that not only promotes its own form elsewhere, but elsewhere another form. If the things mirror one another, it is as the tain in the glass mirrors me—putting there a visual form different from the affective-kinesthetic diagram I feel here. Each thing presents not only itself, the abiding essence that maintains it as a practicable form and a task, but also its doubles, its reflections and shadows, its images and simulacra. It is the thing that produces the monocular images of itself on our retinas, the pool that makes itself visible on the sun-streaked cypresses.

It is by presenting ourselves exposed visibly and palpably in the light that we engender the monstrous shadow that precedes us and soaks into the ground under our feet. The professor who enters the classroom the first day has been preceded by the legend or myth of himself which the students see now materializing before their eyes. They adjust practically to the level of his voice, to the arena of his movements; he knows they are looking at the personage and fits his person into it as he enters the room. They seek to penetrate beneath this mask and their look finds the colors and contours of a caricature. If we recognize our acquaintances in the drawings made by the caricaturist, it is because our seeing was already not anatomical but caricaturizing. The perception that looks under the mask finds another, monstrous mask; the students see the pedant under the pedagogue. The look rebounds between layers of doubles the face engenders. When the professor inspects his own face in a mirror, his eyes are caught between the professoral mask and the pedantic caricature. When in the classroom he slouches over his papers and stifles a yawn, he is not simply shrinking back into a bare anatomy moved by fatigue, he is agitating his masks disdainfully or ironically.

When a face enters the room where people are gathered, borne exposed like an idol over a uniformed and coded body, marked with black and scarlet paint and adorned with flowers and the plumes of dead birds, the glances that turn to it lower or move obliquely across it. It would be hard to justify normalizing the practical imperative, hard to argue that the face whose clearly and distinctly exposed colors, whose firmly grasped carpentry is most palpably evident is the face in which unpracticable forms of that face are absorbed, like monocular images in the real thing. A face is a face by not being a rubbery substance to be grasped and palpated, a skull to be handled gingerly like a costly china bowl; it is a face by commanding the downcast eyes that touch it with respect, it is a face by presenting the coded mask of a social drama. Mouth and cheeks, by idolizing themselves, are not jaws and jowls—or rather, jaws and jowls are the caricature that the mouth and cheeks double into. Is not the idolatrous look that reveres and profanes the face the norm of which the anatomical and practicable intention is a deviant? The face is the place of exposure, of the vulnerability of the organism; one does not look at feathery crystals in the moist membrane of the eye with the focus of a jeweler's eye that guides the precision movement of his adjusting hands; one's look softens before the eyes of another, one's mobilization is disarmed; vulnerability and exposure order tenderness.

Does natural perception believe it is getting closer to the shark in discerning the viscous matter of its flesh under its power, its ferocity, its grace, its dominion in the sea old as and uncontested through three Ice Ages? What kind of primacy would the practical perception have that sees goals and the paths and means to reach them in the cobblestone lanes and moss-covered houses of the medieval town? Would not the vision that penetrates to the practicable layout of the things itself derive from the revery that lets the tones and the rhythms of the tile roofs and amber street lamps lift off in another wave of duration, that of the immemorial toil and repose, legends and festivity that slumber in its trodden paths and shrines worn smooth by innumerable reverent hands?

The gilt door of the thatch-roofed Balinese princely house presents its glory, and its domesticity as a wooden door, in a doubling; the wood is humble and terrestrial only by reason of the gilt it displays; the gilt is glorious only because it is the splendor brought to wood. The home is princely because it is clay bricks, exposed bamboo rafters, from the terrestrial sources of the land, that are carved and gilded to enshrine the luster of the civilization that presides over the island of Bali risen out of the sea in volcanic eruptions and sacred favor.

Does the practical focus that envisions the anatomy of another as a prehensible substance really have ontological primacy over the erotogenic surface, the voluptuous mirages that refract our gaze turned

to strangers? Is the reality in things really that which takes hold of
and is taken hold of by the synergic mobilizations of our practical
postures? Are their sensuous density and substance that resist the
manipulative hand and invite the caress, are their twilight colors
that seduce and soften the focus of the gaze and communicate with
the sensuality of our organism rather than with its postural axis in
some way derivative? Is not to exist as a sector of the geographical
space laid out in perspective simultaneously to exist as a landscape of
revery? The nocturnal trees that rub their twiggy hands and gesticu-
late in monstrous gestures we so readily recognize in old lithographs—
have we not always seen the trees with these caricatural versions of
themselves?

A thing reduced to its simple location in a here-now instant of
presence is not real and is not perceivable, Merleau-Ponty says; a
thing is real by presenting itself in a wave of transcendence, sending
echoes and simulacra of itself back into the past and into the future,
projecting itself in us as a diagram of our own forces. A thing *is*, we
argue, by engendering images of itself, reflections, shadows, masks,
caricatures of itself. Things are not reduced to their reality by being
reduced to facts; the "pure facts" of empirical observation are ab-
stracts of intersecting scientific theories, logics, and effects of techno-
logical engineering. But things are also not reduced to their reality by
being perceived in its practicable format. It is because they engender
carnal, caricatural images of their characteristics, turn phosphores-
cent facades on the levels and horizons of reality, that they also
engender a practicable format. Reality is in this parturition.

The things exist only in a transcendence which does not only
project their integral essences down the tracks of practicable reality;
across a wave of duration they refract off in doubles, masks, veils,
simulacra, shadows, omens. The monocular images, phantasms, lures,
forms made of shadows make the things visible and are the visibility
the things engender. The surfaces of things are not more real than
their facades; the reality that engenders the phantasm is engendered
by it. The face that advances as an idol before which the eyes lower
turns into a mask and a caricature; the idol made of stone or gold
metamorphoses into a face that keeps watch.

Is not the Enlightenment project of an *emendatio mentis* that
would dissipate the dreams, the reveries, the carnal phantasms from
things the project of a mind that would repudiate every imperative
but that of its own autonomous reason? Merleau-Ponty argued that
the universal cosmic order regulating the empirical representation of
objectivity, to which the theoretical reason subjects itself as to its own

imperative, is formulated in obedience to the ordinance of the perceived world in which reality is given. Do not the phosphorescence of the purely visual, the sonorities that do not only signal to a practical prehension but resound for the musical ear, the unwilled course of oneiric and erotic phantasms order the dreaming, the erotic, the artist organism into levels that are directives?

No dream, hallucination, erotic obsession, or psychedelic trip knows itself as the personal construction the philosophical formula "private domain built out of fragments of the macrocosm" explains it to be; the artist who paints a splash of colors that has its own consistency and does not disintegrate before our eyes as so many patches of paint on the surface of the canvas, the composer who arranges sounds in a consonance or dissonance that holds together has no consciousness of being a demiurge who imposes form on amorphous material by an a priori decree of the will. The painter, the dreamer, the libidinous organism find themselves pushed further on by the urgencies by which the dreams, the doubles, the shadows, and resonances materialize an ordinance that commands him or her. Does not everyone that follows his dream, his erotic obsession, his vision, the beat and cadences of his music find that he constructs representations of his dreams, his erotic field, and his artistic visions only by subjecting himself to the fields in which they unfold as to imperatives? No one makes himself a dreamer or a visionary; those we admire—perhaps everyone we admire—are men and women who came upon a field imperative for them, the field of a visionary imperative, a musical imperative, a nocturnal imperative, a passionate imperative.

As one's steps advance, the visible domain laid out as a geographic projection in which things are distributed in lines of perspective turns into a landscape made of the voluptuous contours and hollows of things and of the waves and rain that caress, of mossy forests and nocturnal fragrances that fondle one's surfaces and penetrate one's orifices. The night beyond night summons the insomniac to an abyss that does not lead to the day and its tasks. The unpracticable spaces of visions, of murmurs and melodies in which no one signals another, of the palpable and the impalpable that caresses and the night that engulfs, and the practicable world of objects-objectives are disjoint expanses come upon along the zigzag itinerary of one's nomadic vital space. The space of the purely visual, the range of harmonies and dissonances, the labyrinth of voluptuous contours and seductive hollows, the ether of obsessions and phantasms, the vistas of the essentially nomadic vital space that shows through the grid of the common coordinates—these are not private constructions built out of fragments of the macrocosm, disconnected mirages that ill-focused eyes send to drift over the equator of the practicable world of substantial and graspable things. The practicable world of things is itself suspended within their latitudes. They are not private constructions, which like the invisible and impalpable space in which the community of scientists elaborates a representation of the world given in perception, exist only by hearsay, spaces we do not believe in and cannot inhabit, spaces contained within us. Each is a realm of exteriority not reducible to our own representations, an exteriority that exists with the exteriority of an imperative. The nomad is summoned not by distant things fixed on one equator, but by multiple spaces, multiple ordinances; the equator is itself phantomal.

Sedentary World, Nomadic Vistas

There is about each one a *vital space,* with its auspicious and inauspicious latitudes, its individual geography of passageways and horizons, its directions of ascent and descent. Its levels and paths delineate, in the midst of the avenues and highways where the others circulate, the mountains and valleys in which nature distributes its species, the cosmic vastness in which the inapprehendable ultra-things, moon and stars, navigate, an itinerary for one's own vitality. A space where tasks to the measure of one's forces, landscapes, visions, rhythms and melodies, voluptuous fields and hollows others do not see or hear that haunt one's sensuality, theaters of historical or cosmic dramas to which others are but spectators, make one's body, trained, disciplined, and coded by others, a substance with sensibility and compulsions of its own. It is a space in which the Main Street of one's town is but vaguely marked alongside of the thoroughfare of one's own concerns and pleasures, in which the concert hall figures but not the adjacent power-plant, in which Paris fixes the horizon but not Lyon, in which the sacred mountains summon or the misty clouds hover maternally. It is the space in which continents extend to one's view raw materials and markets or stage great historical dramas of empire and revolution. It is a landscape sultry with voluptuous contours and dark places of intrigue and adventure, danger and security. It is illuminated from dazzling centers where one's eyes one day recognize they were made to see this: the giant sequoia forests, the cave-temples high on the walls of the Agora gorge in Ajanta, the walled medieval town covered with vines and silence between glaciers in the maritime Alps illuminated from the storm clouds. It is recognized when, beneath the map of air-traffic routes and highways, one recognizes the landscapes of intimacy and the enchanted lands of the remote.

In aboriginal Australia the girls are progressively trained in the skills of women; the boys are not educated or trained, but initiated. The decisive stage is the "walkabout"; the youth leaves the camp alone, for a year of wandering. He will learn by himself the terrain and the directions, the places and the ways of finding water, the properties of the plants and the ways to catch and use the animals, the dangers and the exultations. He will find companions in the animals, the stars and the spirits of the desert. When he returns it will be as an equal; he will know the equivalent of what the community has learned and shares.

Among us, in our sedentary empires, there is no initiation; at different stages of our lives we are transferred from post to post in the grids of the modern disciplinary archipelago—hospital, schools, barracks, factory, office, prison or asylum, hospital. We never leave the common paths and workshops, stadiums and marketplaces; the outer deserts, and outer space, are mapped in advance. Yet we too sense the second space of our walkabout lying between the channels and the tracks and the assigned posts. The space of our own desert summons us out of our infancy cradled in the arms and placed in the space of others. From the things at hand there opens a level of vital space that disengages from the levels on which the others are stationed and from the sedentary space where the things repose in their places. The fallen bird nestled in the childish hands will lead one to a post as guard of a nature reserve in Sumatra. The black hand that touches one's child face leads one one day to marry a woman in Agatz. The violin touched one day opens a route that leads to La Scala. The National Geographic paged through, which leads the others to exploratory embraces in the back seats of parked cars, leads one one day to expatriate life in distant ports or rain forests. Vital levels quicken an undisciplined and clairvoyant sensibility to extend before it, on the glowing horizon, the lights of Paris, the Toltec city of Teotihuacan slumbering in the mists of one's America, the great stupa of Borobudur rising against the wall of smoking volcanos to the impermanence, the compassion, and the non-self, the Gate of Nirvana across the sands to the Bay of Bengal from the temple of the Universal Lord Jagannath.

There are those who never locate their vital space, who leave their birthplace only to march in squadrons, or to sit in cubicles their life a dexterity programmed by computers. The land of their collaborators, kin, and intimates is for them a land of exile from a homeland they have never known; they may circulate the planet without ever finding the space of their own walkabout.

To locate one's vital space is to locate in the common world whose latitudes are fixed, where outer space itself is cartographed, an exit, a departure that opens in a wave of time. Somewhere in the midst of the terrestrial that extends beneath one's feet as the provenance of one's first birth and one's births to come a path on the other side of the horizons breaks free. The distances are not seen in a surveying gaze that encompasses, in simultaneity, the remote things present and exhibited; they are divined in a clairvoyance for what draws as it withdraws. The space of the desert is measured by the year of the walkabout. In the fields of one's walkabout one is making one's way to one's own death and to the enterprise, the revolution, the vision and the chant, the hierophany of the sacred that will carry on in its own tides the forces of the life one no longer pilots. The space of one's destiny is a space whose axes are trajectories of time. It is the space of one's own life, but it extends back, for the musician, to the spaces charted by Vivaldi and Beethoven and Bartok, extends back, for the Sandinista militant, to the cloud forests of Nueva Segovia whose paths were open to the mystic Sandino and to the Indian land whose sacred trees and spirits were protected by Nicarauac by his death. It extends ahead beyond the frontiers of one's death, where one's own life forces, without oneself, will be borne on by enterprises, revolutions, by the anonymous discourse of culture.

One's vital space is not plotted from the bird's-eye view, or from the view of the sedentary animal which fixes its dwelling and measures the environs in widening circles that keep the lair in view. It is a landscape where the rivers and the harbors, the deserts and the cliffs and the passes are events not displayed in an array of dimensions and equivalent paths, but located only by the path one oneself takes. The space of destiny is a space extending along a path to be blazed as one goes, across terrain for which there are no eagles to scout the way from the air or cartographers to record the flat projection from helicopters and satellites.

This essentially nomad space is not extended by a goal one has oneself produced, in a space of representation, and projected into the world. The one who determines himself to attain to a post or a throne in the world of music or politics lays out his roads and builds his fences in the common world; he is not commanded by a destiny but aims at a glory or at assets which he will use to traffic for the goods, forces, and caresses of others in the marketplace of the common world. One's vital space is an exteriority whose directions are directives; it is not a web spun out by oneself with which the exterior is recognized only in its appropriation. The axes of vital space are imperatives of expropriation and nomadization; it is the outer desert that summons one to depart divested and alone.

Summons of exteriority, the imperatives are not deducible by one's own calculative reason but arrive as contingencies, as portentous omens, the photograph of a man of the Nuba come upon by chance by Leni Riefenstahl, disgraced Nazi actress, and which led her to a destiny, at the age of 70, as a photographer of the facial paintings of Ethiopia, the seat in the Selma bus that made Rosa Parks pass into the space of non-violent revolution extended from India. The nomad on the solitary walkabout must know what chance encounters are portentous, which hills gleaming on the desert horizons are imperative.

The obedience that recognizes imperatives in the course of its walkabout in the space of destiny elaborates the responses unrepresentable in the scientific discourse of determinism and chance, in the ethical discourse of autarky and decision. The imperatives that extend a space of one's own are vitalizing forces that do not have the form of law but of portentous events. One does not find the space of one's own destiny by an obedience which is only one's commitment to one's own program.

But it is the one that has a hold on his or her own vital space that can then recognize the laws of the practicable world and the deviant axes of the visionary, melodic, phantasmal, oneiric, erotic spaces and the abyssal depths of night and night beyond night. And that can formulate programs which are commitments.

One makes the vital space a private space, whose directions are projected simply out of one's own will or longing, when one understands it as the space in which one finds one's powers come into their own, the space in which one finds one's vitality sustained and harbored, finds one's own sensibility over its extension and depth awakened, the space in which one's body finds its integral mobilization. It is true that when one finds oneself in one's own vital space, one moves in the conviction that one's eyes now see that for which these eyes were made to see, this heart feels what it was made to beat for, thse hands have found the Stradivarius they were made to play, these passions have found the flesh upon which they were made to release all they have of kisses and caresses. But one's flesh is but malleable clay taking on the forms of the common world until it comes to hold itself together through the force of obedience to its imperative. It is because the summons to the space of one's own destiny weighs on one that one finds the force to bring to flush a sensibility for things others do not see or hear or feel, that one finds the force to produce artist fingers, distant vision, the militant vehemence that churns the wells of one's emotions, the reverence that is a reverence of the body and not only of words. It is because one exposes oneself, in one's walkabout, to the portents and necessities that press upon one with the dawn of the day, to the visions that obsess the nights of one's own desert, that one becomes someone on one's own, with something of one's own to tell in the community of those who have each his or her vital space, the community whose camp is not the homeland after the exile but the meeting-place of nomads, itself displaced from day to day or from season to season according to the omens.

Notes

1. This quite ignores the ways that dreams, though not recollected in diurnal consciousness, recur to elaborate their problems in a succession of reiterated and divergent dreams and also haunt and accent the paths and hollows of the perceived world. For Freud the daytime recollection does not give the dream its existence, but effects its cathexis and neutralizes its powers; dreams not recollected extend their forces into the unavowed but active passions of men of action who "have no time for dreaming" and into the work-absorbed trances of artists.

18

Merleau-Ponty and Postmodernism

ﾞ❧ ﾞ❧

Joseph Margolis

One cannot report the relationship between postmodernism and the work of Maurice Merleau-Ponty: there is none, certainly there is none in the ordinary sense in which Jean-François Lyotard embraces postmodernism and Jürgen Habermas rejects it.[1] Furthermore, even under the constraint of philosophical relevance, postmodernism is as much a puzzle as a would-be resolution of deeper puzzles; there is no single formula defining postmodernism that identifies it both accurately and in a philosophically productive way—certainly not Lyotard's notorious jibe:

> I will use the term *modern* [he says] to designate any science that identifies it with reference to a metadiscourse ... making an explicit appeal to some grand narrative, such as the dialectics of Spirit, the hermeneutics of meaning, the emancipation of the rational or working subject, or the creation of wealth. . . . Simplifying to the extreme, I define *postmodern* as incredulity toward metanarratives,[2]

and certainly not in Habermas's implied acceptance of that sort of definition (not, of course, the doctrine that it signifies).[3] The fact is that Lyotard pirates the right to impose an authoritative reading on postmodernism rather than define the form it actually has. To be entirely candid, however, it *has* only the form it is compellingly assigned.

There are many such indeterminate notions—philosophical categories, preeminently—and no single interpreter can hope to fix their meaning by main force. The meaning of "postmodern" depends primarily on its having been first introduced or appropriated in a public

way by some deliberately rhetorical flourish, and then, secondly, on
the dialectical history it acquires once it is released into the stream of
public thought. In this sense, Lyotard has done remarkably well in
defining the notion in a way philosophy has come to favor—and more
or less convincingly attached to other views, Richard Rorty's, for instance, even where such authors have the good sense (though not the
right) to deny the diminished standing the label entails.[4] There are
other loosely formed acceptances of the notion in other conceptual
neighborhoods, in architecture, for instance, in film, painting, literature, culture at large,[5] that similarly tempt one to treat
postmodernism's doctrine as settled enough to justify a straightfor-
wardly matter-of-fact finding of a larger sort. (Also, of course, such
verbal acceptance says nothing about the resolution of the conceptual
puzzles it merely rearranges.)

As it happens, there is at least one sustained attempt to explore
affinities and oppositions involving Merleau-Ponty and
postmodernism—on the reasonable assumption that the phenomenon
antedates the dynamiting of the Pruitt-Igoe housing complex in St.
Louis (1972) and that Merleau-Ponty's philosophical themes were
clear and pertinent enough in his own time to justify extrapolation
now for our own purposes. Gary Madison, who makes the attempt,
has, however, somewhat homogenized the promising affinities and
oppositions that could have been drawn out, so that classical pragmatism (possibly because of Rorty's work) now appears (pejoratively) to
be a sort of postmodernism, and Merleau-Ponty himself is made out
(approvingly) to favor Habermas, in being committed to the uncoerced
universality of a rational consensus and to political liberalism.[6] Both
of these last claims are less than helpful, except in that extravagant
sense in which, after all, they do mark an important site where
correction and clarification may be invited. In any case, Madison's
effort to place Merleau-Ponty in the company of Husserl, Heidegger,
Marxism, pragmatism, postmodernism, and poststructuralism certainly sets the stage for those principal players, even if, in doing that,
we risk losing the precise definition of what Merleau-Ponty's originality comes to. Also, Madison's interpretation has the distinct virtue of
assembling some of the best clues to Merleau-Ponty's philosophical
objective. To propose to reorder these in another way is at least to
acknowledge that debt, and more.

Admirers of Merleau-Ponty ought, also, to admit that his principal undertaking was not merely not finished, but also not sufficiently
well worked out by the end of his life. We *can* define his place, of
course—something of his intention. But we cannot be sure of its full

improvisational possibilities: that would require a second Merleau. We cannot rightly vindicate or discount his project if we cannot rightly establish what it can recover. Its sheer boldness baffles the most sympathetic imagination. In a fair sense, therefore, in linking Merleau-Ponty to the prospects of postmodernism, we play a slippery game: we reshape the latter to favor Merleau-Ponty's pertinence, and we project the powers of the former in order to decide the fate of postmodernism itself. Both maneuvers belong to that twilight rhetoric in which we cannot claim to have merely found the decisive facts of the matter. We insinuate ourselves in a process in which, though originally surrogates, *we* become the principal players: a little like playing chess with oneself, with inherited boards of several abandoned games now made to yield a single homogenized contest already in play. There is nothing for it, as we begin, but to admit the inescapable bias of the philosopher's interpretation; otherwise, there would be no contest at all. There would be no way of understanding our own intellectual history.

I

What we need for form for ourselves, at the start, is a sense of Merleau-Ponty's essential, or at least most mature and promising, themes that might enable us to solve at one and the same time the puzzle of his place among phenomenologists (and perhaps pragmatists and hermeneuts) and the puzzle of how best to construe his contribution to the quarrel regarding modernism and postmodernism (and perhaps Marxism and liberalism as well). It seems a large order, but an effective argument may be drawn from the following remarks:

> [A]. description is not the return to immediate experience; one never returns to immediate experience. It is only a question of whether we are to try to understand it (PhP 30);
>
> [B]. the becoming-nature of man . . . is the becoming-man of nature (VI 185);
>
> [C]. Man is a historical idea and not a natural species. In other words, there is in human existence no unconditional possession, and no fortuitous attribute. Human existence will force us to revise our usual notion of necessity and contingency, because it is the transformation of contingency into necessity by the act of carrying forward (PhP 170).

These are fair samples of Merleau-Ponty's cryptic vision. They do not easily fall into a single felicitous pattern. They *resemble*

postmodernist incursions a little because they do subvert the philosophical canon. But they are not postmodernist, in the straight sense
that they are meant to facilitate a deeper and suppler recovery of
philosophy than the canon would ever care to support: they are opposed to abandoning the philosophical enterprise. Furthermore, that
recovery cannot be expected to be won by appealing to a consensus
among those already committed to the canon (Habermas, say) or to
those who, "postmodernly," reject the canon together with everything
it admits to be a legitimate question (Rorty, for instance). In a word,
Madison cannot be right on either count, for Merleau-Ponty intended
to radicalize philosophy by transforming its governing vision, not by
restoring the canon with minor adjustments (Habermas) and not by
repudiating it altogether (Lyotard and Rorty).

The essential clue cannot be instantly fathomed; we shall have to
return to it a number of times. But it may be put this way: what is
most radical and problematic in *The Visible and the Invisible,* that
still claims philosophical continuity with the boldest features of *Phenomenology of Perception,* depends on what cannot be determinately
specified at all—*spoken*—but can be located with regard to our (or
any) orderly, spontaneously effective conceptual system. If that alone
is true, then Madison's interpretation cannot but fail, because, in
banking on Merleau-Ponty's attention to the liberal and consensual
in the political world (hence the perceived affinities with Habermas),
Madison commits his reading to the *steady extension (or progressive
improvement) of conceptual distinctions already in use;* whereas, surely,
Merleau-Ponty had narrowed his entire effort, approaching the end of
his life, to the task of illuminating the *subterranean* source of all
discovery and the legitimation thereby of discovery that takes a discursive form.

It is only in being drawn to such an option that we are instruc-
tively attracted as well to the possibility that Merleau-Ponty was a
sort of proto-postmodernist. This is not to suggest that Madison takes
him to be a postmodernist. Of course, he does not. He treats him as a
"postmodern" thinker but not as a "postmodernist": Merleau-Ponty
accepts, Madison correctly notes, a "*postmodern* conception of reason
[that] has nothing *postmodernistic* about it, by which I mean that it
in no way involves a rejection of reason or a disavowal of the overriding importance that the Western tradition has always placed on reason. Merleau-Ponty never suggested that 'reason' is nothing more
than the idea-product of our particular historical tradition, merely a
cultural bias of Western man."[7]

True enough, though even that requires fine tuning. He did, you
will remember, say that man was not "a natural species" (PhP 170)

[C]. But it would be a mistake to conclude, as Madison pretty well does, that *that* signifies a commitment to the possibility of a universal progressivism *via* the self-corrective work of reason as it seeks a completely open consensus. That would make Merleau-Ponty out to be a sort of phenomenological Peircean, and hence, an ally of Habermas. "He was [Madison says] most definitely not opposed to the traditional and, in particular, Enlightenment stress on rationality. . . . By 'rationality' Merleau-Ponty understood basically what might be called 'reasonableness': the attempt to reach uncoerced agreement with others by means of unrestricted dialogue. This is a conception of reason that, interestingly enough, is remarkably akin to the conception of reason that a thinker such as Jürgen Habermas has in recent years diligently labored to articulate and which he refers to as 'communicative rationality.' It is a properly hermeneutical conception of reason."[8]

One reason this reading is not likely to be right is simply this: *Habermas* never risks anything like Merleau-Ponty's extreme daring—precisely with respect to the nature of rational discourse. How is it possible, therefore, that, as Merleau-Ponty reaches for the most complete formulation of his obsessing vision, he should prove to have simply joined hands (by an idiosyncratic detour) with Habermas's *modernist* recovery of Enlightenment reason—against, of course, the genuinely subversive (postmodernist) possibilities of the Frankfurt School? Something is wrong here. Certainly, Adorno's negative dialectics suggests an affinity between the Frankfurt radicalizing of Marxist thought and Merleau-Ponty's (and Heidegger's quite different) radicalizing of phenomenology.[9] Let it be said at once, however, that the required correction must pass through something like Madison's original labor.

We must try to make a little more transparent the sense of our specimen remarks. For example, in [A], Merleau-Ponty clearly repudiates any form of cognitive privilege, any form of foundational access to the noumenal order of things: we cannot effect a "return to immediate experience," he says; and yet we must "try to understand it." What could that possibly mean? Surely it is the same point that, in the Preface to *Phenomenology of Perception*, proves to be Merleau-Ponty's abiding puzzle—which, of course, he almost always formulates in a deliberately aporetic way. "The whole universe of science," he says, "is built upon the world as directly experienced, and if we are to subject science itself to rigorous scrutiny and arrive at a precise assessment of its meaning and scope, we must begin by reawakening the basic experience of the world of which science is the second-order expression" (PhP viii).

That single carefully selected term, "second-order," cannot fail, now, to recommend (to the unwary) an intention to recover some form of cognitive privilege. The entire passage playfully insinuates just the reverse of what is meant. The "second-order" is of course the range of all ordinary sensory perception and discourse in which the canonical "objectivist" construes his science: in fact, it marks in a sly way what is "first-order" for the objectivist. Merleau-Ponty is following Husserl here—according to his own lights: he is returning to the "things themselves," to what "is a matter of describing, not of explaining or analyzing" (PhP viii). The "things themselves" cannot be the objects of the latter talents ("explaining and analyzing"), because the "world as directly experienced" is not yet languaged, not yet normalized by the categories of knowledge, consciousness, languaged thought: "To return to things themselves is to return to that world which precedes knowledge, of which knowledge always *speaks,* and in relation to which every scientific schematization is an abstract and derivative sign-language" (PhP ix).

The "world" is that, beyond language and beyond languaged perception, "of which knowledge always speaks." Hence, science is "second-order." Merleau-Ponty is entirely explicit here: he is recovering Husserl's attack on objectivism. But already in the *Phenomenology of Perception,* he recovers Husserl in a way Husserl could never approve: *for,* "description is not the return to immediate experience," to what a deeper reflection might fathom. Could anything be more explicit? The puzzle that remains concerns just how the collecting theme of the late Merleau-Ponty affects and alters the theme of the early Merleau-Ponty.

Merleau-Ponty cannot *return* to the "world," to "things themselves," *in the cognitional way* (in either the objectivist's or the idealist's way). That's just what [A] concedes. (Presumably, that's what makes Merleau-Ponty "postmodern.") Hence, if to "describe" the world that "second-order" discourse speaks about is to *describe* what is not, and can never be, described *in* such second-order discussion, then there is no way to be right about it *in* the second-order way that rightly captures propositional truth (the objectivist's *and* the idealist's way— Husserl's in particular). That's what [B] darkly intimates. Discourse always says more than it knows, "speaks" more than it can say, and *is* more than it can speak. The "wild" nature of the human being is chiasmatically implicated in the "wild" nature of the world. We seek to fathom what is *unsaid* ("unspeakable") in what is said, and in attending to such disclosures, we discover ourselves as well as the world we inhabit ("unspeakably"). "The real [says Merleau-Ponty] does not await our judgement before incorporating the most surprising phenomena, or before rejecting the most plausible figments of our imagination. Perception is not a science of the world, it is not even an act, a deliberate taking up of a position; it is the background from which all acts stand out, and it is presupposed by them. The world is not an object such that I have in my possession the law of its making; it is the natural setting of, and field for, all my thoughts and my explicit perceptions" (PhP xxi).

In speaking, in routinized discursive acts, one must reflect on what signals what is not captured by any utterance or usual perception but amplifies it, as if from beyond, compellingly from the "world" that is not yet tamed by such discourse. That is the marvellous lesson of [C]; there must be a sense in which, in the lived world that forms the background of our explicit (profoundly contingent) discourse, disclosures are glimpsed (not by cognitive privilege but by a sort of necessity in the very process of life, by a certain salience or irresistibility that wells up) that affects *both* what we propositionally affirm and, in what we affirm, what we would legitimate. That sense is the same in which *history* is the brute medium of human life (and the world), in which the deep contingencies of objective science and experience and their transcendental legitimation entail a "transformation . . . into necessity by the act of carrying forward." The "necessity" cannot be discursive or formal in the logical sense. It is historical; for, if it were logical or conceptual, invariantly compelling within its own fixed historical interval, it would simply reinstate the idealism Merleau-Ponty marks as the weakness of his own mentor, Husserl. Also, it must be "contingent" in a deeper sense than that already recognized *in* discourse, for it lies beyond the closure of any (contingent) conceptual scheme we employ, and it "was" (already) the source of whatever propositionalized necessity we now claim to find in our operative categories. That, at any rate, is very close to the lesson of the *Phenomenology*.

History, then, is Merleau-Ponty's clue to overcoming the entire Cartesian world and the deep failure of Husserl's idealism. For Husserl had already blinked, philosophically, in the *Crisis* volume, when, partly responding to what he took to be Max Weber's challenge to the supposed relevance of phenomenology to historical existence, he failed utterly and finally to draw the needed connection between history and subjectivity:

> Our first historical reflection [says Husserl at the beginning of the manuscript] has not only made clear to us the actual situation of the present and its distress as a sober fact; it has also reminded us

that we as philosophers are heirs to the past in respect to the goals
which the word "philosophy" indicates, in terms of concepts, problems, and methods. What is clearly necessary (what else could be of
help here?) is that we *reflect before all decisions,* for a radical self-
understanding: we must inquire back into what was originally and
always sought in philosophy, what was continually sought by all
the philosophers and philosophies that have communicated with
one another historically; but this must include a *critical* consideration of what, in respect to the goals and methods of philosophy, is
ultimate, original, and genuine and which, once seen, apodictically
conquers all.[10]

Husserl's mention of the "apodictic" conveys two ironies: first, it provides an explicit illustration of a sense of universal reason and consensus that is as distant from Habermas's proposal as it is from
Merleau-Ponty's; secondly, it actually identifies what, in Husserl's
idealist reclamation of the canon, Merleau-Ponty could not accept.[11]
Certainly it is clear that Husserl uses "history" to prime a completely
ahistorical exercise of reason; he does not construe reason itself as
radically historicized. That is the meaning of [C].

Still, there is a clue in Husserl's failure that shows the way to a
suppler recovery, shows the permanent limitation of philosophy as
well as its proper viability. Hence, the resolution of his essential
puzzle counts, for Merleau-Ponty, toward reconciling in a novel way
naturalism and phenomenology (all would-be dualisms of ontology
and epistemology, in fact) and also (by an extravagance of applied
reading) it counts toward overcoming the extravagances of both modernism and postmodernism.

This needs some amplification. But the clue is this: Merleau-
Ponty's "return" to the "things themselves" signifies the *redirection* of
philosophy's work beyond objectivism and (idealist) phenomenology
and toward our reclaiming a wild but unitary world that informs all
our discourse but remains beyond it.

It is a redirection of thought, it is not the capture of a privileged
source of knowledge. It is forever implicated in what we claim to
understand and know of the world. But we cannot understand in any
cognitional sense the linkage between the two: *that* cannot be rendered in any way that might yield improved criteria of the cognizing
sort. It is the world's unity, its "flesh" (to which we belong, at a level of
existence deeper than discourse can penetrate), that resists discourse
but informs it—a world already dualized yet prior to any dualism.

That too exposes Husserl's failing. Rightly grasped, it shows at a
stroke the impossibility of ordering first- and second-order
(legitimative) discourse in the canonical way—whether by Descartes's

or by Kant's or by Husserl's lights; *and* it shows, by locating effective discourse itself in the context of what we are calling "history," that there cannot be any hierarchized order between such first- and second-order activity and that neither can exhibit an ultimate necessity that discourse could specify or legitimate. That is a far cry from abandoning philosophy (postmodernism) and from restoring the proper ordering of the levels of discourse between what may rightly be claimed about the world and what may be claimed about all claims about the world (modernism). Madison, as we were saying, sees the danger of the first, but he does not grasp the novelty of the second theme.

II

Madison's mistake is an important one, not at all easy to dislodge. He is right, for instance, to reclaim Merleau-Ponty's insistence on the link between philosophy and the political relevance of its recovery under historical circumstances: for instance, as in the reflection on the relevance of Marxism as philosophy, at the end of the fifties. But Madison is also much too sanguine in his oddly clever reading of Merleau-Ponty's texts. He says that "the conclusion [of Merleau-Ponty's reflection on history] is a prudent and reasonable belief in the possibility of a certain *progress*"; and he grounds that prospect in a textual way in a remark (among similar-sounding remarks), in *Signs,* to the effect that, in spite of the confusions and deadends of history, living societies are able "to pick out the truth of their past in the present" (S 73–74).

Perhaps this does signify a sort of progress—or, better, a sort of energy apt for projects that might redeem us from the errors of what we once claimed to have correctly perceived in history. But what Madison fails to weigh sufficiently is the simple fact that Merleau-Ponty is speaking precisely of the self-understanding of Marxism, *now that it has failed.* Merleau-Ponty says very plainly: "The relationship between philosophy and history is less simple than was believed" (S 13). Certainly it is not as simple as Habermas supposes; and certainly it would be too tepid to maintain, as Madison does, that "[t]o affirm history in this way [Habermas's way, now ascribed to Merleau-Ponty,] amounts to a recognition that there is no definitive solution to human problems."[12]

These two remarks are worlds apart: in the first (Merleau-Ponty's), one finds at least part of the dawning vision that bridges the difference between the *Phenomenology* and *The Visible and the Invisible.* (There is no parallel in Madison's gloss.) When he speaks of "the greatness of a doctrine" (the "classics"—Madison notes the usage), Merleau-Ponty is thinking expressly of Marx's own work; and, in that spirit, he says: "The history of thought does not summarily pronounce: This is true; that is false. Like all history, it has its veiled decisions. It dismantles or embalms certain doctrines, changing them into 'messages' or museum pieces. There are others, on the contrary, which it keeps active. These do not endure because there is some miraculous adequation or correspondence between them and an invariable 'reality'—such an exact and fleshless truth is neither sufficient nor necessary for the greatness of a doctrine—but because, as obligatory steps for those who want to go further, they retain an expressive power which exceeds their statements and propositions. . . . We are saying that a re-examination of Marx would be a meditation upon a classic" (S 10–11).

This line of thinking leads directly to specimen [C], which, let it be noted, is found in the *Phenomenology*. The theory of the "classics" is very close to the central role Merleau-Ponty assigns "perception" in his early work. It is, for instance, very close to the theme, in "The Primacy of Perception," that "perception is a nascent *logos*"—which is to say, that experience moves us to "assist . . . at the birth of . . . knowledge [in the process of knowledge as it takes form, in order to teach us] to recover the consciousness of rationality [rather than merely the 'things, truths, values' that 'are (thereby) constituted for us']" (PhP 25).

That theme might possibly have led us, in some remote way, to suppose that Merleau-Ponty *was* a conventional phenomenologist or a precursor of Habermas. But if there is a sense of progress there, it rests with the recovery of the lesson of that *logos*—in effect, it helps us to gain an escape from the snares of discursive truth—*not* the progressive improvement (*à la* Habermas) of the particular "things, truths, values [therein] constituted for us." For Merleau-Ponty, there is no progress *there*.

Still, wherever Merleau-Ponty means to capture the ontology of *speaking without yet saying* (the *logos* theme), what (by parity of rhetoric) he ultimately collects, particularly in *The Visible and the Invisible*—concerns the deeper theme of the ontology of *being, without yet speaking*. It is this second theme, *not the first*, that tempts us to read Merleau-Ponty as a postmodernist; the first might only tempt us to read him as a poststructuralist. For the first *is* genuinely concerned with the "other" (*l'autre*), in a sense not altogether distant from the master theme of poststructuralism.[13] Yet even that is not entirely accurate; for, unlike the poststructuralists, Merleau-Ponty places the first theme *in* the context of the second—even, incipiently, in the *Phenomenology*. There's the baffling novelty he intends. Consequently, in eclipsing Marxism, in construing Marx in a serious but essentially educative or heuristic way (that is, as a "classic"), Merleau-Ponty cannot merely move on to recover the progressivism of a liberal imagination. He can avail himself of that all right—as, indeed, the poststructuralist often does—but he already senses, there, the deeper lesson of the second theme (which, of course, he never managed to put in final form).

One sees this, for instance, in the Introduction to *Signs* (which Madison draws on), where, having introduced the question of the link between the philosophy and politics of Marxism, Merleau-Ponty explicitly adds the second theme: as if to say, that too is needed to understand what is gained by reclaiming Marx. The issue is introduced in a way that cannot fail to remind one of Heidegger's alternative. Surely, Merleau-Ponty is offering here another option as a way of recovering Husserl's announced purpose: "The philosopher who maintains that the 'historical process' passes through his study is laughed at. . . . Now, as before, philosophy begins with a 'what is thinking?' and is absorbed in the question to begin with. No instruments or organs here. It is pure 'It seems to me that.' He whom all things appear before cannot be hidden from himself. Nevertheless, in the dark night of thought dwells a glimmering of Being" (S 14–15). He offers us a *jeu,* a serious parody of (an alternative to) Heidegger. It agrees with the posing of Heidegger's own question but only in its own sweet way: to make a question of oneself is to call humanism into question; hence, once again, it is to raise an issue that cannot be reconciled with a "liberal" metaphysics (which is not the same, remember, as a liberal politics detached from Merleau-Ponty's second theme). "Man," as he says, "is a historical idea and not a natural species" [C]. To speak thus is not to repudiate humanism (as Heidegger does) in the name of a higher calling, but it is to force humanism to acknowledge its insurmountable limitation.

That the *second* theme is already present in *Signs* is suggested by the phrase, "No instruments or organs here." But the sequel leaves no doubt:

> Take *others* the moment they appear in the world's flesh. They would not exist for me, it is said, unless I recognized them, deciphering in them some sign of the presence to self whose sole model I hold within me. But though my thought is indeed only the other side of my times, of my passive and perceptible being, whenever I try to understand myself the whole fabric of the perceptible world

comes too, and with it comes the others who are caught in it. Before others are or can be subjected to my conditions of possibility and reconstructed in my image, they must already exist as outlines, deviations, and variants of a single Vision in which I too participate. For they are not fictions with which I might people my desert— offspring of my spirit and forever unactualized possibilities—but my twins or the flesh of my flesh. Certainly I do not live their life; they are definitely absent from me and I from them. But that distance becomes a strange proximity as soon as one comes back home to the perceptible world, since the perceptible is precisely that which can haunt more than one body without budging from its place (S 15).

Here, Merleau-Ponty makes a number of telling points, always in the spirit of his immense loyalty to Husserl. First of all, he disallows Husserl's idealism with regard to man's phenomenological powers— the pursuit of the apodictic: my thought "is indeed only the other side of my times." Secondly, the cognitive powers I exercise function only insofar as each of us, others, and the things of the world belong together as distinct precipitated presences within one inclusive Nature: they are all, then, part of "the world's flesh," "flesh of my flesh." Thirdly, all our discursive distinctions function as before, though perhaps with even a heightened sensibility: "I do not live their life [the life of others]." And fourthly (and most important), I need not have thought of them, these "others," or "recognized" them, in order that they should "exist," they are already as much present "in the world's flesh" as I am, and *I* myself cannot "exist" *or* function as I do, except for *their* influencing presence: they are "my twins," "flesh of my flesh," the very power of the encompassing world to draw from me uniquely what appears most intimately my own.

III

It remains true enough, however, that Merleau-Ponty does not quite reach the completion of his vision before *The Visible and the Invisible;* and there, it is not yet fully or felicitously fashioned. The question still nags: What, finally, is gained and lost by that late conception? The details are not our concern, only the right approach to the (second) conception already noted.

In *Signs,* one may say, Merleau-Ponty "places" himself between Heidegger and Sartre (and in that way "recovers" Husserl). The early version of the vision he tests there succeeds in avoiding Heidegger's bankrupt noumenalism, on the one hand, though it experiments with

Heidegger's daring, and repudiates Sartre's disastrous insistence on the total absence of structure in subjectivity, on the other, though it introduces its own bottomless abyss. "The flesh of the world" ensures the co-presence of all articulable things at any moment in which the "I," any "I," *is* present, does function in the way it does, inquires, understands, produces all the changes it effects in things and others: "things *are said* and *are thought* by a Speech and by a Thought which we do not have but which has us" (S 19).

This is not the same philosophical act as Heidegger's abandonment of *Dasein,* in the "Letter on Humanism," or the *Kehre* by which pure structureless noumenal Being "speaks" in its own "language" to certain gifted human mediums. Merleau-Ponty means here to assign thought and speech—*as it determinately obtains in our perceived world*—to the entire "body" of the "world's flesh." The salient possibilities of an objective science and of intersubjective communication are assured *in* that pronouncement but not *by* means of it. (So it affords another clue to Madison's mistake.) It claims no privilege. Certain words *are* said, certain thoughts *are* thought. "Said by whom? Said to whom? [Merleau-Ponty asks]. Not by a mind to a mind, but by a being who has body and language to a being who has body and language, each drawing the other by invisible threads like those who hold the marionettes—*making* the other speak, *think,* and become *what* he is but never would have been by himself" (S 19).

Here, the first theme is being welded to the second, so that it is itself transformed. But not quite fully enough. Similarly, Merleau-Ponty replaces Sartre's deliberate ontological evacuation of the self's structure (its nonbeing) with a profoundly historicized structure—that, once again, invokes the world's flesh: "As a matter of principle," says Merleau-Ponty, "fundamental thought is bottomless. It is, if you wish, an abyss. This means that it is never *with* itself, that we find it next to or setting out from things thought, that it is an opening out—the other invisible extremity of the axis which connects us to ideas and things. Must we say that this extremity is *nothing?* If it were 'nothing,' the difference between the nearby and the far (the contour lines of all existence) would be effaced before it. Dimensionality and opening would no longer make any sense. The absolutely open would be applied completely to an *unrestricted being* . . . the present [. . .] would no longer mean anything" (S 21). (The lesson is indistinguishable from that of one of the Working Notes that belong to the text of *The Visible and the Invisible* (VI 237).

All the chiasmic replacements of the standard dualisms of philosophy—that Husserl should have effected but did not—are, finally, caught up in the world's "unicity": in the sense of the two conceptual lessons Merleau-Ponty promotes. This is what he means, finally, by the "historicity of truth" that *he* finds animating both Husserl and Marx (VI 166)—the counterpart of the historicity of man himself [C]. Even that has its own duality; for, it is the artifactual nature of truth that accounts for the extravagance of Descartes's "infinite horizon of science" as well as of phenomenology and Marxism; and it is the source of our own understanding of truth's nature that purges us of the plausible disorders of the other.

You will have noticed that our specimen [B] was the only one drawn from *The Visible and the Invisible:* it was, plainly, more diffi-cult than the others. What Merleau-Ponty is getting at there, what he is heroically testing, may seem to involve the rejection of any philo-sophically serious conception of truth (the postmodernist's maneuver once again). But that would be a mistake to encourage. Nor can Merleau-Ponty be said to have been theorizing about the symbiosis of subject and object that "precedes" their standard opposition in West-ern philosophy. He was experimenting rather with the conceptual fruitfulness of attributing to "subjects" what *in our discursive practice* is normally attributed to "objects," and vice versa, *as a consequence* of treating the whole of the world as genuinely one, indivisibly such, but not for that reason undifferentiated. Thus:

> *Define* the mind as the other side of the body (VI 259).

> like the chiasm of the eyes, the [chiasm] is also what makes us belong to the same world—a world which is not projective, but forms its unity across incompossibilities such as that of *my* world and the world of the other (VI 215).

> my body is made of the same flesh as the world (it is a perceived), and moreover . . . this flesh of my body is shared by the world, the world *reflects* it, encroaches upon it and it encroaches upon the world (the felt at the same time the culmination of subjectivity and the culmination of materiality (VI 245).

The trick is *not* to test the mere propositional truth of all these utterances one by one. It is rather to allow oneself to entertain them as hints of the infinitely open possibilities of alternative conceptual idioms that may prove fruitful. What Merleau-Ponty is doing, ulti-mately, is introducing us to a kind of fluency we could familiarize ourselves with—that affords the great initial benefit of eliminating the dualisms that have generated all the puzzles of philosophy, and that, in addition, demonstrates just how easy it is to imagine disen-gaging our thought from the formal tyranny of the idiom the old dualisms subtend. He captures all this by improvising a master vision of the "world's flesh," an "ontology" that lies beyond both what we can say and what can be spoken but not said. It is meant to enable us to approach the creative source of whatever—variably, piecemeal, horizontally, contingently and historically, and generally in a regimented way—we finally systematize in thought and language. This is perhaps the meaning of the full passage in which [B] appears:

> It is not we who perceive, it is the thing that perceives itself yonder—it is not we who speak, it is truth that speaks itself at the depths of speech—becoming-nature of man which is the becoming-man of nature—The world is a *field,* and as such is always open (VI 185).

There you have the final chiasm. You may object to such a philosophy. But it is neither modernist not postmodernist. It is an ontology that sets a limit to both.

Notes

1. See Jean-François Lyotard, *The Postmodern Condition: A Report on Knowledge,* trans. Geoff Bennington and Brian Massumi (Minneapolis: University of Minnesota Press, 1984); and Jürgen Habermas, "Modernity versus Postmodernity," *New German Critique,* XXII (1981).

2. Lyotard, *The Postmodern Condition,* pp. xxiii–xxiv.

3. Of course, Lyotard has Habermas specifically in mind in formulating his distinction between the modern and the postmodern: particularly, Jürgen Habermas, *Knowledge and Human Interests,* trans. Jeremy Shapiro (Boston: Beacon, 1971).

4. See Richard Rorty, "Habermas and Lyotard on Postmodernity," in Richard J. Bernstein (ed.), *Habermas and Modernity* (Cambridge: MIT Press, 1985).

5. The following provides a fair sample of the prominent uses of "postmodern" outside of philosophy: Fredric Jameson, *Postmodernism or, The Cultural Logic of Late Capitalism* (Durham: Duke University Press, 1991); Ihab Hassan, *The Postmodern Turn; Essays in Postmodern Theory and Culture* (Columbus: Ohio State University Press, 1987); Matei Calinescu, *Five Faces of Modernity* (Durham: Duke University Press, 1987); Charles Newman, *The Post-modern Aura: The Act of Fiction in an Age of Inflation* (Evanston: Northwestern University Press, 1985); Rosalind E. Krauss, *The Originality of the Avant-Garde and Other Modernists Myths* (Cambridge: MIT Press, 1985); Charles Jencks (ed.), *The Language of Post-Modern Archi-*

Joseph Margolis

tecture, 4th ed. rev. and enl. (New York: Rizzolie, 1984); Linda Hutcheon, *A Poetics of Postmodernism: History, Theory, Fiction* (London: Routledge, 1988).

6. G. B. Madison, *The Hermeneutics of Postmodernity: Figures and Themes* (Bloomington: Indiana University Press, 1988), Ch. 4, particularly pp. 61–62, 71–73.

7. Madison, *The Hermeneutics of Postmodernity,* p. 71.

8. Madison, *The Hermeneutics of Postmodernity,* pp. 71–72.

9. See Theodor Adorno, *Negative Dialectics,* trans. E. B. Ashton (New York: Seabury Press, 1975).

10. Edmund Husserl, *The Crisis of European Sciences and Transcendental Phenomenology: An Introduction to Phenomenological Philosophy,* trans. David Carr (Evanston: Northwestern University Press, 1970), pp. 17–18.

11. Cf. Husserl, *The Crisis of European Sciences and Transcendental Phenomenology,* the rest of p. 18; also, pp. 69, 186, for a brief amplification of Husserl's sense of his own undertaking.

12. Madison, *The Hermeneutics of Postmodernity,* p. 73.

13. See Jean-François Lyotard, *The Differend: Phrases in Dispute,* trans. George Van Den Abbeele (Minneapolis: University of Minnesota Press, 1988).

Contributors

Thomas W. Busch is professor of philosophy at Villanova University. He is author of *The Power of Consciousness and the Force of Circumstance in Sartre's Philosophy* (1990). He has also published numerous articles on Sartre, Marcel, Merleau-Ponty, and Foucault.

M. C. Dillon is professor of philosophy at the State University of New York at Binghamton. He has published extensively on Merleau-Ponty, including *Merleau-Ponty's Ontology* (1988), and is editor of the forthcoming *Merleau-Ponty Vivant* (SUNY Press).

Geraldine Finn is associate professor of cultural studies, Faculty of Arts, Carleton University, Ottawa. She has published widely in the areas of feminism, philosophy, and cultural history. She is co-editor of *Feminism in Canada. From Pressure to Politics* (1982).

Shaun Gallagher is associate professor of philosophy at Canisius College. He is author of *Hermeneutics and Education* (SUNY Press, forthcoming). He has also published articles on Hegel, Husserl, Merleau-Ponty, and Habermas.

Eleanor Godway is assistant professor of philosophy at Central Connecticut State University. Her publications include articles on Merleau-Ponty and Hegel, art and phenomenology, and aspects of Quakerism.

Alfonso Lingis is professor of philosophy at Pennsylvania State University. He is the author of *Excesses: Eros and Culture* (1983), *Libido: The French Existential Theories* (1985) and *Deathbound Subjectivity* (1989) in addition to countless articles on contemporary continental philosophy. He is also the translator of several major works of Emmanuel Levinas.

Gary Brent Madison is professor of philosophy at McMaster University and on the Graduate Faculty at the University of Toronto. He is author of *The Phenomenology of Merleau-Ponty* (1981), *The Logic of Liberty* (1986), and *The Hermeneutics of Postmodernity: Figures and Themes* (1989).

Joseph Margolis is currently Laura H. Carnell Professor of Philosophy at Temple University, Philadelphia, Pennsylvania. His most recent books include the trilogy: *Pragmatism without Foundations* (1986), *Science without Unity* (1987), and *Texts without Referents* (1989); and *The Truth About Relativism* (1991). Soon to appear are: *Life without Principles* a companion volume to the trilogy, and *The New Puzzle of Interpretation.*

Glen A. Mazis is assistant professor of philosophy at St. Lawrence University. He has published articles on continental philosophy, art and literature, temporality and the emotions in journals such as *Philosophy Today, Human Studies,* and *Soundings.* He is currently writing a monograph on emotion and embodiment.

Hugh J. Silverman is professor of philosophy and comparative literature at State University of New York at Stony Brook and is author of *Inscriptions: Between Phenomenology and Structuralism* (1987), as well as translator of Merleau-Ponty's lecture courses *Consciousness and the Acquisition of Language* (1973) and "Philosophy and Non-Philosophy Since Hegel" (1976), and editor of numerous collections in continental philosophy including *Philosophy and Non-Philosophy Since Merleau-Ponty (1988).*

Derek Taylor is a senior doctoral student in the program of Social and Political Thought at York University in Toronto. His doctoral thesis is a critique of contemporary French thought from a phenomenological perspective.

Gail D. Weiss is assistant professor of philosophy at George Washington University. She wrote her doctoral dissertation on Merleau-Ponty, "The Hermeneutics of Gesture," at Yale (1991). She is currently writing a book on gender and the body image.

Michael Yeo is a research associate at the Westminster Institute for Ethics and Values in London, Ontario. He teaches in the department of philosophy at the University of Western Ontario. He wrote his doctoral dissertation (1988) on Merleau-Ponty's understanding of the task of philosophy. His main area of research and publication is applied ethics.

Mark Yount is assistant professor of philosophy at St. Joseph's University in Philadelphia. He has written on Nietzsche and Derrida and is a contributor to the forthcoming *Modernity and Its Discontents* (Fordham University Press) and is co-editor with John D. Caputo of *Institutions, Normalization and Power: Studies in Foucault and the Critique of Institutions* (forthcoming, Pennsylvania State University Press).

Name Index

Adorno, Theodor, 245
Althusser, Louis, 122
Apel, Karl-Otto, 81n22
Atwood, Margaret, 60–61
Augustine, St., 84
Ayatollah, Khomeini, 171

Barthes, Roland, 122, 143
Bartok, Bela, 237
Bates, E., 75, 81n19 n20
Beers, William, 186n14
Beethoven, Ludwig, 237
Benveniste, Emile, 99, 106n40
Bergson, Henri, 53, 58, 156
Bernstein, Richard, 48n3
Bleicher, Josef, 79n1
Borges, Jorge Luis, 224
Bréhier, Emile, 38–42, 50n13
Brunschvicg, León, 42
Bubner, Rüdiger, 80n1
Bühler, Karl, 75, 80n17, 81n21
Busch, Thomas, 6, 93

Caputo, John, 37
Chladenius, J. M., 4, 6
Cezanne, Paul, 56
Claudel, Paul, 98
Cooper, Barry, 164, 172

Dallmayer, Fred, 79n1
Deleuze, Gilles, 110–112, 122, 145–146, 149–158, 159n3 n9
Dennison, George, 75
Depew, David J., 80n1
Derrida, Jacques, 10–11, 37, 46, 52n23, n26, 84, 88, 92, 94–97, 105n35, 106n40, 110, 113–114, 122–123, 131–136, 143–146, 149, 159n8, 160n14, 189–202, 204–210, 213–217, 219–225

De Saussure, Ferdinand, 33, 94–95, 132, 142–143, 152–153, 165, 170n10, 215–217, 221
Descartes, René, 8, 54–55, 92, 99n3, 248, 254
Dillon, Martin C., 50n7 n8, 100n6, 102n19, 110–113, 115, 118–119, 123–127, 140, 142–145

Edie, James, 159n7

Fawcett, Brian, 175, 180
Feyerabend, Paul, 98n3
Finn, Geraldine, 111–112, 165, 168, 184n2, 185n13
Flynn, Bernard C., 103n24
Foucault, Michel, 11, 87, 110, 112, 131, 141, 143–45, 149–151, 154, 157, 158n1, 160n14, 163, 169n4
Frege, Gottlob, 94, 125, 145
Freud, Sigmund, 143, 145, 239
Furth, Hans, 74, 81n20

Gadamer, Hans-Georg, 6, 8–9, 12n4, 30–31, 33, 46, 48, 69–82, 101n18, 117, 142, 145
Gandhi, Mohandas, 166
Geraets, Theodore, 124
Godway, Eleanor, 111–112, 180, 183
Gordimer, Nadine, 178, 181, 185n12
Greer, Germaine, 166
Guattari, Felix, 149–150

Habermas, Jurgen, 9, 69–82, 112, 115, 151, 164, 169n8, 171, 241–242, 244–245, 248–250
Havel, Vaclav, 186n20
Hayek, Friedrich A., 100n16
Hegel, G. W. F., 33, 46, 162, 171–173

261